GLENCOE Grammar & Composition HANDBOOK

McGraw Hill Education

Bothell, WA • Chicago, IL • Columbus, OH • New York, NY

McGraw-Hill Education

Send all inquiries to:
McGraw-Hill Education
8787 Orion Place
Columbus, OH 43240

ISBN: 978-0-07-662447-8
MHID: 0-07-662447-1

Printed in the United States of America.

3 4 5 6 7 8 9 QTN 15 14

The McGraw·Hill Companies

Table of Contents at a Glance

Table of Contents

Chapter 3 Verbs 94

Chapter 4 Pronouns 121

Chapter 5 Adjectives 142

Chapter 6 Adverbs 156

Chapter 7 Prepositions, Conjunctions, and Interjections 171

Chapter 8 Clauses and Complex Sentences 190

Chapter 9 Subject-Verb Agreement 205

Chapter 10 Diagraming Sentences 217

Chapter 11 Capitalization 234

Chapter 12 Punctuation 246

Part One

Ready Reference

The **Ready Reference** consists of three parts. The **Glossary of Terms** is a list of language arts terms with definitions and examples. Page references show you where to find more information about the terms elsewhere in the book. The **Usage Glossary** lists words that are easily confused or often used incorrectly and explains how to use the words correctly. The third part is **Abbreviations**, which consists of lists of many commonly used abbreviations.

By day and night
I sing this song:
"All right's all right,
Alright's all wrong."

– Willard R. Espy,
Say It My Way

continuously
Regardless
[not irregardless]
neither . . . nor
either . . . or
correlative conjunction
both . . . and
not only . . . but also
this
demonstrative adjective
those
these
Tues.
RSVP
abbreviations
AVE
CST
B.C.

GLOSSARY OF TERMS

A

abbreviation An abbreviation is a shortened form of a word or phrase. Many abbreviations are followed by periods (pages 264–266).

EXAMPLES Mrs., Tues., Dec., NBA, ft., St., RI

abstract noun An abstract noun names an idea, a quality, or a feeling that can't be seen or touched (page 82).

EXAMPLE Her **bravery** and **courage** filled us with **admiration.**

action verb An action verb is a verb that expresses action. An action verb may consist of more than one word (pages 97–98).

EXAMPLES The director **shouts** at the members of the cast.

The lights **are flashing** above the stage.

The play **has begun.**

active voice A verb is in the active voice when the subject performs the action of the verb (pages 111–112).

EXAMPLE Thornton Wilder **composed** that play.

adjective An adjective is a word that describes, or modifies, a noun or a pronoun (pages 144–152, 164–165).

HOW ADJECTIVES MODIFY NOUNS	
WHAT KIND?	We studied **ancient** history.
HOW MANY?	I read **four** chapters.
WHICH ONE?	**That** invention changed history.

adjective clause An adjective clause is a subordinate clause that modifies, or describes, a noun or a pronoun in the main clause of a complex sentence (pages 195, 197).

EXAMPLE The Aqua-Lung, **which divers strap on,** holds oxygen.

READY REFERENCE

adjective phrase An adjective phrase is a prepositional phrase or a participial phrase that modifies, or describes, a noun or a pronoun (pages 178, 206–207).

EXAMPLES The servers **at the new restaurant** are courteous. **[prepositional phrase modifying *servers*]**

The musician **seated at the piano** is Erik. **[participial phrase modifying *musician*]**

adverb An adverb is a word that modifies a verb, an adjective, or another adverb (pages 158–167, 179–180).

WHAT ADVERBS MODIFY

VERBS	People *handle* old violins **carefully.**
ADJECTIVES	**Very** *old* violins are valuable.
ADVERBS	Orchestras **almost** *always* include violins.

WAYS ADVERBS MODIFY VERBS

ADVERBS TELL	EXAMPLES
HOW	grandly, easily, completely, neatly, gratefully, sadly
WHEN	soon, now, immediately, often, never, usually, early
WHERE	here, there, everywhere, inside, downstairs, above

adverb clause An adverb clause is a subordinate clause that often modifies the verb in the main clause of a complex sentence. It tells *how, when, where, why,* or *under what conditions* the action occurs (pages 198–199).

EXAMPLE **After we won the meet,** we shook hands with our opponents.

An adverb clause can also modify an adjective or an adverb.

EXAMPLES Carson is younger **than I am. [The adverb clause *than I am* modifies the adjective *younger*.]**

Sherry walks faster **than her brother runs. [The adverb clause *than her brother runs* modifies the adverb *faster*.]**

adverb phrase An adverb phrase is a prepositional phrase that modifies a verb, an adjective, or another adverb (page 178).

	ADVERB PHRASES
MODIFIES A VERB	The servers *dress* **like movie characters.**
MODIFIES AN ADJECTIVE	The restaurant is *popular* **with young people.**
MODIFIES AN ADVERB	The restaurant opens *early* **in the morning.**

agreement Agreement is the match between grammatical forms. A verb must agree with its subject. A pronoun must agree with its antecedent (pages 73, 132–133, 181, 206–214).

EXAMPLES Both **ducks** and **swans swim** in this lake. **[subject-verb agreement]**

Jerry and his **brother** visited **their** grandparents. **[pronoun-antecedent agreement]**

antecedent An antecedent is the word a pronoun refers to. The word *antecedent* means "going before" (pages 128–130).

EXAMPLE **Max** likes to read books. **He** particularly likes novels. **[*He* refers to *Max*. *Max* is the antecedent of *He*.]**

apostrophe An apostrophe (') is a punctuation mark used in possessive nouns, possessive indefinite pronouns, and contractions. In contractions an apostrophe shows that one or more letters have been left out (pages 86–88, 261–262).

EXAMPLES Shefali's friends don't always understand her.

Cameron's asking for everyone's help.

appositive An appositive is a noun that is placed next to another noun to identify it or add information about it (pages 89–90).

EXAMPLE James Madison's wife, **Dolley,** was a famous first lady.

appositive phrase An appositive phrase is a group of words that includes an appositive and other words that modify the appositive (pages 89–90).

EXAMPLE Madison, **our fourth president,** held many other offices.

article The words *a, an,* and *the* make up a special group of adjectives called articles. *A* and *an* are called **indefinite articles** because they refer to one of a general group of people, places, things, or ideas. *A* is used before words beginning with a consonant sound. *An* is used before words beginning with a vowel sound (page 147).

EXAMPLES **a** union **a** picture **an** hour **an** easel

The is called the **definite article** because it identifies specific people, places, things, or ideas (page 147).

auxiliary verb *See helping verb.*

B

base form A base form is the simplest form of a word. *Small* is a base form; other forms of *small* are *smaller* and *smallest. Be* is a base form; other forms of *be* are *am, is, are, was, were, being,* and *been* (pages 104, 113–116, 149–150, 163).

C

clause A clause is a group of words that has a subject and a verb (pages 192–201). *See also adjective clause, adverb clause, main clause, noun clause, and subordinate clause.*

closing A closing is a way to end a letter. It begins with a capital letter and is followed by a comma (page 237).

EXAMPLES

Yours truly, Sincerely, With love, Your friend,

collective noun A collective noun names a group of people, animals, or things. It may be singular or plural, depending on the meaning of the sentence (pages 85, 210–211).

EXAMPLES The **team** shares the field with its opponent.

The **team** share their jokes with one another.

colon A colon (:) is a punctuation mark. It's used to introduce a list and to separate the hour and the minutes when you write the time of day. It's also used after the salutation of a business letter (page 257).

EXAMPLES Please buy these fruits**:** apples, bananas, grapes, peaches.

It's now exactly 2**:**43 P.M.

Dear Editor**:**

comma A comma (,) is a punctuation mark that's used to separate items or to set them off from the rest of a sentence (pages 250–255).

EXAMPLES Shoes**,** socks**,** hats**,** and gloves lay in the bottom of the closet.

Tessa's great-grandmother**,** who is ninety**,** loves to travel.

common noun A common noun names any person, place, thing, or idea. Common nouns can be either concrete or abstract (pages 81–82).

EXAMPLE **Children** learn **handwriting** in **school.**

comparative form The comparative form of an adjective compares one person or thing with another. The comparative form of an adverb compares one action with another (pages 149–152, 162–163).

EXAMPLES Is Venezuela **larger** than Peru? **[adjective]**

The pianist arrived **earlier** than the violinist. **[adverb]**

complete predicate *See predicate.*

complete subject *See subject.*

complex sentence A complex sentence has one main clause and one or more subordinate clauses (pages 193–194).

EXAMPLE Since Mariah moved to Springfield, she has made many new friends. **[*She has made many new friends* is a main clause. *Since Mariah moved to Springfield* is a subordinate clause.]**

compound-complex sentence A compound-complex sentence has two or more main clauses and one or more subordinate clauses (page 194).

EXAMPLE Ahmal has never scored a goal, but he plays soccer because he loves the game. **[The two main clauses are *Ahmal has never scored a goal* and *he plays soccer. Because he loves the game* is a subordinate clause.]**

compound noun A compound noun is a noun made of two or more words (pages 82, 85).

EXAMPLES storybook, showcase, bookmark
ice cream, dining room, high school
sister-in-law, sixth-grader, push-ups

compound predicate A compound predicate consists of two or more simple predicates, or verbs, that have the same subject. The verbs may be connected by *and, or, but, both . . . and, either . . . or,* or *neither . . . nor* (page 73).

EXAMPLE Many students **read** the novel *Jane Eyre* and **enjoy** it.

compound sentence A compound sentence is a sentence that contains two or more main clauses joined by a comma and a coordinating conjunction or by a semicolon (pages 75, 181, 183–184, 192).

EXAMPLES **Eudora Welty is a novelist,** but **she also writes essays.** **[A comma and the coordinating conjunction *but* join the two main clauses, *Eudora Welty is a novelist* and *she also writes essays.*]**

Eudora Welty is a novelist; she also writes essays.

compound subject A compound subject consists of two or more simple subjects that have the same predicate. The subjects may be joined by *and, or, both . . . and, either . . . or,* or *neither . . . nor* (pages 73, 181, 213–214).

EXAMPLE **Charlotte Brontë** and **Emily Brontë** were sisters.

compound verb *See compound predicate.*

concrete noun A concrete noun names something you can see or touch (page 82).

EXAMPLE **Julio** wore a **cap** on his **head** and a **scarf** around his **neck.**

conjunction A conjunction is a connecting word. *See coordinating conjunction, correlative conjunction, and subordinating conjunction.*

conjunctive adverb A conjunctive adverb may be used to join the simple sentences in a compound sentence (pages 183–184).

EXAMPLE The school cafeteria sometimes serves Chinese food; **however,** other cafeteria meals are not very tasty.

contraction A contraction is a word formed from one or more words by omitting one or more letters and substituting an apostrophe (pages 87–88, 166, 262).

EXAMPLES We **can't** find the map. **[*Can't* is a contraction of *cannot.*]**

Carmella's visited every state. **[*Carmella's* is a contraction of *Carmella has.*]**

coordinating conjunction A coordinating conjunction is a word used to connect compound parts of a sentence. *And, but, or, nor,* and *for* are coordinating conjunctions. *So* and *yet* are also sometimes used as coordinating conjunctions (pages 181, 213–214).

EXAMPLE Juan **or** Lisa collects the money **and** distributes the tickets.

correlative conjunction Correlative conjunctions are pairs of words used to connect compound parts of a sentence. Correlative conjunctions include *both . . . and, either . . . or, neither . . . nor,* and *not only . . . but also* (pages 181, 213–214).

EXAMPLE Examples of great architecture exist in **both** New York **and** Paris.

D

dash A dash (—) is a punctuation mark. It's usually used in pairs to set off a sudden break or change in thought or speech (page 263).

EXAMPLE Billy Adams—he lives next door—is our team manager.

declarative sentence A declarative sentence makes a statement. It ends with a period (pages 66, 249).

EXAMPLE Edgar Allan Poe wrote suspenseful short stories.

demonstrative adjective A demonstrative adjective points out something and modifies a noun by answering the question *which one?* or *which ones? This, that, these,* and *those* are demonstrative adjectives when they modify nouns (page 147).

EXAMPLES Take **this** umbrella with you. **That** answer is wrong.
Take **these** boots too. **Those** clouds are lovely.

READY REFERENCE

demonstrative pronoun A demonstrative pronoun is a pronoun that points out something. *This, that, these,* and *those* are demonstrative pronouns when they take the place of nouns (pages 136, 148).

EXAMPLES Take **this** with you. **That** is the wrong answer.

Take **these** too. **Those** are lovely clouds.

dependent clause *See subordinate clause.*

direct address Direct address is a name used in speaking directly to a person. Direct address may also be a word or a phrase used in place of a name. Words used in direct address are set off by commas (page 251).

EXAMPLES **Suzy,** please hand me a dish towel.

Here**, my dear mother,** is your birthday present.

Don't do that again**, Samson.**

direct object A direct object receives the action of a verb. It answers the question *whom?* or *what?* after an action verb (pages 98–100).

EXAMPLE The actor rehearsed his **lines** from the play.

direct quotation A direct quotation gives a speaker's exact words (pages 236, 258).

EXAMPLE **"Spiders,"** explained Raul, **"have eight legs."**

double negative A double negative is the use of two negative words to express the same idea. Only one negative word is necessary (pages 166–167).

EXAMPLES

INCORRECT I **don't** have **no** homework.

CORRECT I **don't** have **any** homework.

CORRECT I have **no** homework.

E

end mark An end mark is a punctuation mark used at the end of a sentence. Periods, question marks, and exclamation points are end marks (pages 66–67, 249).

EXAMPLES Tell me a story.

Where have you been?

What a hot day this has been!

essential clause An essential clause is a clause that is necessary to make the meaning of a sentence clear. Don't use commas to set off essential clauses (page 197).

EXAMPLE The girl **who is standing beside the coach** is our best swimmer.

essential phrase An essential phrase is a phrase that is necessary to make the meaning of a sentence clear. Don't use commas to set off essential phrases (page 279).

EXAMPLE The boy **seated at the piano** is Erik.

exclamation point An exclamation point (!) is a punctuation mark used to end a sentence that shows strong feeling (exclamatory). It's also used after strong interjections (pages 67, 249).

EXAMPLES My! What a hot day it is!

exclamatory sentence An exclamatory sentence expresses strong feeling. It ends with an exclamation point (pages 67, 249).

EXAMPLES What a great writer Poe was!

How I enjoy his stories!

F

future perfect tense The future perfect tense of a verb expresses action that will be completed before another future event begins (page 110).

EXAMPLE The production **will have closed** by next week.

future tense The future tense of a verb expresses action that will take place in the future (page 110).

EXAMPLE Mr. and Mrs. Pao **will attend** the performance.

G

gender The gender of a noun may be masculine (male), feminine (female), or neuter (referring to things) (page 130).

EXAMPLES boy (male), woman (female), desk (neuter)

gerund A gerund is a verb form that ends in *-ing* and is used as a noun.

EXAMPLE **Exercising** builds strength, endurance, and flexibility.

gerund phrase A gerund phrase is a group of words that includes a gerund and other words that complete its meaning.

EXAMPLE **Exercising on a bike** is fun for all ages.

H

helping verb A helping verb is a verb that helps the main verb express action or make a statement (pages 104–106, 207).

EXAMPLES Telma **is acting** in another play today. **[*Is* is the helping verb; *acting* is the main verb.]**

Emilio **has written** a story. **[*Has* is the helping verb; *written* is the main verb.]**

hyphen A hyphen (-) is a punctuation mark that's used in some compound words (page 263).

EXAMPLE Mrs. Gilmore's **mother-in-law** is **sixty-two** years old.

I

imperative sentence An imperative sentence gives a command or makes a request. It ends with a period (pages 66, 72, 249).

EXAMPLE Read "The Pit and the Pendulum."

indefinite pronoun An indefinite pronoun is a pronoun that does not refer to a particular person, place, or thing (pages 132–133, 212, 262).

SOME INDEFINITE PRONOUNS

SINGULAR			PLURAL
another	everybody	no one	both
anybody	everyone	nothing	few
anyone	everything	one	many
anything	much	somebody	others
each	neither	someone	several
either	nobody	something	

SINGULAR OR PLURAL all, any, most, none, some

indirect object An indirect object answers the question *to whom?* or *for whom?* or *to what?* or *for what?* an action is done (page 100).

EXAMPLE Friends sent the **actors** flowers.

indirect quotation An indirect quotation does not give a speaker's exact words (page 236).

EXAMPLE Raul said **that spiders have eight legs.**

infinitive An infinitive is formed with the word *to* and the base form of a verb. Infinitives are often used as nouns in sentences.

EXAMPLE **To write** is Alice's ambition.

infinitive phrase An infinitive phrase is a group of words that includes an infinitive and other words that complete its meaning.

EXAMPLE **To write a great novel** was Alice's ambition.

intensive pronoun An intensive pronoun ends with *-self* or *-selves* and is used to draw special attention to a noun or a pronoun already named (page 134).

EXAMPLE Yolanda **herself** repaired the engine.

interjection An interjection is a word or group of words that expresses emotion. It has no grammatical connection to other words in a sentence (pages 185–186, 249).

EXAMPLE **Good grief!** My favorite restaurant has closed.

interrogative pronoun An interrogative pronoun is a pronoun used to introduce an interrogative sentence. *Who, whom, which, what,* and *whose* are interrogative pronouns (pages 135–136).

EXAMPLE **Who** borrowed the book?

interrogative sentence An interrogative sentence asks a question. It ends with a question mark (pages 66, 71–72, 209, 249).

EXAMPLE Did Poe also write poetry?

intransitive verb An intransitive verb is a verb that does not have a direct object (pages 98–99).

EXAMPLE The audience **applauds** loudly.

inverted sentence An inverted sentence is a sentence in which the subject follows the verb (pages 72, 208–209).

EXAMPLES There **are** many **immigrants** among my ancestors.

Across the ocean **sailed** the three **ships.**

irregular verb An irregular verb is a verb whose past and past participle are formed in a way other than by adding *-d* or *-ed* to the base form (pages 113–116).

SOME IRREGULAR VERBS

BASE	PAST	PAST PARTICIPLE
go	went	gone
write	wrote	written
begin	began	begun

italics Italics are printed letters that slant to the right. *This sentence is printed in italic type.* Italics are used for the titles of certain kinds of published works and works of art. In handwriting, underlining is a substitute for italics (page 260).

EXAMPLE On the desk were a copy of *Robinson Crusoe* and several issues of *Time* magazine.

L

linking verb A linking verb connects the subject of a sentence with a noun or an adjective in the predicate (pages 101–102).

EXAMPLE Juana Ortiz **was** the director.

M

main clause A main clause has a subject and a predicate and can stand alone as a sentence (pages 192–194).

EXAMPLE After the storm passed, **the governor surveyed the damage.**

main verb A main verb is the last word in a verb phrase. If a verb stands alone, it's a main verb (pages 104–106, 207).

EXAMPLES The professor is **studying** ancient history.
The professor **studies** ancient history.

N

negative word A negative word expresses the idea of "no" or "not" (pages 166–167).

SOME COMMON NEGATIVE WORDS

barely	no	no one	nowhere
hardly	nobody	not	scarcely
never	none	nothing	

nonessential clause A nonessential clause is a clause that is not necessary to make the meaning of a sentence clear. Use commas to set off nonessential clauses (pages 197, 253).

EXAMPLE Janice**, who is standing beside the coach,** is our best swimmer.

nonessential phrase A nonessential phrase is a phrase that is not necessary to make the meaning of a sentence clear. Use commas to set off nonessential phrases (pages 251, 252).

EXAMPLE Erik**, dreaming of fame,** sits at the piano.

nonrestrictive clause *See nonessential clause.*

nonrestrictive phrase *See nonessential phrase.*

noun A noun is a word that names a person, a place, a thing, or an idea (pages 81–90).

NOUNS

PERSONS	sister, mayor, player, coach, pianist, children
PLACES	park, zoo, lake, school, playground, desert, city
THINGS	magazine, boots, rose, pencil, peach, baseball, car
IDEAS	honesty, truth, democracy, pride, maturity, progress

noun clause A noun clause is a subordinate clause used as a noun (pages 200–201).

EXAMPLE **Whoever plays hockey** wears protective equipment.

number Number is the form of a word that shows whether it's singular or plural (page 130).

EXAMPLES **This book is a mystery.** [singular words]
These books are mysteries. [plural words]

READY REFERENCE

O

object An object is a noun or a pronoun that follows a verb or a preposition. *See direct object, indirect object, and object of a preposition.*

EXAMPLE Mario gave the **horse** a **carrot** for a **treat.** [*Horse* is an indirect object; *carrot* is a direct object; *treat* is the object of a preposition.]

object of a preposition The object of a preposition is the noun or pronoun that ends a prepositional phrase (pages 175, 176–177).

EXAMPLE Hang the painting outside the **auditorium.**

object pronoun *Me, us, you, him, her, it, them,* and *whom* are object pronouns. Object pronouns are used as direct objects, indirect objects, and objects of prepositions (pages 125–127, 176–177).

EXAMPLE Sally gave **her** and **me** a picture of **them.**

P

parentheses Parentheses ( ) are punctuation marks used to set off words that define or explain another word (page 264).

EXAMPLE This container holds one gallon **(**3.785 liters**)**.

participial phrase A participial phrase is a group of words that includes a participle and other words that complete its meaning (page 251).

EXAMPLE **Sitting at the piano,** Erik loses himself in the music.

participle A participle is a verb form that can act as the main verb in a verb phrase or as an adjective to modify a noun or a pronoun (page 251). *See also past participle and present participle.*

EXAMPLES Erik has **played** several pieces on the piano. **[main verb]**

His **playing** skill improves daily. **[adjective]**

passive voice A verb is in the passive voice when the subject receives the action of the verb (pages 111–112).

EXAMPLE That play **was composed** by Thornton Wilder.

past participle A past participle is usually formed by adding *-d* or *-ed* to the base form of a verb. Some past participles are formed irregularly. When the past participle acts as a verb, one or more helping verbs are always used before the past participle. A past participle may also be used as an adjective (pages 104–105, 113–116, 145).

EXAMPLES Kimi has **baked** cookies for us. **[*Baked* is the past participle of *bake*.]**

Mrs. Gonzales had **planted** tomatoes in the spring. **[*Planted* is the past participle of *plant*.]**

Two students have **written** a play. **[*Written* is the past participle of *write*.]**

Erik practices on a **rented** piano. **[*Rented* is an adjective modifying *piano*.]**

past perfect tense The past perfect tense of a verb expresses action that happened before another action or event in the past (page 109).

EXAMPLES The actors **had rehearsed** for many weeks.

We **had** just **arrived** when the play started.

past progressive The past progressive form of a verb expresses action or a condition that was continuing at some time in the past (page 107).

EXAMPLE We **were watching** a scary show.

past tense The past tense of a verb expresses action that already happened (pages 103, 113–116).

EXAMPLE The actors **rehearsed.**

perfect tenses The perfect tenses are the present perfect tense, the past perfect tense, and the future perfect tense. The perfect tenses consist of a form of the verb *have* and a past participle (pages 108–110).

EXAMPLES Lynn **has played** the trumpet for three years. **[present perfect]**

His father **had played** the trumpet as a boy. **[past perfect]**

By the end of high school, Lynn **will have played** the trumpet for seven years. **[future perfect]**

period A period (.) is a punctuation mark used to end a sentence that makes a statement (declarative) or gives a command (imperative). It's also used at the end of many abbreviations (pages 66, 249, 264–266).

EXAMPLES The day was hot and humid**.** **[declarative]**

Bring me some lemonade**.** **[imperative]**

personal pronoun A personal pronoun is a pronoun that refers to people or things. *I, me, you, he, she, him, her, it, we, us, they,* and *them* are personal pronouns (pages 125–126).

EXAMPLE **I** saw **you** with **her** and **him.**

phrase A phrase is a group of words that is used as a single part of speech and does not contain a verb and its subject. *See adjective phrase, adverb phrase, appositive phrase, prepositional phrase, and verb phrase.*

EXAMPLE Three students **were hiking through the woods.**

[*Were hiking* is a verb phrase. *Through the woods* is a prepositional phrase acting as an adverb to modify the verb *were hiking*.]

plural noun A plural noun is a noun that means more than one of something (pages 83–88).

EXAMPLE The **students** and their **parents** heard the **candidates** give their **speeches.**

possessive noun A possessive noun is a noun that shows ownership (pages 86–88, 261).

EXAMPLE **Tiffany's** friend distributed the **children's** toys.

possessive pronoun A possessive pronoun is a pronoun that shows ownership. *My, mine, our, ours, your, yours, his, her, hers, its, their, theirs,* and *whose* are possessive pronouns (pages 131, 262).

predicate The predicate part of a sentence tells what the subject does or has. It can also tell what the subject is or is like. The **complete predicate** includes all the words in the predicate of a sentence. The **simple predicate** is the main word or word group in the complete predicate. The simple predicate is always a verb (pages 68–73).

EXAMPLE Emily Dickinson **wrote hundreds of poems. [The complete predicate is *wrote hundreds of poems.* The simple predicate is *wrote*.]**

predicate adjective A predicate adjective is an adjective that follows a linking verb and modifies the subject of the sentence (pages 101–102, 145).

EXAMPLE Ms. Ortiz is **stern** but **fair.**

predicate noun A predicate noun is a noun that follows a linking verb and renames or identifies the subject of the sentence (pages 101–102).

EXAMPLE Ms. Ortiz is the **director.**

preposition A preposition is a word that relates a noun or a pronoun to another word in a sentence (pages 174–180).

EXAMPLE A boy **with** red hair stood **near** the window.

prepositional phrase A prepositional phrase is a group of words that begins with a preposition and ends with a noun or a pronoun, which is called the **object of the preposition** (pages 174–180, 208–209, 251).

EXAMPLE Hang the painting **outside the new auditorium.**

present participle A present participle is formed by adding *-ing* to the base form of a verb. A helping verb is always used with the present participle when it acts as a verb. (pages 104–105, 145).

EXAMPLES Mr. Omara is **teaching** algebra this year. **[*Teaching* is the present participle of *teach*.]**

The students were **making** decorations. **[*Making* is the present participle of *make*.]**

present perfect tense The present perfect tense of a verb expresses action that happened at an indefinite time in the past (page 108).

EXAMPLE The actors **have rehearsed** for many hours.

READY REFERENCE

present progressive The present progressive form of a verb expresses action or a condition that is continuing in the present (pages 106–107, 110).

EXAMPLE Althea **is finishing** her song.

present tense The present tense of a verb expresses action that happens regularly. It can also express a general truth (pages 103, 110).

EXAMPLE A great actor **wins** awards.

principal parts of a verb The principal parts of a verb are the base form, the present participle, the past, and the past participle. The principal parts are used to form verb tenses (pages 104, 113–116).

BASE	PRESENT PARTICIPLE	PAST	PAST PARTICIPLE
play	playing	played	played
go	going	went	gone

progressive forms Progressive forms of verbs express continuing action. They consist of a form of the verb *be* and a present participle (pages 106–107). *See also past progressive and present progressive.*

EXAMPLES Carla **is leaving,** but Mr. and Mrs. Tsai **are staying.**

Ahmed **was studying,** but his brothers **were playing** basketball.

pronoun A pronoun is a word that takes the place of one or more nouns (pages 125–136).

EXAMPLE Max likes books. **He** particularly enjoys novels. **[The pronoun *He* takes the place of the noun *Max*.]**

proper adjective A proper adjective is an adjective formed from a proper noun. It begins with a capital letter (pages 145–146, 242).

EXAMPLE The **Florida** sun beat down on the **Japanese** tourists.

proper noun A proper noun names a particular person, place, thing, or idea. The first word and all other important words in a proper noun are capitalized (pages 81–82, 238–242).

EXAMPLE Did **Edgar Allan Poe** ever see the **Statue of Liberty**?

Q

question mark A question mark (?) is a punctuation mark used to end a sentence that asks a question (interrogative) (pages 66, 249).

EXAMPLE Do you like green eggs and ham**?**

quotation marks Quotation marks (“ ”) are punctuation marks used to enclose the exact words of a speaker. They're also used for certain titles (pages 258–259).

EXAMPLES **“**A spider,**”** said Sean, **“**has eight legs.**”**

Have you read the story **“**To Build a Fire**”**?

R

reflexive pronoun A reflexive pronoun ends with *-self* or *-selves* and refers to the subject of a sentence. In a sentence with a reflexive pronoun, the action of the verb returns to the subject (page 134).

EXAMPLE Yolanda bought **herself** a book on engine repair.

regular verb A regular verb is a verb whose past and past participle are formed by adding *-d* or *-ed* (page 103).

EXAMPLES I **believed** her.

The twins **have learned** a lesson.

relative pronoun A relative pronoun is a pronoun that may be used to introduce an adjective clause (page 195).

EXAMPLE Divers prefer equipment **that** is lightweight.

restrictive clause *See essential clause.*

restrictive phrase *See essential phrase.*

run-on sentence A run-on sentence is two or more sentences incorrectly written as one sentence (page 75).

EXAMPLES Welty wrote novels, she wrote essays. **[run-on]**
Welty wrote novels she wrote essays. **[run-on]**
Welty wrote novels. She wrote essays. **[correct]**
Welty wrote novels, and she wrote essays. **[correct]**
Welty wrote novels; she wrote essays. **[correct]**

S

salutation A salutation is the greeting in a letter. The first word and any proper nouns in a salutation should be capitalized (pages 237, 255).

EXAMPLES My dear aunt Julia, Dear Professor Higgins:

semicolon A semicolon (;) is a punctuation mark used to join the main clauses of a compound sentence (pages 256–257).

EXAMPLE Kendra weeded the garden**;** Geronimo mowed the lawn.

sentence A sentence is a group of words that expresses a complete thought (pages 66–68).

EXAMPLE Edgar Allan Poe wrote many short stories.

sentence fragment A sentence fragment does not express a complete thought. It may also be missing a subject, a predicate, or both (page 68).

EXAMPLES The poems. **[fragment]**
Lay in Dickinson's bureau for years. **[fragment]**
The poems lay in Dickinson's bureau for years. **[sentence]**

simple predicate *See predicate.*

simple sentence A simple sentence has one subject and one predicate (pages 74, 192).

EXAMPLE Eudora Welty lived in Jackson, Mississippi.

simple subject *See subject.*

singular noun A singular noun is a noun that means only one of something (pages 83–86).

EXAMPLE The **child** and his **father** saw a **rabbit** in the **garden.**

subject The subject part of a sentence names whom or what the sentence is about. The **complete subject** includes all the words in the subject of a sentence. The **simple subject** is the main word or word group in the complete subject (pages 68–73, 206–214).

EXAMPLE **A large ship with many sails** appeared on the horizon. **[The complete subject is *A large ship with many sails.* The simple subject is *ship*.]**

subject pronoun *I, we, you, he, she, it, they,* and *who* are subject pronouns. Subject pronouns are used as subjects and predicate pronouns (pages 125–127).

EXAMPLE **He** and **I** know **who you** are.

subordinate clause A subordinate clause is a group of words that has a subject and a predicate but does not express a complete thought and cannot stand alone as a sentence. A subordinate clause is always combined with a main clause in a sentence (pages 193–201).

EXAMPLE Mariah**, who moved here from Montana,** is very popular.

subordinating conjunction A subordinating conjunction is a word that is used to introduce a subordinate clause (page 199).

SUBORDINATING CONJUNCTIONS

after	because	though	whenever
although	before	till	where
as	if	unless	whereas
as if	since	until	wherever
as though	than	when	while

superlative form The superlative form of an adjective compares one person or thing with several others. The superlative form of an adverb compares one action with several others (pages 149–152, 162–163).

EXAMPLES Is Brazil the **richest** country in South America? **[adjective]**

The drummer arrived **earliest** of all the players. **[adverb]**

T

tense Tense shows the time of the action of a verb (pages 103–110).

EXAMPLES The team often **wins** games. **[present tense]**

The team **won** the game. **[past tense]**

The team **will win** this game. **[future tense]**

transitive verb A transitive verb is an action verb that transfers action to a direct object (pages 98–99).

EXAMPLE The audience **applauds** the actors.

V

verb A verb is a word that expresses action or a state of being (pages 97–116, 206–214).

EXAMPLES Juanita **plays** soccer.

Kwami **is** a good student.

verbal A verbal is a verb form used as a noun, an adjective, or an adverb. Participles, gerunds, and infinitives are verbals.

EXAMPLES The **swimming** instructor showed us **diving** techniques. **[participles used as adjectives]**

Mr. McCoy teaches **swimming** and **diving. [gerunds used as nouns]**

Mr. McCoy taught us **to swim** and **to dive. [infinitives used as nouns]**

verb phrase A verb phrase consists of one or more helping verbs followed by a main verb (page 105).

EXAMPLE Telma **is acting** in another play today. **[*Is* is the helping verb; *acting* is the main verb.]**

voice *See active voice and passive voice.*

USAGE GLOSSARY

This glossary will guide you in choosing between words that are often confused. It will also tell you about certain words and expressions you should avoid when you speak or write for school or business.

A

a, an Use *a* before words that begin with a consonant sound. Use *an* before words that begin with a vowel sound.

EXAMPLES **a** poem, **a** house, **a** yacht, **a** union, **a** one-track mind

an apple, **an** icicle, **an** honor, **an** umbrella, **an** only child

accept, except *Accept* is a verb that means "to receive" or "to agree to." *Except* is a preposition that means "but." *Except* may also be a verb that means "to leave out or exclude."

EXAMPLES Please **accept** this gift.

Will you **accept** our decision?

Everyone will be there **except** you. **[preposition]**

Some students may be **excepted** from taking physical education. **[verb]**

advice, advise *Advice,* a noun, means "an opinion offered as a guide." *Advise,* a verb, means "to give advice."

EXAMPLE Why should I **advise** you when you never accept my **advice**?

affect, effect *Affect* is a verb that means "to cause a change in" or "to influence the emotions of." *Effect* may be a noun or a verb. As a noun, it means "result." As a verb, it means "to bring about or accomplish."

EXAMPLES The mayor's policies have **affected** every city agency.

The mayor's policies have had a positive **effect** on every city agency. **[noun]**

READY REFERENCE

The mayor has **effected** positive changes in every city agency. **[verb]**

ain't *Ain't* is unacceptable in speaking and writing unless you're quoting someone's exact words or writing dialogue. Use *I'm not; you, we,* or *they aren't; he, she,* or *it isn't.*

all ready, already *All ready* means "completely ready." *Already* means "before" or "by this time."

EXAMPLE The band was **all ready** to play its last number, but the fans were **already** leaving the stadium.

all right, alright The spelling *alright* is not acceptable in formal writing. Use *all right.*

EXAMPLE Don't worry; everything will be **all right.**

all together, altogether Use *all together* to mean "in a group." Use *altogether* to mean "completely" or "in all."

EXAMPLES Let's cheer **all together.**

You are being **altogether** silly.

I have three dollars in quarters and two dollars in dimes; that's five dollars **altogether.**

almost, most Don't use *most* in place of *almost.*

EXAMPLE Marty **almost** **[*not* most]** always makes the honor roll.

a lot, alot *A lot* should always be written as two words. It means "a large number or amount." Avoid using *a lot* in formal writing; be specific.

EXAMPLES **A lot** of snow fell last night.

Ten inches of snow fell last night.

altar, alter An *altar* is a raised structure at which religious ceremonies are performed. *Alter* means "to change."

EXAMPLES The bride and groom approached the **altar.**

Mom **altered** my old coat to fit my little sister.

among, between Use *among* to show a relationship in which more than two persons or things are considered as a group.

EXAMPLES The committee will distribute the used clothing **among** the poor families in the community.

There was confusion **among** the players on the field.

In general, use *between* to show a relationship involving two persons or things, to compare one person or thing with an entire group, or to compare more than two items within a single group.

EXAMPLES Mr. and Mrs. Ohara live halfway **between** Seattle and Portland. **[relationship involving two places]**

What was the difference **between** Elvis Presley and other singers of the twentieth century? **[one person compared with a group]**

Emilio could not decide **between** the collie, the cocker spaniel, and the beagle. **[items within a group]**

anxious, eager *Anxious* means "fearful." It is not a synonym for *eager,* which means "filled with enthusiasm."

EXAMPLES Jean was **anxious** about her test results.

Kirk was **eager [*not* anxious]** to visit his cousin.

anyways, anywheres, everywheres, nowheres, somewheres Write these words without the final *s: anyway, anywhere, everywhere, nowhere, somewhere.*

a while, awhile Use *a while* after a preposition. Use *awhile* as an adverb.

EXAMPLES She read for **a while.**

She read **awhile.**

READY REFERENCE

B

bad, badly *Bad* is an adjective; use it before nouns and after linking verbs to modify the subject. *Badly* is an adverb; use it to modify action verbs.

EXAMPLES Clara felt **bad** about the broken vase.

The team performed **badly** in the first half.

bare, bear *Bare* means "naked." A *bear* is an animal.

EXAMPLES Don't expose your **bare** skin to the sun.

There are many **bears** in Yellowstone National Park.

base, bass One meaning of *base* is "a part on which something rests or stands." *Bass* pronounced to rhyme with *face* is a type of voice. When *bass* is pronounced to rhyme with *glass,* it's a kind of fish.

EXAMPLES Who is playing first **base**?

We need a **bass** singer for the part.

We caught several **bass** on our fishing trip.

beside, besides *Beside* means "at the side of" or "next to." *Besides* means "in addition to."

EXAMPLES Katrina sat **beside** her brother at the table.

Besides apples and bananas, the lunchroom serves dry cereal and bagels.

blew, blue *Blue* is the color of a clear sky. *Blew* is the past tense of *blow.*

EXAMPLES She wore a **blue** shirt.

The dead leaves **blew** along the driveway.

boar, bore A *boar* is a male pig. *Bore* means "to tire out with dullness"; it can also mean "a dull person."

EXAMPLES Wild **boars** are common in parts of Africa.

Please don't **bore** me with your silly jokes.

bow When *bow* is pronounced to rhyme with *low,* it means "a knot with two loops" or "an instrument for shooting arrows." When *bow* rhymes with *how,* it means "to bend at the waist."

EXAMPLES Can you tie a good **bow**?

Have you ever shot an arrow with a **bow**?

Actors **bow** at the end of a play.

brake, break As a noun, a *brake* is a device for stopping something or slowing it down. As a verb, *brake* means "to stop or slow down"; its principal parts are *brake, braking, braked,* and *braked.* The noun *break* has several meanings: "the result of breaking," "a fortunate chance," "a short rest." The verb *break* also has many meanings. A few are "to smash or shatter," "to destroy or disrupt," "to force a way through or into," "to surpass or excel." Its principal parts are *break, breaking, broke,* and *broken.*

EXAMPLES Rachel, please put a **brake** on your enthusiasm. **[noun]**

He couldn't **brake** the car in time to avoid the accident. **[verb]**

To fix the **break** in the drainpipe will cost a great deal of money. **[noun]**

Don't **break** my concentration while I'm studying. **[verb]**

bring, take *Bring* means "to carry from a distant place to a closer one." *Take* means "to carry from a nearby place to a more distant one."

EXAMPLES Will you **bring** me some perfume when you return from Paris?

Remember to **take** your passport when you go to Europe.

bust, busted Don't use these words in place of *break, broke, broken,* or *burst.*

EXAMPLES Don't **break** [*not* bust] that vase!

Who **broke** [*not* busted] this vase?

Someone has **broken** [*not* busted] this vase.

The balloon **burst** [*not* busted] with a loud pop.

The child **burst** [*not* busted] into tears.

buy, by *Buy* is a verb. *By* is a preposition.

EXAMPLES I'll **buy** the gift tomorrow.

Stand **by** me.

C

can, may *Can* indicates ability. *May* expresses permission or possibility.

EXAMPLES I **can** tie six kinds of knots.

"You **may** be excused," said Dad. [permission]

Luanna **may** play in the band next year. [possibility]

capital, capitol A *capital* is a city that is the seat of a government. *Capitol,* on the other hand, refers only to a building in which a legislature meets.

EXAMPLES What is the **capital** of Vermont?

The **capitol** has a gold dome.

cent, scent, sent A *cent* is a penny. A *scent* is an odor. *Sent* is the past tense and past participle of *send.*

EXAMPLES I haven't got one **cent** in my pocket.

The **scent** of a skunk is unpleasant.

I **sent** my grandma a birthday card.

choose, chose *Choose* is the base form; *chose* is the past tense. The principal parts are *choose, choosing, chose,* and *chosen.*

EXAMPLES Please **choose** a poem to recite in class.

Brian **chose** to recite a poem by Emily Dickinson.

cite, sight, site *Cite* means "to quote an authority." *Sight* is the act of seeing or the ability to see; it can also mean "to see" and "something seen." A *site* is a location; it also means "to place or locate."

EXAMPLES Consuela **cited** three sources of information in her report.

My **sight** is perfect.

The board of education has chosen a **site** for the new high school.

clothes, cloths *Clothes* are what you wear. *Cloths* are pieces of fabric.

EXAMPLES Please hang all your **clothes** in your closet.

Use these **cloths** to wash the car.

coarse, course *Coarse* means "rough." *Course* can mean "a school subject," "a path or way," "order or development," or "part of a meal." *Course* is also used in the phrase *of course.*

EXAMPLES To begin, I'll need some **coarse** sandpaper.

I'd like to take a photography **course.**

The hikers chose a difficult **course** through the mountains.

complement, complementary; compliment, complimentary As a noun, *complement* means "something that completes"; as a verb, it means "to complete." As a noun, *compliment* means "a flattering remark"; as a verb, it means "to praise." *Complementary* and *complimentary* are the adjective forms of the words.

EXAMPLES This flowered scarf will be the perfect **complement** for your outfit. **[noun]**

This flowered scarf **complements** your outfit perfectly. **[verb]**

Phyllis received many **compliments** on her speech. **[noun]**

Many people **complimented** Phyllis on her speech. **[verb]**

consul; council, councilor; counsel, counselor A *consul* is a government official living in a foreign city to protect his or her country's interests and citizens. A *council* is a group of people gathered for the purpose of giving advice. A *councilor* is one who serves on a council. As a noun, *counsel* means "advice." As a verb, *counsel* means "to give advice." A *counselor* is one who gives counsel.

EXAMPLES The **consul** protested to the foreign government about the treatment of her fellow citizens.

The city **council** met to discuss the lack of parking facilities at the sports field.

The defendant received **counsel** from his attorney. **[noun]**

The attorney **counseled** his client to plead innocent. **[verb]**

could of, might of, must of, should of, would of After the words *could, might, must, should,* and *would,* use the helping verb *have* or its contraction, *'ve,* not the word *of.*

EXAMPLES **Could** you **have** prevented the accident?

You **might have** swerved to avoid the other car.

You **must have** seen it coming.

I **should've** warned you.

D

dear, deer *Dear* is a word of affection and is used to begin a letter. It can also mean "expensive." A *deer* is an animal.

EXAMPLES Talia is my **dear** friend.

We saw a **deer** at the edge of the woods.

desert, dessert *Desert* has two meanings. As a noun, it means "dry, arid land" and is stressed on the first syllable. As a verb, it means "to leave" or "to abandon" and is stressed on the second syllable. A *dessert* is something sweet eaten after a meal.

EXAMPLES This photograph shows a sandstorm in the **desert.** **[noun]**

I won't **desert** you in your time of need. **[verb]**

Strawberry shortcake was served for **dessert.**

diner, dinner A *diner* is someone who dines or a place to eat. A *dinner* is a meal.

EXAMPLES The **diners** at the corner **diner** enjoy the friendly atmosphere.

Dinner will be served at eight.

doe, dough A *doe* is a female deer. *Dough* is a mixture of flour and a liquid.

EXAMPLES A **doe** and a stag were visible among the trees.

Knead the **dough** for three minutes.

doesn't, don't *Doesn't* is a contraction of *does not.* It is used with *he, she, it,* and all singular nouns. *Don't* is a contraction of *do not.* It is used with *I, you, we, they,* and all plural nouns.

EXAMPLES She **doesn't** know the answer to your question.

The twins **don't** like broccoli.

E

eye, I An *eye* is what you see with; it's also a small opening in a needle. *I* is a personal pronoun.

EXAMPLE **I** have something in my **eye.**

F

fewer, less Use *fewer* with nouns that can be counted. Use *less* with nouns that can't be counted.

EXAMPLES There are **fewer** students in my English class than in my math class.

I used **less** sugar than the recipe recommended.

flour, flower *Flour* is used to bake bread. A *flower* grows in a garden.

EXAMPLES Sift two cups of **flour** into a bowl.

A daisy is a **flower.**

for, four *For* is a preposition. *Four* is a number.

EXAMPLES Wait **for** me.

I have **four** grandparents.

formally, formerly *Formally* is the adverb form of *formal,* which has several meanings: "according to custom, rule, or etiquette," "requiring special ceremony or fancy clothing," "official." *Formerly* means "previously."

EXAMPLES The class officers will be **formally** installed on Thursday.

Mrs. Johnson was **formerly** Miss Malone.

G

go, say Don't use forms of *go* in place of forms of *say*.

EXAMPLES I tell her the answer, and she **says [*not* goes]**, "I don't believe you."

I told her the news, and she **said [*not* went]**, "Are you serious?"

good, well *Good* is an adjective; use it before nouns and after linking verbs to modify the subject. *Well* is an adverb; use it to modify action verbs. *Well* may also be an adjective meaning "in good health."

EXAMPLES You look **good** in that costume.

Joby plays the piano **well.**

You're looking **well** in spite of your cold.

grate, great A *grate* is a framework of bars set over an opening. *Grate* also means "to shred by rubbing against a rough surface." *Great* means "wonderful" or "large."

EXAMPLES The little girl dropped her lollipop through the **grate.**

Will you **grate** this cheese for me?

You did a **great** job!

H

had of Don't use *of* between *had* and a past participle.

EXAMPLE I wish I **had known [*not* had of known]** about this sooner.

had ought, hadn't ought, shouldn't ought *Ought* never needs a helping verb. Use *ought* by itself.

EXAMPLES You **ought** to win the match easily.

You **ought** not to blame yourself. *or* You **shouldn't** blame yourself.

hardly, scarcely *Hardly* and *scarcely* have negative meanings. They shouldn't be used with other negative words, like *not* or the contraction *n't*, to express the same idea.

EXAMPLES I **can** [*not* can't] **hardly** lift this box.

The driver **could** [*not* couldn't] **scarcely** see through the thick fog.

he, she, it, they Don't use a pronoun subject immediately after a noun subject, as in *The **girls they** baked the cookies.* Omit the unnecessary pronoun: *The **girls** baked the cookies.*

hear, here *Hear* is a verb meaning "to be aware of sound by means of the ear." *Here* is an adverb meaning "in or at this place."

EXAMPLES I can **hear** you perfectly well.

Please put your books **here.**

how come In formal speech and writing, use *why* instead of *how come.*

EXAMPLE **Why** weren't you at the meeting? [*not* How come you weren't at the meeting?]

I

in, into, in to Use *in* to mean "inside" or "within." Use *into* to show movement from the outside to a point within. Don't write *into* when you mean *in to.*

EXAMPLES Jeanine was sitting outdoors **in** a lawn chair.

When it got too hot, she went **into** the house.

She went **in to** get out of the heat.

its, it's *Its* is the possessive form of *it. It's* is a contraction of *it is* or *it has.*

EXAMPLES The dishwasher has finished **its** cycle.

It's [It is] raining again.

It's [It has] been a pleasure to meet you, Ms. Donatello.

K

kind of, sort of Don't use these expressions as adverbs. Use *somewhat* or *rather* instead.

EXAMPLE We were **rather** sorry to see him go. [*not* We were kind of sorry to see him go.]

knead, need *Knead* means "to mix or work into a uniform mass." As a noun, a *need* is a requirement. As a verb, *need* means "to require."

EXAMPLES **Knead** the clay to make it soft.

I **need** a new jacket.

knew, new *Knew* is the past tense of *know. New* means "unused" or "unfamiliar."

EXAMPLES I **knew** the answer.

I need a **new** pencil.

There's a **new** student in our class.

knight, night A *knight* was a warrior of the Middle Ages. *Night* is the time of day during which it is dark.

EXAMPLES A handsome **knight** rescued the fair maiden.

Night fell, and the moon rose.

L

lay, lie *Lay* means "to put" or "to place." Its principal parts are *lay, laying, laid,* and *laid.* Forms of *lay* are usually followed by a direct object. *Lie* means "to recline" or "to be positioned." Its principal parts are *lie, lying, lay,* and *lain.* Forms of *lie* are never followed by a direct object.

EXAMPLES **Lay** your coat on the bed.

The children are **laying** their beach towels in the sun to dry.

Dad **laid** the baby in her crib.

Myrna had **laid** the book beside her purse.

Lie down for a few minutes.

The lake **lies** to the north.

The dog is **lying** on the back porch.

This morning I **lay** in bed listening to the birds.

You have **lain** on the couch for an hour.

lead, led As a noun, *lead* has two pronunciations and several meanings. When it's pronounced to rhyme with *head,* it means "a metallic element." When it's pronounced to rhyme with *bead,* it can mean "position of being in first place in a race or contest," "example," "clue," "leash," or "the main role in a play."

EXAMPLES **Lead** is no longer allowed as an ingredient in paint.

Jason took the **lead** as the runners entered the stadium.

Follow my **lead.**

The detective had no **leads** in the case.

Only dogs on **leads** are permitted in the park.

Who will win the **lead** in the play?

As a verb, *lead* means "to show the way," "to guide or conduct," "to be first." Its principal parts are *lead, leading, led,* and *led.*

EXAMPLES Ms. Bachman **leads** the orchestra.

The trainer was **leading** the horse around the track.

An usher **led** us to our seats.

Gray has **led** the league in hitting for two years.

learn, teach *Learn* means "to receive knowledge." *Teach* means "to give knowledge."

EXAMPLES Manny **learned** to play the piano at the age of six.

Ms. Guerrero **teaches** American history.

leave, let *Leave* means "to go away." *Let* means "to allow to."

EXAMPLES I'll miss you when you **leave.**

Let me help you with those heavy bags.

like, as, as if, as though *Like* can be a verb or a preposition. It should not be used as a subordinating conjunction. Use *as*, *as if*, or *as though* to introduce a subordinate clause.

EXAMPLES I **like** piano music. **[verb]**

Teresa plays the piano **like** a professional. **[preposition]**

Moira plays **as** **[*not* like]** her teacher taught her to play.

He looked at me **as if** **[*not* like]** he'd never seen me before.

loose, lose The adjective *loose* means "free," "not firmly attached," or "not fitting tightly." The verb *lose* means "to misplace" or "to fail to win."

EXAMPLES Don't **lose** that **loose** button on your shirt.

If we **lose** this game, we'll be out of the tournament.

M

mail, male *Mail* is what turns up in your mailbox. *Mail* also means "send." A *male* is a boy or a man.

EXAMPLES We received four pieces of **mail** today.

Sunny **mailed** a gift to her aunt Netta.

The **males** in the chorus wore red ties.

main, mane *Main* means "most important." A *mane* is the long hair on the neck of certain animals.

EXAMPLES What is your **main** job around the house?

The horse's **mane** was braided with colorful ribbons.

many, much Use *many* with nouns that can be counted. Use *much* with nouns that can't be counted.

EXAMPLES **Many** of the events are entertaining.

Much of the money goes to charity.

meat, meet *Meat* is food from an animal. Some meanings of *meet* are "to come face to face with," "to make the acquaintance of," and "to keep an appointment."

EXAMPLES Some people don't eat **meat.**

Meet me at the library at three o'clock.

minute The word *minute* (min´it) means "sixty seconds" or "a short period of time." The word *minute* (mī nōōt´) means "very small."

EXAMPLES I'll be with you in a **minute.**

Don't bother me with **minute** details.

O

object *Object* is stressed on the first syllable when it means "a thing." *Object* is stressed on the second syllable when it means "oppose."

EXAMPLES Have you ever seen an unidentified flying **object**?

Mom **objected** to the proposal.

of Don't use *of* after the prepositions *off, inside,* and *outside.*

EXAMPLES He jumped **off** [*not* **off of**] the diving board.

The cat found a mouse **inside** [*not* **inside of**] the garage.

Outside [*not* **outside of**] the school, there is an old-fashioned drinking fountain.

off Don't use *off* in place of *from.*

EXAMPLE I'll borrow some money **from** [*not* **off**] my brother.

ought to of Don't use *of* in place of *have* after *ought to.*

EXAMPLE You **ought to have** [*not* **ought to of**] known better.

P

pair, pare, pear A *pair* is two. *Pare* means "to peel." A *pear* is a fruit.

EXAMPLES I bought a new **pair** of socks.

Pare the potatoes and cut them in quarters.

Would you like a **pear** or a banana?

passed, past *Passed* is the past tense and the past participle of the verb *pass. Past* can be an adjective, a preposition, an adverb, or a noun.

EXAMPLES We **passed** your house on the way to school. [verb]

The **past** week has been a busy one for me. [adjective]

We drove **past** your house. [preposition]

At what time did you drive **past**? [adverb]

I love Great-grandma's stories about the **past.** [noun]

pause, paws A *pause* is a short space of time. *Pause* also means "to wait for a short time." *Paws* are animal feet.

EXAMPLES We will **pause** now to reflect for a moment.

I wiped the dog's muddy **paws.**

peace, piece *Peace* means "calmness" or "the absence of conflict." A *piece* is a part of something.

EXAMPLES We enjoy the **peace** of the countryside.

The two nations have finally made **peace.**

May I have another **piece** of pie?

plain, plane *Plain* means "not fancy," "clear," or "a large area of flat land." A *plane* is an airplane or a device for smoothing wood; it can also mean "a two-dimensional figure."

EXAMPLES He wore a **plain** blue tie.

The solution is perfectly **plain** to me.

Buffalo once roamed the **plains.**

We took a **plane** to Chicago.

Jeff used a **plane** to smooth the rough wood.

How do you find the area of a **plane** with four equal sides?

precede, proceed *Precede* means "to go before" or "to come before." *Proceed* means "to continue" or "to move along."

EXAMPLE Our band **preceded** the decorated floats as the parade **proceeded** through town.

principal, principle As a noun, *principal* means "head of a school." As an adjective, *principal* means "main" or "chief." *Principle* is a noun meaning "basic truth or belief" or "rule of conduct."

EXAMPLES Mr. Washington, our **principal,** will speak at the morning assembly. **[noun]**

What was your **principal** reason for joining the club? **[adjective]**

The **principle** of fair play is important in sports.

Q

quiet, quit, quite The adjective *quiet* means "silent" or "motionless." The verb *quit* means "to stop" or "to give up or resign." The adverb *quite* means "very" or "completely."

EXAMPLES Please be **quiet** so I can think.

Shirelle has **quit** the swim team.

We were **quite** sorry to lose her.

raise, rise *Raise* means "to cause to move upward." It can also mean "to breed or grow" and "to bring up or rear." Its principal parts are *raise, raising, raised,* and *raised.* Forms of *raise* are usually followed by a direct object. *Rise* means "to move upward." Its principal parts are *rise, rising, rose,* and *risen.* Forms of *rise* are never followed by a direct object.

EXAMPLES **Raise** your hand if you know the answer.

My uncle is **raising** chickens.

Grandma and Grandpa Schwartz **raised** nine children.

Steam **rises** from boiling water.

The sun is **rising.**

The children **rose** from their seats when the principal entered the room.

In a short time, Loretta had **risen** to the rank of captain.

rap, wrap *Rap* means "to knock." *Wrap* means "to cover."

EXAMPLES **Rap** on the door.

Wrap the presents.

read, reed *Read* means "to understand the meaning of something written" or "to speak aloud something that is written or printed." A *reed* is a stalk of tall grass.

EXAMPLES Will you **read** Jimmy a story?

We found a frog in the **reeds** beside the lake.

real, really *Real* is an adjective; use it before nouns and after linking verbs to modify the subject. *Really* is an adverb; use it to modify action verbs, adjectives, and other adverbs.

EXAMPLES Winona has **real** musical talent.

She is **really** talented.

real, reel *Real* means "actual." A *reel* is a spool to wind something on, such as a fishing line.

EXAMPLES I have a **real** four-leaf clover.

My dad bought me a new fishing **reel.**

reason is because Don't use *because* after *reason is.* Use *that* after *reason is,* or use *because* alone.

EXAMPLES The **reason** I'm tired is **that** I didn't sleep well last night.

I'm tired **because** I didn't sleep well last night.

row When *row* is pronounced to rhyme with *low,* it means "a series of things arranged in a line" or "to move a boat by using oars." When *row* is pronounced to rhyme with *how,* it means "a noisy quarrel."

EXAMPLES We sat in the last **row** of the theater.

Let's **row** across the lake.

My sister and I had a serious **row** yesterday, but today we've forgotten about it.

S

sail, sale A *sail* is part of a boat. It also means "to travel in a boat." A *sale* is a transfer of ownership in exchange for money.

EXAMPLES As the boat **sails** away, the crew raise the **sails.**

The **sale** of the house was completed on Friday.

sea, see A *sea* is a body of water. *See* means "to be aware of with the eyes."

EXAMPLES The **sea** is rough today.

I can **see** you.

set, sit *Set* means "to place" or "to put." Its principal parts are *set, setting, set,* and *set.* Forms of *set* are usually followed by a direct object. *Sit* means "to place oneself in a seated position." Its principal parts are *sit, sitting, sat,* and *sat.* Forms of *sit* are not followed by a direct object.

EXAMPLES Lani **set** the pots on the stove.

The children **sit** quietly at the table.

sew, sow *Sew* means "to work with needle and thread." When *sow* is pronounced to rhyme with *how,* it means "a female pig." When *sow* is pronounced to rhyme with *low,* it means "to plant."

EXAMPLES Can you **sew** a button on a shirt?

The **sow** has five piglets.

Some farmers **sow** corn in their fields.

shined, shone, shown Both *shined* and *shone* are past tense forms and past participles of *shine.* Use *shined* when you mean "polished"; use *shone* in all other instances.

EXAMPLES Clete **shined** his shoes.

The sun **shone** brightly.

Her face **shone** with happiness.

Shown is the past participle of *show;* its principal parts are *show, showing, showed,* and *shown.*

EXAMPLES You **showed** me these photographs yesterday.

You have **shown** me these photographs before.

some, somewhat Don't use *some* as an adverb in place of *somewhat.*

EXAMPLE The team has improved **somewhat** [*not* some] since last season.

son, sun A *son* is a male child. A *sun* is a star.

EXAMPLES Kino is Mr. and Mrs. Akawa's **son.**

Our **sun** is 93 million miles away.

stationary, stationery *Stationary* means "fixed" or "unmoving." *Stationery* is writing paper.

EXAMPLES This classroom has **stationary** desks.

Rhonda likes to write letters on pretty **stationery.**

sure, surely *Sure* is an adjective; use it before nouns and after linking verbs to modify the subject. *Surely* is an adverb; use it to modify action verbs, adjectives, and other adverbs.

EXAMPLES Are you **sure** about that answer?

You are **surely** smart.

T

tail, tale A *tail* is what a dog wags. A *tale* is a story.

EXAMPLES The dog's **tail** curled over its back.

Everyone knows the **tale** of Goldilocks and the three bears.

tear When *tear* is pronounced to rhyme with *ear,* it's a drop of fluid from the eye. When *tear* is pronounced to rhyme with *bear,* it means "a rip" or "to rip."

EXAMPLES A **tear** fell from the child's eye.

Tear this rag in half.

than, then *Than* is a conjunction used to introduce the second part of a comparison. *Then* is an adverb meaning "at that time."

EXAMPLES LaTrisha is taller **than** LaToya.

My grandmother was a young girl **then.**

that, which, who *That* may refer to people or things. *Which* refers only to things. *Who* refers only to people.

EXAMPLES The poet **that** wrote *Leaves of Grass* is Walt Whitman.

I have already seen the movie **that** is playing at the Palace.

The new play, **which** closed after a week, received poor reviews.

Students **who** do well on the test will receive scholarships.

that there, this here Don't use *there* or *here* after *that, this, those,* or *these.*

EXAMPLES I can't decide whether to read **this [*not* this here]** magazine or **that [*not* that there]** book.

Fold **these [*not* these here]** towels and hang **those [*not* those there]** shirts in the closet.

their, there, they're *Their* is a possessive form of *they;* it's used to modify nouns. *There* means "in or at that place." *They're* is a contraction of *they are.*

EXAMPLES A hurricane damaged **their** house.

Put your books **there.**

They're our next-door neighbors.

theirs, there's *Theirs* is a possessive form of *they* used as a pronoun. *There's* is a contraction of *there is* or *there has.*

EXAMPLES **Theirs** is the white house with the green shutters.

There's [There is] your friend Chad.

There's [There has] been an accident.

them Don't use *them* as an adjective in place of *those.*

EXAMPLE I'll take one of **those [*not* them]** hamburgers.

this kind, these kinds Use the singular forms *this* and *that* with the singular nouns *kind, sort,* and *type.* Use the plural forms *these* and *those* with the plural nouns *kinds, sorts,* and *types.*

EXAMPLES Use **this kind** of lightbulb in your lamp.

Do you like **these kinds** of lamps?

READY REFERENCE

Many Pakistani restaurants serve **that sort** of food.

Those sorts of foods are nutritious.

This type of dog makes a good pet.

These types of dogs are good with children.

thorough, through *Thorough* means "complete." *Through* is a preposition meaning "into at one side and out at another."

EXAMPLES We gave the bedrooms a **thorough** cleaning.

A breeze blew **through** the house.

threw, through *Threw* is the past tense of *throw. Through* is a preposition meaning "into at one side and out at another." *Through* can also mean "finished."

EXAMPLES Lacey **threw** the ball.

Ira walked **through** the room.

At last I'm **through** with my homework.

to, too, two *To* means "in the direction of"; it is also part of the infinitive form of a verb. *Too* means "very" or "also." *Two* is the number after *one.*

EXAMPLES Jaleela walks **to** school.

She likes **to** study.

The soup is **too** salty.

May I go **too**?

We have **two** kittens.

try and Use *try to.*

EXAMPLE Please **try to** [*not* **try and**] be on time.

U

unless, without Don't use *without* in place of *unless.*

EXAMPLE **Unless** [*not* **Without**] I clean my room, I can't go to the mall.

used to, use to The correct form is *used to.*

EXAMPLE We **used to [*not* use to]** live in Cleveland, Ohio.

W

waist, waste Your *waist* is where you wear your belt. As a noun, *waste* means "careless or unnecessary spending" or "trash." As a verb, it means "to spend or use carelessly or unnecessarily."

EXAMPLES She tied a colorful scarf around her **waist.**

Buying that computer game was a **waste** of money.

Put your **waste** in the dumpster.

Don't **waste** time worrying.

wait, weight *Wait* means "to stay or remain." *Weight* is a measurement.

EXAMPLES **Wait** right here.

Her **weight** is 110 pounds.

wait for, wait on *Wait for* means "to remain in a place looking forward to something expected." *Wait on* means "to act as a server."

EXAMPLES **Wait for** me at the bus stop.

Nat and Tammy **wait on** diners at The Golden Griddle.

way, ways Use *way,* not *ways,* in referring to distance.

EXAMPLE It's a long **way [*not* ways]** to Tipperary.

weak, week *Weak* means "feeble" or "not strong." A *week* is seven days.

EXAMPLE She felt **weak** for a **week** after the operation.

READY REFERENCE

weather, whether *Weather* is the condition of the atmosphere. *Whether* means "if"; it is also used to introduce the first of two choices.

EXAMPLES The **weather** in Portland is mild and rainy.

Tell me **whether** you can go.

I can't decide **whether** to go or stay.

when, where Don't use *when* or *where* incorrectly in writing a definition.

EXAMPLES A compliment is a flattering remark. **[*not* A compliment is when you make a flattering remark.]**

Spelunking is the hobby of exploring caves. **[*not* Spelunking is where you explore caves.]**

where Don't use *where* in place of *that.*

EXAMPLE I see **that [*not* where]** the Yankees are in first place in their division.

where . . . at Don't use *at* after *where.*

EXAMPLE **Where** is your mother? **[*not* Where is your mother at?]**

who's, whose *Who's* is a contraction of *who is* or *who has. Whose* is the possessive form of *who.*

EXAMPLES **Who's [Who is]** conducting the orchestra?

Who's [Who has] read this book?

Whose umbrella is this?

wind When *wind* has a short-*i* sound, it means "moving air." When *wind* has a long-*i* sound, it means "to wrap around."

EXAMPLES The **wind** is strong today.

Wind the bandage around your ankle.

wood, would *Wood* comes from trees. *Would* is a helping verb.

EXAMPLE **Would** you prefer a **wood** bookcase or a metal one?

wound When *wound* is pronounced to rhyme with *sound,* it is the past tense of *wind.* The word *wound* (wo͞ond) means "an injury in which the skin is broken."

EXAMPLE I **wound** the bandage around my ankle to cover the **wound.**

Y

your, you're *Your* is a possessive form of *you. You're* is a contraction of *you are.*

EXAMPLES **Your** arguments are convincing.

You're doing a fine job.

ABBREVIATIONS

An abbreviation is a short way to write a word or a group of words. Abbreviations should be used sparingly in formal writing except for a few that are actually more appropriate than their longer forms. These are *Mr., Mrs.,* and *Dr. (doctor)* before names, *A.M.* and *P.M.*, and *B.C.* and *A.D.*

Some abbreviations are written with capital letters and periods, and some with capital letters and no periods; some are written with lowercase letters and periods, and some with lowercase letters and no periods. A few may be written in any one of these four ways and still be acceptable. For example, to abbreviate *miles per hour,* you may write *MPH, M.P.H., mph,* or *m.p.h.*

Some abbreviations may be spelled in more than one way. For example, *Tuesday* may be abbreviated *Tues.* or *Tue. Thursday* may be written *Thurs.* or *Thu.* In the following lists, only the most common way of writing each abbreviation is given.

When you need information about an abbreviation, consult a dictionary. Some dictionaries list abbreviations in a special section in the back. Others list them in the main part of the book.

MONTHS

Jan.	January	none	July
Feb.	February	Aug.	August
Mar.	March	Sept.	September
Apr.	April	Oct.	October
none	May	Nov.	November
none	June	Dec.	December

DAYS

Sun.	Sunday	Thurs.	Thursday
Mon.	Monday	Fri.	Friday
Tues.	Tuesday	Sat.	Saturday
Wed.	Wednesday		

TIME AND DIRECTION

CDT	central daylight time
CST	central standard time
DST	daylight saving time
EDT	eastern daylight time
EST	eastern standard time
MDT	mountain daylight time
MST	mountain standard time
PDT	Pacific daylight time
PST	Pacific standard time
ST	standard time
NE	northeast
NW	northwest
SE	southeast
SW	southwest
A.D.	in the year of the Lord (Latin *anno Domini*)
B.C.	before Christ
B.C.E.	before the common era
C.E.	common era
A.M.	before noon (Latin *ante meridiem*)
P.M.	after noon (Latin *post meridiem*)

MEASUREMENT

The same abbreviation is used for both the singular and the plural meaning of measurements. Therefore, *ft.* stands for both *foot* and *feet,* and *in.* stands for both *inch* and *inches.* Note that abbreviations of metric measurements are commonly written without periods. U.S. measurements, on the other hand, are usually written with periods.

Metric System

Mass and Weight

t	metric ton
kg	kilogram
g	gram
cg	centigram
mg	milligram

Capacity

kl	kiloliter
l	liter
cl	centiliter
ml	milliliter

Length

km	kilometer
m	meter
cm	centimeter
mm	millimeter

U.S. Weights and Measures

Weight

wt.	weight
lb.	pound
oz.	ounce

Capacity

gal.	gallon
qt.	quart
pt.	pint
c.	cup
tbsp.	tablespoon
tsp.	teaspoon
fl. oz.	fluid ounce

Length

mi.	mile
rd.	rod
yd.	yard
ft.	foot
in.	inch

MISCELLANEOUS MEASUREMENTS

p.s.i.	pounds per square inch
MPH	miles per hour
MPG	miles per gallon
rpm	revolutions per minute
C	Celsius, centigrade
F	Fahrenheit
K	Kelvin
kn	knot

COMPUTER AND INTERNET

CPU	central processing unit
CRT	cathode ray tube
DOS	disk operating system
e-mail	electronic mail
GB	gigabyte
URL	uniform resource locator
DVD	digital video disc
d.p.i.	dots per inch
WWW	World Wide Web
ISP	internet service provider
DNS	domain name system

ADDITIONAL ABBREVIATIONS

ac	alternating current
dc	direct current
AM	amplitude modulation
FM	frequency modulation
ASAP	as soon as possible
e.g.	for example (Latin *exempli gratia*)
etc.	and others, and so forth (Latin *et cetera*)
i.e.	that is (Latin *id est*)
Inc.	incorporated
ISBN	International Standard Book Number

lc	lowercase
misc.	miscellaneous
p.	page
pp.	pages
R.S.V.P.	please reply (French *répondez s'il vous plaît*)
SOS	international distress signal
TM	trademark
uc	uppercase
vs.	versus
w/o	without

UNITED STATES (U.S.)

In most cases, state names and street addresses should be spelled out. The postal abbreviations in the following list should be used with ZIP codes in addressing envelopes. They may also be used with ZIP codes for return addresses and inside addresses in business letters. The traditional state abbreviations are seldom used nowadays, but occasionally it's helpful to know them.

State	Traditional	Postal
Alabama	Ala.	AL
Alaska	none	AK
Arizona	Ariz.	AZ
Arkansas	Ark.	AR
California	Calif.	CA
Colorado	Colo.	CO
Connecticut	Conn.	CT
Delaware	Del.	DE
District of Columbia	D.C.	DC
Florida	Fla.	FL
Georgia	Ga.	GA
Hawaii	none	HI
Idaho	none	ID
Illinois	Ill.	IL
Indiana	Ind.	IN

Iowa	none	IA
Kansas	Kans.	KS
Kentucky	Ky.	KY
Louisiana	La.	LA
Maine	none	ME
Maryland	Md.	MD
Massachusetts	Mass.	MA
Michigan	Mich.	MI
Minnesota	Minn.	MN
Mississippi	Miss.	MS
Missouri	Mo.	MO
Montana	Mont.	MT
Nebraska	Nebr.	NE
Nevada	Nev.	NV
New Hampshire	N.H.	NH
New Jersey	N.J.	NJ
New Mexico	N. Mex.	NM
New York	N.Y.	NY
North Carolina	N.C.	NC
North Dakota	N. Dak.	ND
Ohio	none	OH
Oklahoma	Okla.	OK
Oregon	Oreg.	OR
Pennsylvania	Pa.	PA
Rhode Island	R.I.	RI
South Carolina	S.C.	SC
South Dakota	S. Dak.	SD
Tennessee	Tenn.	TN
Texas	Tex.	TX
Utah	none	UT
Vermont	Vt.	VT
Virginia	Va.	VA
Washington	Wash.	WA
West Virginia	W. Va.	WV
Wisconsin	Wis.	WI
Wyoming	Wyo.	WY

Part Two

Grammar, Usage, and Mechanics

Your first discipline is your vocabulary; then your grammar and your punctuation. . . .Then you add rhyme and meter. And your delight is in that power.

—Robert Frost

PHOTO: Mark Steinmetz; (bkgd)Ryan McVay/Photodisc/Getty Images.

Chapter 1

Subjects, Predicates, and Sentences

PRETEST Kinds of Sentences

Write declarative, interrogative, imperative, *or* exclamatory *to identify each sentence.*

1. Fencing is an old sport.
2. Will a fencing team compete in the Olympics?
3. The character of Zorro was known for fencing.
4. What a fast moving sport fencing is!
5. Wear a mask when you fence.

PRETEST Sentences and Sentence Fragments

Write sentence *or* fragment *for each item. Rewrite each fragment to make it a sentence.*

6. In the spring and summer.
7. The back of the quarter is getting fifty new designs.

8. George Washington is still pictured on the quarter.
9. Collected coins for many years.
10. My sister works in a bank.
11. Enjoys her work very much.
12. I have a checking and a savings account at the bank.
13. Baby-sat every summer.
14. Florida and South Carolina.
15. I read many books during the trip.

PRETEST Subjects and Predicates

Write each sentence. Underline the simple subjects once and the simple predicates twice.

16. The train left twenty minutes ago.
17. The girls practice shooting baskets every afternoon.
18. Last week George passed his driving test.
19. Put the dishes on the shelf.
20. Did you find your key?
21. Mom and Dad came to the concert.
22. Over the hill ran the fox.
23. Locate and label your folder.
24. Do you play tennis, softball, or soccer?
25. There is the jacket.

PRETEST Simple, Compound, and Run-on Sentences

Write simple, compound, *or* run-on *to identify each numbered item. If an item is a run-on, rewrite it correctly.*

26. Eighteen-year-old residents can apply for American citizenship.
27. Applicants must have lived in the United States for at least five years, and they must understand English.
28. Every year many people come to the United States.
29. Years ago, large numbers of people arrived at Ellis Island and went through screening there.

30. Many immigrants wanted a better life, or they were looking for greater freedom.
31. Ellis Island closed in 1954 it reopened in 1990.
32. It reopened as a museum and tells the story of immigrants.
33. The Statue of Liberty is in New York Harbor, and it still welcomes visitors to the United States.
34. My grandparents came from Mexico now they are citizens.
35. They went through hardships, but they live happily here.

1.1 KINDS OF SENTENCES

A **sentence** is a group of words that expresses a complete thought.

Different kinds of sentences have different purposes. A sentence can make a statement, ask a question, or give a command. A sentence can also express strong feeling. All sentences begin with a capital letter and end with a punctuation mark. The punctuation mark depends on the purpose of the sentence.

A **declarative sentence** makes a statement. It ends with a period.

EXAMPLE Edgar Allan Poe wrote suspenseful short stories.

An **interrogative sentence** asks a question. It ends with a question mark.

EXAMPLE Did Poe also write poetry?

An **imperative sentence** gives a command or makes a request. It ends with a period.

EXAMPLE Read "The Pit and the Pendulum."

An **exclamatory sentence** expresses strong feeling. It ends with an exclamation point.

EXAMPLE What a great writer Poe was!

EXAMPLE How I enjoy his stories!

PRACTICE Identifying Kinds of Sentences

Write declarative, interrogative, imperative, *or* exclamatory *to identify each sentence.*

1. How excited we are about our trip to Maine!
2. Have you ever traveled to Maine?
3. Send me a postcard.
4. Will you take a bus or a train?
5. What a beautiful beach this is!
6. The ocean water is very cold.
7. I see a loon on the water.
8. Be very quiet.
9. Loons are diving birds.
10. Loon calls sound like laughter.

1.2 SENTENCES AND SENTENCE FRAGMENTS

Every sentence has two parts: a subject and a predicate.

Sentence

EXAMPLE Emily Dickinson wrote poetry.

Subject Predicate

The **subject part** of a sentence names whom or what the sentence is about.

The **predicate part** of a sentence tells what the subject does or has. It can also tell what the subject is or is like.

A **sentence fragment** does not express a complete thought. It may also be missing a subject, a predicate, or both.

CORRECTING SENTENCE FRAGMENTS

FRAGMENT	PROBLEM	SENTENCE
The poems.	The fragment lacks a predicate. *What did the poems do?*	The poems lay in Dickinson's bureau for years.
Wrote about her emotions.	The fragment lacks a subject. *Who wrote about her emotions?*	This famous poet wrote about her emotions.
Of meaning.	The fragment lacks a subject and a predicate.	Her poems contain many layers of meaning.

PRACTICE Identifying Sentences and Fragments

Write sentence *or* fragment *for each item. Write each sentence and underline the subject part once and the predicate part twice. For each fragment, add a subject or a predicate or both to make it a sentence.*

1. Many animals live in the sea.
2. Always under water.
3. Whales and dolphins breathe air.
4. Sponges and corals look like plants.
5. Borrowed a book about the sea.
6. A starfish has thick arms around its body.
7. Its feet are under its arms.
8. Starfish see only dark and light.
9. Millions of tiny plants.
10. Different types of whales.

1.3 SUBJECTS AND PREDICATES

A sentence consists of a subject and a predicate that together express a complete thought. Both a subject and a predicate may consist of more than one word.

	Complete Subject	Complete Predicate
EXAMPLE	Charles Dickens's **novels**	**are** still popular today.
EXAMPLE	My English **teacher**	**wrote** an article about Dickens.

The **complete subject** includes all the words in the subject of a sentence.

The **complete predicate** includes all the words in the predicate of a sentence.

Not all words in the subject or the predicate are equally important.

EXAMPLE The young **Charles Dickens** **wrote** many articles.

(Complete Subject: The young Charles Dickens; Simple Subject: Charles Dickens. Complete Predicate: wrote many articles; Simple Predicate: wrote.)

The **simple subject** is the main word or word group in the complete subject.

The simple subject is usually a noun or a pronoun. A **noun** is a word that names a person, a place, a thing, or an idea. A **pronoun** is a word that takes the place of one or more nouns.

The **simple predicate** is the main word or word group in the complete predicate.

The simple predicate is always a verb. A **verb** is a word that expresses action or a state of being.

Sometimes the simple subject is the same as the complete subject. Sometimes the simple predicate is the same as the complete predicate.

PRACTICE Identifying Complete Subjects and Complete Predicates

Write each sentence. Underline the complete subject once and the complete predicate twice.

1. Jaimie goes to camp every summer.
2. The camp is located in the mountains.
3. Jack Ranos is the head counselor.
4. Many activities are planned each week.
5. Most of the campers stay in cabins.
6. Several cats live at the camp.
7. The rain started this morning.

8. I learned how to sail.
9. The campers cook the meals.
10. The new sign showed us the trail.

PRACTICE Identifying Simple Subjects and Simple Predicates

Write each sentence. Underline the simple subject once and the simple predicate twice.

1. The party begins at 8:00.
2. Twenty students rode in the bus.
3. Some football players practice every day.
4. Her large suitcase has wheels.
5. Jon's desk is too small for the computer.
6. The long road stretched ahead of us.
7. Performers in the dance company moved gracefully to the drumming.
8. Our computer broke last week.
9. That restaurant usually changes its menu weekly.
10. The tree bark felt rough.

1.4 IDENTIFYING THE SUBJECT

In most sentences, the subject comes before the predicate.

	Subject	Predicate
EXAMPLE	Washington Irving	described New York in his stories.

Other kinds of sentences, such as questions, begin with part or all of the predicate. The subject comes next, followed by the rest of the predicate.

	Predicate	Subject	Predicate
EXAMPLE	Are	people	still reading his stories?

To locate the subject of a question, rearrange the words to form a statement.

PREDICATE	SUBJECT	PREDICATE
Did	Irving	write many funny stories?
	Irving	did write many funny stories.

The predicate also comes before the subject in sentences with inverted word order and in declarative sentences that begin with *Here is, Here are, There is,* and *There are.*

EXAMPLE Over the paper raced (Predicate) Irving's pen. (Subject)

EXAMPLE There is (Predicate) Irving's original manuscript. (Subject)

In imperative sentences (requests and commands), the subject is usually not stated. The predicate is the entire sentence. The word *you* is understood to be the subject.

EXAMPLE (You) (Understood Subject) Look for the author's name on the cover. (Predicate)

GRAMMAR / USAGE / MECHANICS

PRACTICE Identifying the Subject

Write each sentence. Underline the complete subject. Write (You) *before any sentence with an understood subject.*

1. Students wear uniforms in some schools.
2. Do you agree with this idea?
3. Into the pool ran the children.
4. Write a list of materials for the project.
5. Mars has two tiny moons.
6. The sky on Mars appears red.
7. Here is a poster of Mars.
8. Have space explorations found water on Mars?
9. Study chapter 2 of your science text.
10. Will your science class be studying about the planets?

1.5 COMPOUND SUBJECTS AND COMPOUND PREDICATES

A sentence may have more than one simple subject or simple predicate.

A **compound subject** consists of two or more simple subjects that have the same predicate. The subjects may be joined by *and, or, both . . . and, either . . . or,* or *neither . . . nor.*

Compound Subject

EXAMPLE **Charlotte Brontë** and **Emily Brontë** were sisters.

When the two simple subjects are joined by *and* or by *both . . . and,* the compound subject is plural. Use the plural form of the verb to agree with the plural compound subject.

When simple subjects are joined by *or, either . . . or,* or *neither . . . nor,* the verb must agree with the nearer simple subject.

EXAMPLE Neither **Charlotte** nor **Emily is** my favorite author.

EXAMPLE Neither her **sisters** nor **Charlotte was** outgoing.

EXAMPLE Neither **Charlotte** nor her **sisters were** outgoing.

In the first sentence, *Emily* is the nearer subject, so the singular form of the verb is used. In the second sentence, *Charlotte* is the nearer subject, so the singular form of the verb is used here too. In the third sentence, *sisters* is the nearer subject, so the plural form of the verb is used.

A **compound predicate** consists of two or more simple predicates, or verbs, that have the same subject. The verbs may be connected by *and, or, but, both . . . and, either . . . or,* or *neither . . . nor.*

Compound Predicate

EXAMPLE Many students **read** and **enjoy** novels.

The compound predicate in this sentence consists of *read* and *enjoy.* Both verbs agree with the plural subject, *students.*

GRAMMAR / USAGE / MECHANICS

PRACTICE Identifying Compound Subjects and Compound Predicates

Write each sentence, using the correct form of the verb in parentheses. Then underline the compound subjects once and the compound predicates twice.

1. Grace and Erin (is, are) twins.
2. Some twins (looks, look) and (acts, act) different.
3. Either Brad or Zak (feeds, feed) and (walks, walk) the dogs.
4. Both whales and dolphins (breathes, breathe) air.
5. The teacher or the children (cleans, clean) the board.
6. The passengers either (buys, buy) tickets or (pays, pay) on the train.
7. Alex (writes, write) the copy and (draws, draw) the pictures.
8. Neither the books nor this magazine (gives, give) the information.
9. The teachers or the parents (presents, present) the award.
10. Many students (plays, play) an instrument and (sings, sing) in the chorus.

1.6 SIMPLE, COMPOUND, AND RUN-ON SENTENCES

A **simple sentence** has one subject and one predicate.

Simple Sentence

EXAMPLE Eudora Welty lived in Jackson, Mississippi.

A simple sentence may have a compound subject, a compound predicate, or both, as in the following example.

Simple Sentence

EXAMPLE **Jeff** and **I** **read** and **enjoy** Welty's stories.

Compound Subject Compound Predicate

A **compound sentence** is a sentence that contains two or more simple sentences joined by a comma and a coordinating conjunction (*and, but, or*) or by a semicolon.

Compound Sentence

EXAMPLE Welty is a novelist, but she also writes essays.

EXAMPLE Welty is a novelist; she also writes essays.

Simple Sentence Simple Sentence

A run-on sentence is two or more sentences incorrectly written as one sentence. To correct a run-on, write separate sentences or combine the sentences.

CORRECTING RUN-ON SENTENCES

RUN-ON	CORRECT
Welty wrote novels she wrote essays.	Welty wrote novels**. S**he wrote essays.
Welty wrote novels, she wrote essays.	Welty wrote novels**, and** she wrote essays.
	Welty wrote novels**;** she wrote essays.

GRAMMAR / USAGE / MECHANICS

PRACTICE Identifying Simple, Compound, and Run-on Sentences

Write simple, compound, *or* run-on *to identify each numbered item. If an item is a run-on, rewrite it correctly.*

1. Loud noises can cause hearing damage.
2. Protect yourself from hearing loss turn down the volume on your media player.
3. You can take the elevator or walk up the stairs to the third floor.
4. Jan plays soccer; she also plays field hockey.
5. The theater group rehearsed in the morning, and they performed the play in the afternoon.

6. All of the sailboats and canoes are in the water or on the shore.
7. Will the package be delivered, or will you pick it up at the post office?
8. This morning Moira and I planted and watered the flower garden.
9. Beverly Cleary is an award-winning children's author have you read any of her books?
10. In 1984 Cleary won the Newbery Medal for her book *Dear Mr. Henshaw* she has also written two autobiographies.

PRACTICE Proofreading

Rewrite the following passage, correcting errors in spelling, capitalization, grammar, and usage. Add any missing punctuation. Write legibly to be sure one letter is not mistaken for another. There are ten mistakes.

Sally Ride

[1]Have you ever heard of Sally Ride. [2]In 1983 Ride became the first American woman in space.

[3]Ride have a doctorate degree in astrophysics, a branch of astronomy. [4]in 1977 she saw a newspaper want ad. [5]Looking for NASA mission specialists. [6]More than 8,000 people applied for the program, with 34 other people, Ride was hired by NASA. [7]She attended space training school. [8]For two years, she worked on a robot arm for the space shuttles?

[9]Her first space mission was aboard the space shuttle Challenger. [10]Ride helped with experiments, she tested the robot arm. [11]On this mission, the crew traveled 2.5 million miles. [12]In 1984, Ride made a second shuttle flight

[13]In 1986 the Challenger broke apart after take-off Ride investigated the accident. [14]In 1987 retired from NASA.

POSTTEST Kinds of Sentences

Write declarative, interrogative, imperative, *or* exclamatory *to identify each sentence.*

1. Will you take good care of a pet?
2. What a lot of work it is!
3. Feeding and caring for a pet takes time.
4. Walk your dog every day.
5. How much does a pet cost?

POSTTEST Sentences and Sentence Fragments

Write sentence *or* fragment *for each item. Rewrite each fragment to make it a sentence.*

6. Flew to Florida.
7. I met my friend at the library.
8. The soccer game started early.
9. The new computer on my desk.
10. We bought tickets for the concert.
11. Under the table.
12. Bought a new bike.
13. Please pick up the trash.
14. The long walk to the park.
15. We saw the shooting star.

POSTTEST Subjects and Predicates

Write each sentence. Underline the simple subjects once and the simple predicates twice.

16. Did Will and Molly see the film about reptiles?
17. Reptiles eat and digest big meals.
18. Lizards can regulate their body temperature.
19. Do most reptiles live in warm areas?
20. The Gila monster and beaded lizard are poisonous.

21. Many snakes and lizards have forked tongues.
22. Write about a poisonous lizard.
23. Many reptiles fool their enemies.
24. Some snakes give off a terrible smell.
25. Their enemies think they are dead.

POSTTEST Simple, Compound, and Run-on Sentences

Write simple, compound, *or* run-on *to identify each numbered item. If an item is a run-on, rewrite it correctly.*

26. My new car has antilock brakes.
27. I looked at it last week then I decided to buy it.
28. My coach helps me during the week, and my mother works with me over the weekend.
29. Most of the dogs and all of the cats need medical checkups.
30. Mom and Dad planned the menu, and Jake and I cooked the food.
31. Julia read the book, but Alex saw the movie.
32. Did Juanita paint her room alone, or did her sister help her?
33. The baby whined and cried, his mother comforted him.
34. Susan does her homework right after school Steven waits until after dinner.
35. Dan and Ellen cleaned their rooms and swept the floor.

Chapter 2

Nouns

PRETEST Kinds of Nouns

Write each noun. Label the common nouns C *and the proper nouns* P.

1. In the small town of Kalona, Uncle George and his son own a bakery.
2. The trip to Europe will be too expensive unless the travelers tour the countryside by train.
3. The group of scientists understood the importance of the discovery.
4. Dian Fossey told about her research of gorillas in her book *Gorillas in the Mist.*
5. Every year, Milwaukee, Wisconsin, has a festival in late June and early July.

PRETEST Possessive Nouns

Write the possessive form of the noun in parentheses.

6. The (cat) toy is behind the couch.
7. (Jess) baseball game starts at 7:00 P.M.

8. The (women) locker room is around the corner.
9. The mechanic repaired (Nick) car.
10. You should always follow your (doctor) orders.
11. The (Jacksons) new house is bigger than their old one.
12. The conductor asked to see the (tourists) tickets as they boarded the train.
13. Angela helped prepare her (boss) presentation for the meeting.
14. The (girls) swimming lesson is held in the indoor pool.
15. The teacher displayed the (children) pictures.

PRETEST Recognizing Plurals, Possessives, and Contractions

Identify the italicized word in each sentence by writing plural noun, singular possessive noun, plural possessive noun, *or* contraction.

16. Two-thirds of *Earth's* surface is covered by water.
17. Does anyone know where *Megan's* dog is?
18. *Matt's* had a lot of work to do lately.
19. The *parents* wanted their children to play together.
20. Their *daughters'* music teacher sang in the choir.
21. Sheila was unable to attend the *teachers'* conference.
22. Your skin is part of your *body's* immune defense system.
23. The *guests'* coats are in the closet.
24. *He's* going to the recreation center after school.
25. The storm damaged the *Gomez's* house.

PRETEST Appositives

Write the appositive or appositive phrase in each sentence.

26. Jason, an avid skier, hopes to win a gold medal some day.
27. Kendra flew to Minnesota to visit Aunt Josephine, her favorite aunt.

28. My dog, Riley, likes to retrieve tennis balls.
29. After returning from her vacation, a two-week trip to Hawaii, Colleen was ready to get back to work.
30. Have you seen the movie *My Pal Pauly*?
31. Benjamin Franklin, a printer and journalist, contributed greatly to the founding of the United States.
32. On Thursday, the day before my birthday, I went to the zoo with my cousins.
33. The author Roald Dahl wrote *Charlie and the Chocolate Factory.*
34. A talented singer and guitar player, Billy performs three times a week at the community theater.
35. Chlorine, a greenish-yellow gas, is poisonous in large quantities.

2.1 KINDS OF NOUNS

A **noun** is a word that names a person, a place, a thing, or an idea.

NOUNS	
PERSONS	sister, mayor, player, coach, pianist, children
PLACES	park, zoo, lake, school, playground, desert, city
THINGS	magazine, boots, rose, pencil, peach, baseball, car
IDEAS	honesty, truth, democracy, pride, maturity, progress

A **common noun** names *any* person, place, thing, or idea.
A **proper noun** names a *particular* person, place, thing, or idea.

The first word and all other important words in a proper noun are capitalized: *Edgar Allan Poe, Statue of Liberty.*

Common nouns can be either concrete or abstract.

Concrete nouns name things you can see or touch.

Abstract nouns name ideas, qualities, and feelings that can't be seen or touched.

KINDS OF NOUNS		
COMMON NOUNS		**PROPER NOUNS**
Abstract	**Concrete**	
truth	document	Supreme Court
courage	crown	Queen Elizabeth I
time	snow	December
history	museum	Museum of Modern Art
entertainment	actor	Meryl Streep
education	school	Howard University
comedy	comedian	Jerry Seinfeld
friendship	friend	Jessica
tragedy	ship	*Titanic*

GRAMMAR / USAGE / MECHANICS

Compound nouns are nouns made of two or more words.

A compound noun can be one word, like *storybook*, or more than one word, like *ice cream.* A compound noun can also be joined by one or more hyphens, like *runner-up.*

COMPOUND NOUNS	
ONE WORD	housekeeper, showcase, bookmark, outdoors, teammate
MORE THAN ONE WORD	post office, dining room, maid of honor, high school
HYPHENATED	sister-in-law, great-aunt, kilowatt-hour, walkie-talkie

PRACTICE Identifying Common and Proper Nouns

Write each noun. Label the common nouns C *and the proper nouns* P.

1. Lake Michigan is the only Great Lake entirely in the United States.
2. Elena bought fifteen postcards during her trip from Mexico to Florida.
3. Freedom of speech is a right named in the Bill of Rights.
4. My favorite uncle is a firefighter and paramedic in North Carolina.
5. The new chef at the Gateway Restaurant makes the best chili in town.
6. Every year golfers compete at the Masters Tournament in Georgia.
7. After visiting Universal Studios in California, Kelsey decided she wanted to be an actor.
8. John F. Kennedy was the youngest person ever elected president.
9. The view from the top of the Washington Monument is fantastic.
10. The fossils of the dinosaur named Sue are at the Field Museum in Chicago.

2.2 SINGULAR AND PLURAL NOUNS

A **singular noun** names one person, place, thing, or idea. A **plural noun** names more than one.

To form the plural of most nouns, you simply add *-s*. Other plural nouns are formed in different ways.

FORMING PLURAL NOUNS

NOUNS ENDING WITH	TO FORM PLURAL	EXAMPLES		
s, z, ch, sh, x	Add ***-es.***	bus bus**es**	buzz buzz**es**	box box**es**
o preceded by a vowel	Add ***-s.***	rodeo rodeo**s**	studio studio**s**	radio radio**s**
o preceded by a consonant	Usually add ***-es.***	hero hero**es**	potato potato**es**	echo echo**es**
	Sometimes add ***-s.***	zero zero**s**	photo photo**s**	piano piano**s**
y preceded by a vowel	Add ***-s.***	day day**s**	turkey turkey**s**	toy toy**s**
y preceded by a consonant	Usually change ***y*** to ***i*** and add ***-es.***	city cit**ies**	diary diar**ies**	penny penn**ies**
f or ***fe***	Usually change ***f*** to ***v*** and add ***-s*** or ***-es.***	wife wi**ves**	leaf lea**ves**	half hal**ves**
	Sometimes add ***-s.***	roof roof**s**	chief chief**s**	belief belief**s**

To form the plural of compound nouns written as one word, usually add *-s* or *-es.* To form the plural of compound nouns that are written as more than one word or are hyphenated, make the main noun in the compound word plural, or check a dictionary.

COMPOUND NOUNS	
ONE WORD	doorbell**s**, necklace**s**, rosebush**es**; Exception: passer**s**by
MORE THAN ONE WORD	post office**s**, dining room**s**, maid**s** of honor, high school**s**
HYPHENATED	brother**s**-in-law, great-aunt**s**, eighth-grader**s**, push-up**s**

Words such as *family* and *team* are called collective nouns.

A **collective noun** names a group of people, animals, or things.

A collective noun subject may be followed by a singular verb or a plural verb, depending on the meaning. The subject is singular when the members of the group act as a single unit. The subject is plural when each member of the group acts separately. Other words in a sentence can sometimes help you decide whether a collective noun is singular or plural.

EXAMPLE The **team shares** the field with **its** opponent. **[shares, its, singular]**

EXAMPLE The **team share their** jokes with one another. **[share, their, plural]**

GRAMMAR / USAGE / MECHANICS

PRACTICE Forming Plural Nouns

Write the plural form of each noun.

1. sister-in-law
2. elephant
3. computer
4. leash
5. tomato
6. shelf
7. ratio
8. family
9. reef
10. monkey

PRACTICE Identifying Collective Nouns

Write each collective noun. Label it S *if it's singular and* P *if it's plural.*

1. The company offers many different services.
2. The pilots association chooses its representatives.
3. The Peterson family lives on Tenth Street.
4. The class paint pictures for the art show.
5. The whale pod migrates south in the winter.
6. The team are introduced before the game.
7. The group eats lunch outside.
8. The band performs every weekend.
9. The audience becomes silent.
10. The colony works hard to provide their own food.

2.3 POSSESSIVE NOUNS

A noun can show ownership or possession of things or qualities. This kind of noun is called a possessive noun.

A **possessive noun** tells who or what owns or has something.

Possessive nouns may be common nouns or proper nouns. They may also be singular or plural. Notice the possessive nouns in the following sentences:

SINGULAR NOUN	**Rita** has a book about baseball.
SINGULAR POSSESSIVE NOUN	**Rita's** book is about baseball.
PLURAL NOUN	Several **cities** have baseball teams.
PLURAL POSSESSIVE NOUN	These **cities'** teams attract fans.

Possessive nouns are formed in one of two ways. To form the possessive of singular nouns and plural nouns not ending in *s*, add an apostrophe and *s ('s).* To form the possessive of plural nouns ending in *s*, add just an apostrophe at the end of the word.

FORMING POSSESSIVE NOUNS

NOUNS	TO FORM POSSESSIVE	EXAMPLES
All singular nouns; plural nouns not ending in ***s***	Add an apostrophe and ***s*** (**'s**).	a girl–a girl**'s** name Germany–Germany**'s** exports the bus–the bus**'s** capacity Ms. Ames–Ms. Ames**'s** class children–children**'s** toys women–women**'s** coats
Plural nouns ending in ***s***	Add just an apostrophe (**'**) at the end of the plural noun.	babies–babies**'** birth weight the Joneses–the Joneses**'** car

PRACTICE **Writing Possessive Nouns**

Write the possessive form of the noun in parentheses.

1. The (coach) daughter has just joined the team.
2. (Janis) essay won first prize.
3. The (trees) roots were exposed.
4. The (teachers) lounge was locked.
5. (Oregon) coastline is very rugged.
6. The third floor houses the (men) department.
7. (Columbus) voyage across the ocean took about seventy days.
8. How big is your (computer) memory?
9. The (families) combined garage sale is this weekend.
10. (Sir Isaac Newton) theory of gravity describes how the universe is held together.

2.4 RECOGNIZING PLURALS, POSSESSIVES, AND CONTRACTIONS

Most plural nouns, all possessive nouns, and certain contractions end with the sound of *s*. These words may sound alike, but their spellings and meanings are different.

NOUN FORMS AND CONTRACTIONS

	EXAMPLE	MEANING
Plural Noun	The **students** wrote a play.	more than one student
Plural Possessive Noun	The **students'** play is good.	the play by several students
Singular Possessive Noun	I saw the **student's** performance.	the performance of one student
Contraction	This **student's** the author. This **student's** written other plays.	This student is the author. This student has written other plays.

A **contraction** is a word made by combining two words and leaving out one or more letters. An apostrophe shows where the letters have been omitted.

Plural nouns don't have an apostrophe. Contractions and singular possessive nouns look exactly alike. Some plural possessive nouns end with *'s,* and some end with just an apostrophe. You can tell these words apart by the way they're used in a sentence.

NOUN FORMS AND CONTRACTIONS

PLURAL NOUNS	CONTRACTIONS	SINGULAR POSSESSIVE NOUNS	PLURAL POSSESSIVE NOUNS
speakers	speaker's	speaker's	speakers'
women	woman's	woman's	women's
echoes	echo's	echo's	echoes'
countries	country's	country's	countries'

PRACTICE Identifying Plurals, Possessives, and Contractions

Identify the italicized word in each sentence by writing plural noun, singular possessive noun, plural possessive noun, *or* contraction.

1. The *doctors'* convention will last four days.
2. *Tyler's* animals depend on him.
3. There are many *squirrels* in the park.
4. He was riding in *Katrina's* car.
5. *Miguel's* doing his homework.
6. *Wendy's* never been to London.
7. The angle of *Earth's* tilt is about twenty-three degrees.
8. The *Davises'* new home is in Boulder.
9. You should get your *parents'* permission first.
10. Jolene and her *brothers* attended the soccer game.

2.5 APPOSITIVES

An **appositive** is a noun that is placed next to another noun to identify it or add information about it.

EXAMPLE James Madison's wife, **Dolley,** was a famous first lady.

The noun *Dolley* identifies the noun next to it, *wife.* In this sentence, *Dolley* is an appositive.

An **appositive phrase** is a group of words that includes an appositive and other words that modify the appositive.

EXAMPLE Madison, **our fourth president,** held many other offices.

The words *our* and *fourth* modify the appositive *president.* The phrase *our fourth president* is an appositive phrase. It identifies the noun *Madison.*

An appositive or an appositive phrase can appear anywhere in a sentence as long as it appears next to the noun it identifies.

EXAMPLE **Our fourth president,** Madison held many other offices.

EXAMPLE Many historians have studied the life of Madison, **our fourth president.**

Appositives and appositive phrases are usually set off with commas. If the appositive is essential to the meaning of the sentence, however, commas are not used.

EXAMPLE Madison's friend **Thomas Jefferson** was president before Madison.

EXAMPLE Madison's father, **James Madison,** was a plantation owner.

Obviously, Madison had more than one friend, so the appositive, *Thomas Jefferson,* is needed to identify this particular friend. No commas are needed. However, Madison had only one father. The father's name is not needed to identify him. Therefore, commas are needed.

PRACTICE Identifying Appositives

Write each sentence. Underline the appositive or appositive phrase and add appropriate commas. Circle the noun the appositive identifies.

1. Mt. Everest the world's highest peak is 29,028 feet high.
2. In addition to writing music, the composer Johann Sebastian Bach worked as a musician and conductor.
3. The waiter a friend of mine is also a college student.
4. In rugby a rough sport many players are injured.
5. A serious student Rebecca will graduate early from college.
6. *Gone with the Wind* now a movie classic will be on television tonight.
7. I was five when I went to my first sporting event a baseball game.
8. My father's friend Carlos is a well-known chef.
9. Her hero is Michelle Kwan a skating superstar.
10. My car a blue Toyota is at the repair shop.

PRACTICE Proofreading

Rewrite the following passage, correcting errors in spelling, capitalization, grammar, and usage. Add any missing punctuation. Write legibly to be sure one letter is not mistaken for another. There are ten mistakes.

Leonardo da Vinci

[1]The life and work of Leonardo da Vinci the great Italian Renaissance painter have interested people for over five hundred years. [2]Leonardo was born in 1452 near Florence, italy. [3]Leonardos artistic talents were revealed early. [4]He worked with a leading Renaissance painter.

[5]In 1482, Leonardo left Florence for the City of Milan. [6]He worked there for nearly eighteen year's. [7]It was then that he painted *The Last Supper* one of his best-known paintings. [8]Leonardo returned to florence in 1499. [9]There he painted *Mona Lisa* perhaps his most famous painting.

[10]Leonardo was also an engineer and a scientist. [11]Long before there was airplanes and helicopters, he drew designs for them. [12]He studied the bodies of humans and animals. [13]He kept notes and drawings of his work. [14]Leonardo was one of the Renaissance's great genius.

POSTTEST Kinds of Nouns

Write each noun. Label the common nouns C *and the proper nouns* P.

1. Canadian geese migrate every winter to find open ground near wetlands.
2. A powerful earthquake shook northern California on the first day of the 1989 World Series.
3. Marial plays soccer in the summer, baseball in the fall, and hockey in the winter.
4. There were four blue eggs in the nest that Stacey found in the tree.
5. The equator runs through Kenya, a country in Africa.

POSTTEST Possessive Nouns

Write the possessive form of the noun in parentheses.

6. The (Thomases) backyard is full of weeds.
7. Did you hear reports of (today) weather?
8. The (dancers) costumes were beautiful.
9. (Ben) puppy has grown a lot.
10. The (Earth) revolution around the sun takes one year.
11. The (announcer) voice was strong and clear.
12. My (class) musical presentation is third on the program this evening.
13. The (children) laughter echoed down the hall.
14. The (cities) agreement was signed by both mayors.
15. That is the (district) newest school.

POSTTEST Recognizing Plurals, Possessives, and Contractions

Identify the italicized word in each sentence by writing plural noun, singular possessive noun, plural possessive noun, *or* contraction.

16. We are making *Mother's* Day cards to sell at the craft show.
17. *Michael's* been a police officer for twenty-five years.
18. The *chickens* are eating corn in the barnyard.
19. The *diplomats'* flight was canceled due to thunder storms.
20. We waited for our friends at the *park's* entrance.
21. *Martin's* staying for dinner tonight.
22. How many *shoes* are in your closet?
23. I read my poem at the *writers'* workshop.
24. *Samantha's* grades pleased her parents.
25. My *grandparents'* cottage is in Wisconsin.

POSTTEST Appositives

Write the appositive or appositive phrase in each sentence.

26. We spent the whole day at the Mall of America, the largest mall in the United States.

27. The coach, a retired soccer player himself, knows how to motivate players.

28. My best friend, Tara, wants to go to the movie too.

29. Every summer my friend's family goes to Lake Superior, the largest freshwater lake in the world.

30. Everyone likes my new puppy, a golden retriever.

31. Greg, the best athlete in our school, scored the most points.

32. Tokyo, the capital of Japan, is a heavily populated city.

33. The school principal, Mrs. Flaherty, made the announcement.

34. A Native American of the Pueblo San Ildefonso, Maria Martinez became well-known for her beautiful pottery.

35. This is Marcela, the newest member of our basketball team.

Chapter 3

Verbs

PRETEST Action Verbs and Linking Verbs

Write each verb. Label the action verbs A *and the linking verbs* L.

1. Cats come in many different sizes.
2. All of them are good hunters.
3. They pounce on their prey.
4. Cats see well in dim light.
5. The whiskers of all cats seem very sensitive.
6. Small cats purr.
7. Some large cats roar.
8. The cheetah, a large cat, is the fastest land animal.
9. It runs seventy miles an hour.
10. The cheetah's flexible spine acts as a spring.

PRETEST Direct Objects, Indirect Objects, Predicate Nouns, and Predicate Adjectives

Identify the italicized word in each sentence by writing direct object, indirect object, predicate noun, *or* predicate adjective.

11. Noise during a movie is a *nuisance.*
12. The children made a *mural* of dinosaurs.
13. That movie is *fabulous!*
14. The teacher gave the *class* a writing assignment.
15. The bank sent the *customer* a detailed statement.
16. The witness was *honest.*
17. During the convention, the vice-president became his party's *choice* for president.
18. We heard the weather *report* on the radio.
19. Some parents asked *questions* at the meeting.
20. We bought a *ticket* to New Orleans.

PRETEST Present and Past Tenses and Progressive Forms

Write the verb. Then write present tense, past tense, present progressive, *or* past progressive *to identify it.*

21. I was staying after school for help with my math homework.
22. In my freshman year, I joined the school's marching band.
23. Jared and his friends were playing basketball.
24. This jug holds two gallons, or eight quarts, of water.
25. The Secretary of State was preparing a report about the progress of the talks.
26. Those dogs bark all day.
27. We are writing a skit for our class play.
28. Samantha is learning how to ski.
29. I am cooking breakfast for my parents.
30. Someone borrowed my camera.

PRETEST Perfect and Future Tenses

Write the verb. Then write present perfect, past perfect, future, *or* future perfect *to identify its tense.*

31. We had listened to all the songs several times.
32. We will bring pasta salad to the picnic.
33. Hillary's brother has written a magazine article.
34. Who will work at the fair?
35. Her parents have paid for the movie tickets.
36. I will have fixed the printer by tonight.
37. The book had disappeared from the shelf.
38. We have read that news magazine in class.
39. The children will have finished the game by that time.
40. The team had practiced all summer.

PRETEST Irregular Verbs

Write the correct verb form from the choices in parentheses.

41. During their swimming lesson, the children (swam, swum) the length of the pool.
42. The students have (knew, known) about the competition for weeks.
43. He (lose, lost) them yesterday.
44. Have you (pay, paid) for the food?
45. I have (driven, drove) the 500 miles to Omaha several times this year.
46. Karen Mayfield (ran, run) for state senator.
47. The base runner (stole, stolen) second base.
48. She has (took, taken) the book back to the library.
49. I (did, done) most of my homework during study hall.
50. Ms. Franklin had (teach, taught) social studies at Avery School.

3.1 ACTION VERBS

You may have heard the movie director's call for "lights, camera, *action!*" The actions in movies and plays can be expressed by verbs. If a word expresses action and tells what a subject does, it's an action verb.

An **action verb** is a word that expresses action. An action verb may be made up of more than one word.

Notice the action verbs in the following sentences.

EXAMPLE The director **shouts** at the members of the cast.

EXAMPLE The lights **are flashing** above the stage.

EXAMPLE The audience **arrived** in time for the performance.

EXAMPLE Several singers **have memorized** the lyrics of a song.

Action verbs can express physical actions, such as *shout* and *arrive*. They can also express mental activities, such as *memorize* and *forget*.

ACTION VERBS	
PHYSICAL	shout, flash, arrive, talk, applaud, act, sing, dance
MENTAL	remember, forget, think, memorize, read, dream, appreciate

Have, *has*, and *had* are often used before other verbs. They can also be used as action verbs when they tell that the subject owns or holds something.

EXAMPLE The actors already **have** their costumes.

EXAMPLE The director **has** a script in her back pocket.

EXAMPLE Rosa **had** a theater program from 1920.

PRACTICE Identifying Action Verbs

Write the action verbs.

1. Heather and Lisa heard a crashing sound.
2. They ran to the kitchen window.
3. The girls turned on the outdoor lights.
4. They looked out into the night.
5. They listened for more noise.
6. Then Heather remembered a similar noise.
7. She grabbed a flashlight.
8. The girls walked into the backyard.
9. They saw Heather's cat, Angus.
10. It had knocked over a flowerpot.

3.2 TRANSITIVE AND INTRANSITIVE VERBS

In some sentences, the predicate consists of only an action verb.

EXAMPLE The actor **rehearsed.**

Most sentences provide more information. The predicate often names who or what receives the action of the verb.

EXAMPLE The actor rehearsed his **lines** from the play.

The word *lines* tells what the actor rehearsed. *Lines* is a direct object.

A **direct object** receives the action of a verb. It answers the question *whom?* or *what?* after an action verb.

A sentence may have a compound direct object. That is, a sentence may have more than one direct object.

EXAMPLE We saw **Maurice** and **Inez** in the audience.

When an action verb transfers action to a direct object, the verb is transitive. When an action verb has no direct object, the verb is intransitive.

A **transitive verb** has a direct object.

An **intransitive verb** does not have a direct object.

Most action verbs can be transitive or intransitive. A verb can be labeled transitive or intransitive only by examining its use in a particular sentence.

EXAMPLE The audience **applauds** the actors. **[transitive]**

EXAMPLE The audience **applauds** loudly. **[intransitive]**

GRAMMAR / USAGE / MECHANICS

PRACTICE Recognizing Transitive and Intransitive Verbs

For each sentence, write the action verb. Then write T *if the verb is transitive or* I *if the verb is intransitive. If the verb is transitive, write the direct object or objects.*

1. Flowers produce seeds.
2. The seeds grow into new plants.
3. Flowers vary in size, shape, and color.
4. The color of petals attracts insects.
5. Insects carry pollen.
6. The pollen sticks to parts of their bodies.
7. Birds transfer pollen as well.
8. Palms grow small flowers.
9. I saw the dates and coconuts on the palm trees.
10. Most trees blossom in spring or summer.

3.3 INDIRECT OBJECTS

A direct object answers the question *whom?* or *what?* after an action verb.

EXAMPLE Friends sent **flowers.**

In some sentences, an indirect object also follows an action verb.

An **indirect object** answers the question *to whom?* or *for whom?* or *to what?* or *for what?* an action is done.

EXAMPLE Friends sent the **actors** flowers.

The direct object in the sentence is *flowers.* The indirect object is *actors. Actors* answers the question *to whom?* after the action verb *sent.*

A sentence may have a compound indirect object. In the sentence below, *cast* and *orchestra* are indirect objects. The direct object is *thanks.*

EXAMPLE Ms. Ortiz gave the **cast** and the **orchestra** her thanks.

An indirect object appears only in a sentence that has a direct object. Two clues can help you recognize an indirect object. First, an indirect object always comes between the verb and the direct object. Second, you can put the word *to* or *for* before an indirect object and change its position. The sentence will still have the same meaning, but it will no longer have an indirect object.

EXAMPLE Friends **sent** the **director flowers.** **[*Director* is an indirect object.]**

EXAMPLE Friends sent flowers **to the director.** **[*Director* is not an indirect object.]**

You know that in the first sentence *director* is the indirect object because it comes between the verb and the direct object and because it can be placed after the word *to,* as in the second sentence.

PRACTICE Identifying Direct and Indirect Objects

Write the indirect objects and underline them. Then write the direct objects.

1. Janna baked the class muffins.
2. The teacher read the students an original poem.
3. The magazine offers its readers a discount.
4. I gave the dog a can of food.
5. Patrick made his friends lunch.
6. Ms. Juarez brought the family a beautiful gift.
7. Mai has written her father a note.
8. Sarah sold her sister the old bike.
9. Jacob gave his cousin the media player.
10. Terence bought the children stickers.

GRAMMAR / USAGE / MECHANICS

3.4 LINKING VERBS AND PREDICATE WORDS

A **linking verb** connects the subject of a sentence with a noun or an adjective in the predicate.

EXAMPLE Juana Ortiz **was** the **director.**

EXAMPLE Ms. Ortiz **is imaginative.**

In the first sentence, the verb *was* links the noun *director* to the subject. *Director* identifies the subject. In the second sentence, the verb *is* links the adjective *imaginative* to the subject. *Imaginative* describes the subject.

A **predicate noun** is a noun that follows a linking verb. It renames or identifies the subject.

A **predicate adjective** is an adjective that follows a linking verb. It describes, or modifies, the subject.

A sentence may contain a compound predicate noun or a compound predicate adjective.

EXAMPLE Ms. Ortiz is a **teacher** and a **musician.** **[compound predicate noun]**

EXAMPLE Ms. Ortiz is **stern** but **fair.** **[compound predicate adjective]**

COMMON LINKING VERBS			
be (am, is, are,	seem	taste	sound
was, were)	appear	feel	grow
become	look	smell	turn

Most of these verbs can also be used as action verbs.

EXAMPLE The director **sounded** angry. **[linking verb]**

EXAMPLE The director **sounded** the alarm. **[action verb]**

NOTE Two other linking verbs are *remain* and *stay.*

PRACTICE Identifying Verbs, Predicate Nouns, and Predicate Adjectives

For each sentence, write the verb. Label the verb A *if it's an action verb or* L *if it's a linking verb. If it's a linking verb, write the predicate noun or the predicate adjective. Label a predicate noun* PN. *Label a predicate adjective* PA.

1. Some sharks are dangerous.
2. Most sharks have slits on the sides of their heads.
3. The skeleton of a shark is cartilage.
4. Cartilage feels softer than bone.
5. Hard, tiny scales cover sharkskin.
6. Long ago, people used dried sharkskin for sandpaper.
7. Shark teeth look pointy and sharp.

8. They cut and rip meat.
9. Sharks sense movement.
10. Many sharks are fierce hunters.

3.5 PRESENT AND PAST TENSES

The verb in a sentence expresses action. It also tells when the action takes place. The form of a verb that shows the time of the action is called the **tense** of the verb.

The **present tense** of a verb expresses action that happens regularly. It can also express a general truth.

EXAMPLE A great actor **wins** awards.

In the present tense, the base form of a verb is used with all plural subjects and the pronouns *I* and *you.* For singular subjects other than *I* and *you, -s* or *-es* is usually added to the base form of the verb. Remember that a verb must agree in number with its subject.

PRESENT TENSE FORMS

SINGULAR	PLURAL
I **walk.**	We **walk.**
You **walk.**	You **walk.**
He, she, *or* it **walks.**	They **walk.**

The **past tense** of a verb expresses action that already happened.

The past tense of many verbs is formed by adding *-d* or *-ed* to the base form of the verb.

EXAMPLE The actors **rehearsed.** Ms. Ortiz **directed.**

GRAMMAR / USAGE / MECHANICS

PRACTICE **Identifying Present and Past Tenses**

For each sentence, write the verb. Then write present *or* past *to identify its tense.*

1. I enjoy mysteries.
2. Johanna and Jack walked to the store.
3. Many people recycle paper and cans.
4. Janice shopped at a used clothing store.
5. The store opens every day at 8:00 A.M.
6. I appreciate the cards and letters.
7. The teachers arrive at school before the students.
8. I mailed the letters yesterday.
9. Susan or Tara baby-sits the children.
10. In 1940 Americans elected Franklin D. Roosevelt to a third term as president.

3.6 MAIN VERBS AND HELPING VERBS

Verbs have four principal parts that are used to form all tenses. Notice how the principal parts of a verb are formed.

PRINCIPAL PARTS OF VERBS

BASE FORM	PRESENT PARTICIPLE	PAST	PAST PARTICIPLE
act	acting	acted	acted

You can use the base form and the past alone to form the present and past tenses. The present participle and the past participle can be combined with helping verbs to form other tenses.

A **helping verb** helps the main verb express action or make a statement.

A **verb phrase** consists of one or more helping verbs followed by a main verb.

EXAMPLE Telma **is acting** in another play today.

The word *is* is the helping verb, and the present participle *acting* is the main verb. Together they form a verb phrase.

The most common helping verbs are *be, have,* and *do.* Forms of the helping verb *be* are *am, is,* and *are* in the present and *was* and *were* in the past. These helping verbs often combine with the present participle of the main verb.

GRAMMAR / USAGE / MECHANICS

BE AND THE PRESENT PARTICIPLE

SINGULAR	PLURAL	SINGULAR	PLURAL
I **am** learning.	We **are** learning.	I **was** learning.	We **were** learning.
You **are** learning.	You **are** learning.	You **were** learning.	You **were** learning.
She **is** learning.	They **are** learning.	He **was** learning.	They **were** learning.

The helping verb *have* combines with the past participle of the main verb. Forms of the helping verb *have* are *have* and *has* in the present and *had* in the past.

HAVE AND THE PAST PARTICIPLE

SINGULAR	PLURAL	SINGULAR	PLURAL
I **have** learned.	We **have** learned.	I **had** learned.	We **had** learned.
You **have** learned.	You **have** learned.	You **had** learned.	You **had** learned.
She **has** learned.	They **have** learned.	He **had** learned.	They **had** learned.

Forms of the helping verb *do* are *do* and *does* in the present and *did* in the past. The helping verb *do* combines with the base form of a verb: *I do believe you. She does believe you. They did believe you.*

NOTE Other helping verbs are *can, could, may, might, must, should,* and *would.*

PRACTICE Identifying Main Verbs and Helping Verbs

Write each verb phrase. Underline the helping verb. Write base form, present participle, *or* past participle *to identify the main verb.*

1. We are learning about birds.
2. Birds live all over the world.
3. They maintain a steady body temperature.
4. Have you read the book about birds?
5. We have watched birds in parks and gardens.
6. We were using binoculars.
7. Some birds like different parts of the forest.
8. We do view many different birds at the nature reserve.
9. An eagle was flying above high mountains.
10. Did you see it?

3.7 PROGRESSIVE FORMS

You know that the present tense of a verb can express action that occurs repeatedly. To express action that is taking place at the present time, use the present progressive form of the verb.

The **present progressive form** of a verb expresses action or a condition that is continuing in the present.

EXAMPLE Althea **is finishing** her song.

The present progressive form of a verb consists of the helping verb *am, are,* or *is* and the present participle of the main verb.

PRESENT PROGRESSIVE FORMS

SINGULAR	PLURAL
I **am watching.**	We **are watching.**
You **are watching.**	You **are watching.**
He, she, *or* it **is watching.**	They **are watching.**

The **past progressive form** of a verb expresses action or a condition that was continuing at some time in the past.

EXAMPLE We **were watching** a scary show.

The past progressive form of a verb consists of the helping verb *was* or *were* and the present participle of the main verb.

PAST PROGRESSIVE FORMS

SINGULAR	PLURAL
I **was working.**	We **were working.**
You **were working.**	You **were working.**
He, she, *or* it **was working.**	They **were working.**

PRACTICE Using Progressive Forms

Rewrite the sentence using the progressive form of the verb. If the verb is in the present tense, change it to the present progressive form. If the verb is in the past tense, change it to the past progressive form.

1. This week Alison's class visits the botanic gardens.
2. The children watched the play.
3. Ponce de León looked for the Fountain of Youth.
4. Mika leaves for school at 8:15 A.M.
5. Steven practiced the trumpet this afternoon.
6. Cora and Raymond sing in the youth choir.
7. John and Ben attend most of the football games.
8. Nine planets revolve around the Sun.
9. I ride my horse every Saturday.
10. Sarah visited me in the hospital.

3.8 PRESENT PERFECT AND PAST PERFECT TENSES

The **present perfect tense** of a verb expresses action that happened at an indefinite time in the past.

EXAMPLE The actor **has rehearsed** for many hours.

EXAMPLE Lori and Pam **have watched** *Grease* five times.

The present perfect tense consists of the helping verb *have* or *has* and the past participle of the main verb.

PRESENT PERFECT TENSE

SINGULAR	PLURAL
I **have watched.**	We **have watched.**
You **have watched.**	You **have watched.**
He, she, *or* it **has watched.**	They **have watched.**

The **past perfect tense** of a verb expresses action that happened before another action or event in the past.

The past perfect tense is often used in sentences that contain a past-tense verb in another part of the sentence.

EXAMPLE The actors **had rehearsed** for many weeks.

EXAMPLE We **had** just **arrived** when the play **started.**

The past perfect tense of a verb consists of the helping verb *had* and the past participle of the main verb.

PAST PERFECT TENSE	
SINGULAR	**PLURAL**
I **had started.**	We **had started.**
You **had started.**	You **had started.**
He, she, *or* it **had started.**	They **had started.**

GRAMMAR / USAGE / MECHANICS

PRACTICE Identifying Perfect Tenses

Write the verb. Then write present perfect *or* past perfect *to identify the tense.*

1. I have driven to Albuquerque in three hours.
2. I had watched several track meets last year.
3. Gabriel has saved enough money for guitar lessons.
4. Tom Cruise has starred in two *Mission Impossible* movies.
5. You have packed too many clothes.
6. I had washed my car before the rainstorm.
7. The wait staff had cleaned all the tables before the evening dinner rush.
8. I had worried about the test all weekend.

9. Gina and Michael have collected all of the tickets.
10. Al has counted the money twice.

3.9 EXPRESSING FUTURE TIME

The **future tense** of a verb expresses action that will take place in the future.

EXAMPLE We **shall attend** the performance.

EXAMPLE The actors **will show** their talents.

The future tense of a verb is formed by using the helping verb *will* before the base form of a verb. The helping verb *shall* is sometimes used when the subject is *I* or *we.*

There are other ways to show that an action will happen in the future. *Tomorrow, next year,* and *later* are all words that indicate a future time. These words are called **time words,** and they may be used with the present tense to express future time.

EXAMPLE Our show **opens next week.**

EXAMPLE **Tomorrow** we **start** rehearsals.

The present progressive form can also be used with time words to express future actions.

EXAMPLE Our show **is opening next week.**

EXAMPLE **Tomorrow** we **are starting** rehearsals.

Another way to talk about the future is with the future perfect tense.

The **future perfect tense** of a verb expresses action that will be completed before another future event begins.

EXAMPLE By Thursday I **shall have performed** six times.

EXAMPLE The production **will have closed** by next week.

The future perfect tense is formed by using *will have* or *shall have* before the past participle of a verb.

PRACTICE Identifying Verb Tenses

Write the verb. Then write present, future, present progressive, *or* future perfect *to identify the verb tense.*

1. We shall come to the airport an hour early.
2. By the end of the week, our class will have finished reading the book.
3. Hanna and Jo will dance first in the show.
4. I shall have completed my assignment by the end of the day.
5. I go to the library on Tuesday for an interview with the director of the library.
6. Tonight Norm is preparing a special dinner as a surprise for his parents.
7. Students in our class will plan the dance.
8. By summer the gardeners will have planted the new garden.
9. Marissa begins the course this afternoon.
10. The last flight for Houston is leaving at 9:00 P.M.

3.10 ACTIVE AND PASSIVE VOICE

A verb is in the **active voice** when the subject performs the action of the verb.

EXAMPLE Thornton Wilder **composed** that play.

A verb is in the **passive voice** when the subject receives the action of the verb.

EXAMPLE That play **was composed** by Thornton Wilder.

In the first example, the author, Thorton Wilder, seems more important because *Thornton Wilder* is the subject of the sentence. In the second example, the play seems more important because *play* is the subject of the sentence.

Notice that verbs in the passive voice consist of a form of *be* and the past participle. Often a phrase beginning with *by* follows the verb in the passive voice.

EXAMPLE I am puzzled **by your question.** **[passive voice]**

EXAMPLE Your question puzzles me. **[active voice]**

EXAMPLE The puppy is frightened **by loud noises.** **[passive voice]**

EXAMPLE Loud noises frighten the puppy. **[active voice]**

EXAMPLE Plays are performed **by actors.** **[passive voice]**

EXAMPLE Actors perform plays. **[active voice]**

EXAMPLE This painting was purchased **by Ms. Jones.** **[passive voice]**

EXAMPLE Ms. Jones purchased this painting. **[active voice]**

The active voice is usually a stronger, more direct way to express ideas. Use the passive voice if you want to stress the receiver of the action or if you don't know who performed the action.

EXAMPLE *Our Town* **was performed.** **[You may want to stress the play.]**

EXAMPLE The actors **were fired.** **[You may not know who fired the actors.]**

GRAMMAR / USAGE / MECHANICS

PRACTICE Using Active and Passive Voice

Rewrite each sentence, changing the verb from active to passive or from passive to active.

1. Benjamin Franklin published an almanac.
2. Athens, Greece, hosted the first modern Olympics.
3. Beethoven composed the music for "Ode to Joy."
4. The school newspaper is edited by students.
5. The president signed the agreement in the Oval Office.
6. Cosmas Ndeti completed the Boston Marathon in 2 hours, 7 minutes, and 15 seconds in 1994.
7. The prism separated the light into rainbow colors.
8. Amanda and her sister share a room.
9. The "Model T" was introduced by Ford in 1908.
10. Maria showed pictures of Mexico.

3.11 IRREGULAR VERBS

The irregular verbs listed here are grouped according to the way their past and past participle are formed.

IRREGULAR VERBS

PATTERN	BASE FORM	PAST	PAST PARTICIPLE
One vowel changes to form the past and the past participle.	begin	began	begun
	drink	drank	drunk
	ring	rang	rung
	shrink	shrank *or* shrunk	shrunk
	sing	sang	sung
	sink	sank	sunk
	spring	sprang *or* sprung	sprung
	swim	swam	swum
The past and the past participle are the same.	bring	brought	brought
	build	built	built
	buy	bought	bought
	catch	caught	caught
	creep	crept	crept
	feel	felt	felt
	fight	fought	fought
	find	found	found
	get	got	got *or* gotten
	have	had	had
	hold	held	held
	keep	kept	kept
	lay	laid	laid
	lead	led	led
	leave	left	left
	lend	lent	lent
	lose	lost	lost
	make	made	made
	meet	met	met
	pay	paid	paid
	say	said	said

PATTERN	BASE FORM	PAST	PAST PARTICIPLE
The past and the past participle are the same.	seek	sought	sought
	sell	sold	sold
	send	sent	sent
	sit	sat	sat
	sleep	slept	slept
	spend	spent	spent
	spin	spun	spun
	stand	stood	stood
	sting	stung	stung
	swing	swung	swung
	teach	taught	taught
	tell	told	told
	think	thought	thought
	win	won	won

PRACTICE Using Irregular Verbs I

Write the correct verb form from the choices in parentheses.

1. Sami (buyed, bought) fish and vegetables at the market every Saturday.
2. The French (fought, fighted) with American patriots during the Revolutionary War.
3. Julia (sang, sung) in the concert.
4. The baby (crept, creeped) across the room.
5. I (leaved, left) my postcards on the plane.
6. My jeans had (shrank, shrunk) in the dryer.
7. I (made, maked) my own costume for the play.
8. Julio (payed, paid) for tickets for tonight's baseball game.
9. The toy boat (sank, sunk) after several minutes.
10. Abraham Lincoln's speech (began, begun) with the words, "Four score and seven years ago."

3.12 MORE IRREGULAR VERBS

Here are some more irregular verbs.

IRREGULAR VERBS

PATTERN	BASE FORM	PAST	PAST PARTICIPLE
The base form and the past participle are the same.	become	became	become
	come	came	come
	run	ran	run
The past ends in *ew*, and the past participle ends in *wn*.	blow	blew	blown
	draw	drew	drawn
	fly	flew	flown
	grow	grew	grown
	know	knew	known
	throw	threw	thrown
The past participle ends in *en*.	bite	bit	bitten *or* bit
	break	broke	broken
	choose	chose	chosen
	drive	drove	driven
	eat	ate	eaten
	fall	fell	fallen
	freeze	froze	frozen
	give	gave	given
	ride	rode	ridden
	rise	rose	risen
	see	saw	seen
	shake	shook	shaken
	speak	spoke	spoken
	steal	stole	stolen
	take	took	taken
	write	wrote	written

PATTERN	BASE FORM	PAST	PAST PARTICIPLE
The past and the past participle don't follow any pattern.	be	was, were	been
	do	did	done
	go	went	gone
	lie	lay	lain
	tear	tore	torn
	wear	wore	worn
The base form, the past, and the past participle are the same.	burst	burst	burst
	cost	cost	cost
	cut	cut	cut
	hit	hit	hit
	hurt	hurt	hurt
	let	let	let
	put	put	put
	read	read	read
	set	set	set
	spread	spread	spread

PRACTICE Using Irregular Verbs II

Write the correct verb form from the choices in parentheses.

1. The kitten has (broken, broke) the new vase.
2. Joel has (run, ran) in the race every year.
3. Patrick (seen, saw) the play at school.
4. I (tore, torn) my sleeve on the nail.
5. Have you (wore, worn) your new shoes yet?
6. Sandy has (fell, fallen) on the ice.
7. I have (shaken, shook) the mixture for twenty seconds.
8. Percy has (read, readed) many of Gary Paulsen's books, including *Hatchet*.
9. The lake had (froze, frozen) during the night.
10. The left fielder had (threw, thrown) the ball to the shortstop.

PRACTICE Proofreading

Rewrite the following passage, correcting errors in spelling, capitalization, grammar, and usage. Add any missing punctuation. Write legibly to be sure one letter is not mistaken for another. There are ten mistakes.

Theodor Seuss Geisel

[1]Do you know the name Theodor Seuss Giesel. [2]That was the real name of the well-known children's author Dr. seuss. [3]Dr. Seuss had plan for a career as an English professor. [4]He become a cartoonist and writer instead.

[5]His first children's book begun as a nonsense poem. [6]He had wrote it while on a voyage in 1936. [7]Later, he drawed pictures for the poem. [8]The pictures and poem was published as the book *And to Think That I Saw It on Mulberry Street.* [9]This was the beginning of his career as a children's author.

[10]Seuss' book *The Cat in the Hat* changed children's book publishing. [11]He used jist a few easy-to-read words in the story. [12]Because of *The Cat in the Hat's* popularity, Seuss published many other delightful books that are now classics.

POSTTEST Action Verbs and Linking Verbs

Write each verb. Label the action verbs A *and the linking verbs* L.

1. Sound waves enter our ears.
2. They strike the eardrum.
3. The eardrum vibrates.
4. Signals reach the brain.
5. Then we hear sounds.
6. Some sounds are too high-pitched to be heard by humans.
7. The process of hearing is complicated.
8. Sir Francis Galton invented a whistle to call dogs.
9. The sound was too high for people to hear.
10. Dogs heard it clearly.

POSTTEST Direct Objects, Indirect Objects, Predicate Nouns, and Predicate Adjectives

Identify the italicized word in each sentence by writing direct object, indirect object, predicate noun, *or* predicate adjective.

11. All nuts have *shells*.
12. A cashew is a *seed* of a cashew apple.
13. My friend brought *me* a bag of cashews.
14. Cashews are my favorite *nuts*.
15. The children fly *kit*es in the spring.
16. Some construct their own *kites* from different materials.
17. The children win *prizes* for their kite designs.
18. Some kites are *complicated*
19. One type of kite is the *box kite.*
20. My sister showed her *friends* our homemade kite.

POSTTEST Present and Past Tenses and Progressive Forms

Write the verb. Then write present tense, past tense, present progressive, *or* past progressive *to identify the tenses.*

21. Race participants ran for ten miles.
22. Friends are distributing water every mile.
23. I am taking pictures of the race.
24. The race earns money for special causes.
25. The posters give information about the race.
26. The race was stopping traffic along its route.
27. The runners were talking about the course.
28. They wear special shirts.
29. Ian was hoping to win first prize.
30. Emily and other participants are walking.

GRAMMAR / USAGE / MECHANICS

POSTTEST Perfect and Future Tenses

Write the verb. Then write present perfect, past perfect, future, *or* future perfect *to identify its tense.*

31. I shall write the letter tomorrow.
32. I had returned the broken camera yesterday.
33. By next month, I will have saved enough money for a new digital camera.
34. Surely the electronics store will have closed before eight o'clock this evening.
35. The director has chosen the cast members for this year's school play.
36. Ms. Collins had forgotten her wallet.
37. The judges have given the scores for the first skater.
38. By next week, the teachers will have agreed on a program.
39. The students had ordered the books yesterday.
40. The farmhand will feed the horses.

POSTTEST Irregular Verbs

Write the correct verb form from the choices in parentheses.

41. They (sang, sung) the national anthem at the opening of the games.

42. The mice (creep, crept) along the rug.

43. I had (lend, lent) my brother the jacket.

44. The contestant (knew, known) the answers to all questions but one.

45. The news of the election results (spread, spreaded) quickly.

46. Have you (took, taken) the exam?

47. *The Wizard of Oz* has (become, became) a classic children's movie.

48. Knights (wore, worn) armor as a means of protection.

49. James (ate, eaten) lunch at 11:30 A.M. today.

50. Dad has (wrote, written) the grocery list.

Chapter 4

Pronouns

PRETEST Personal Pronouns

Write each personal pronoun. Then write one of the following phrases to identify the pronoun: subject pronoun as subject, subject pronoun as predicate pronoun, object pronoun as direct object, object pronoun as indirect object.

1. I saw you at the concert.
2. He gave her tickets for Saturday night's first show at the theater.
3. She offered him a seat, but he refused it.
4. Today's song leader is he.
5. The author of my favorite book series is she, and I have read all of the books.

PRETEST Using Pronouns

Write the correct word or phrase from the choices in parentheses.

6. The photographer gave Terrell, Alfie, and (they, them) a special price for the photographs.

7. The winner of the local newspaper's essay contest was (she, her).

8. The coach timed Becca and (him, he) as they ran laps around the track.

9. (We, Us) writers are always looking for new ideas for our stories.

10. (Sandy and I, Sandy and me, Me and Sandy, I and Sandy) met for lunch last week.

11. Susan and (him, he) ride the bus to school every day but Friday.

12. Ms. Michaud and (she, her) plan and direct the school play every year.

13. (You and I, You and me) can build the playhouse with the help of our parents.

14. The piano teacher gave (she and I, she and me, her and I, her and me) a duet to learn.

15. Grandpa gave (he and she, him and her, he and her, him and she) some old photos.

PRETEST Pronouns and Antecedents

Write each personal pronoun and its antecedent. If a pronoun doesn't have a clear antecedent, rewrite the numbered item to make the meaning clear.

16. Gail Carson Levine won a Newbery Medal for her first book. It was called *Ella Enchanted.*

17. Ms. Levine worked in an office. She took writing classes at night.

18. Walter Dean Myers grew up in Harlem, New York. He loved to read as a child.

19. Myers wrote a book about the place. It's called *Harlem.*

20. Myers's son drew the pictures for the book. He made the memories come alive.

PRETEST Identifying Pronouns

Write each pronoun. Then write possessive, indefinite, personal, reflexive, intensive, interrogative, *or* demonstrative *to identify it.*

21. His exercise equipment includes weights and a rowing machine.

22. Please be sure to wear your warm jacket, gloves, and hat.

23. The bicycle over there is mine.

24. Everyone will participate in the play as actors, directors, or stage crew.

25. Will you be giving yourself enough time to get to the theater before the show starts?

26. Who bought the stamps?

27. Many voted for the proposal to raise taxes for the schools.

28. They set up the chairs themselves.

29. These are beautiful flowers.

30. What is the capital city of Alaska?

PRETEST Indefinite Pronouns

Write the subjects and the correct words from the choices in parentheses.

31. Some of the drinks (is, are) warm, but other drinks are still cold.

32. Everything in this closet (belong, belongs) to my sister or me.

33. Some of the parents (has, have) volunteered to help with the class project.
34. Many of the children (plan, plans) to accept the principal's reading challenge.
35. Both (has, have) decided to take a computer course during the summer.
36. Someone (has, have) written an essay about going to the dentist.
37. Everyone (want, wants) to come to the street party.
38. Something large (is, are) in the gift bag.
39. Nobody on the team (like, likes) the new uniforms.
40. Others (travel, travels) in the afternoon.

PRETEST Personal, Reflexive, Intensive, Interrogative, and Demonstrative Pronouns

Write the correct word from the choices in parentheses.

41. (Whose, Who's) playing the trumpet in the school jazz band this year?
42. Jane and (me, I) will compete in next week's swimming meet.
43. (This, Those) is an adventure story about looking for a missing treasure.
44. Do (those, that) books belong on the bookshelf or in the cabinet?
45. The ending of the short story by Saki surprised (us, ourselves).
46. The drivers (theirselves, themselves) set up the course.
47. (Who, Whom) did Ms. Sullivan choose for the solo?
48. Do (this, these) match the hat?
49. Brad built the clock (himself, hisself).
50. We found (us, ourselves) thinking about the idea.

4.1 PERSONAL PRONOUNS CCSS L.6.1a, c, d

A **pronoun** is a word that takes the place of one or more nouns.

EXAMPLE Max likes books. **He** particularly enjoys novels.

EXAMPLE Max and Irma like books. **They** particularly enjoy novels.

In the first example, the pronoun *He* replaces the noun *Max* as the subject of the sentence. In the second example, *They* replaces *Max and Irma.*

Pronouns that refer to people or things are called **personal pronouns.**

Some personal pronouns are used as the subjects of sentences. Others are used as the objects of verbs.

A **subject pronoun** is used as the subject of a sentence. It may also be used like a predicate noun, in which case it's called a predicate pronoun.

EXAMPLE **I** enjoy a good book in my spare time. **[subject]**

EXAMPLE **We** belong to a book club. **[subject]**

EXAMPLE **She** gave a good book report. **[subject]**

EXAMPLE **It** was about Andrew Jackson. **[subject]**

EXAMPLE **They** especially like adventure stories. **[subject]**

EXAMPLE The most popular author was **he. [predicate pronoun]**

An **object pronoun** may be a direct object or an indirect object.

EXAMPLE The teacher praised **us. [direct object]**

EXAMPLE Tell **me** a story. **[indirect object]**

EXAMPLE The movie frightened **them. [direct object]**

EXAMPLE The class wrote **her** a letter. **[indirect object]**

EXAMPLE The story amuses **you. [direct object]**

EXAMPLE The plot gives **him** an idea. **[indirect object]**

PERSONAL PRONOUNS		
	SINGULAR	**PLURAL**
Subject Pronouns	I you he, she, it	we you they
Object Pronouns	me you him, her, it	us you them

PRACTICE Identifying Personal Pronouns

Write each personal pronoun. Then write one of the following phrases to identify the pronoun: subject pronoun as subject, subject pronoun as predicate pronoun, object pronoun as direct object, object pronoun as indirect object.

1. The waiter gave her the menu.
2. I brought him the book.
3. We sent them a letter.
4. The girl on the bus was you!
5. They enjoy taking care of animals.
6. The neighbors hire me to mow lawns.
7. He and she make a good working team.
8. She gave him the money.
9. You are inviting me to the party.
10. The driver of the car was he.

4.2 USING PRONOUNS CCSS L.6.1a, d

Use subject pronouns in compound subjects. Use object pronouns in compound objects.

EXAMPLE **He** and Carmen wrote the report. **[not *Him and Carmen*]**

EXAMPLE Tell John and **me** about the report. **[not *John and I*]**

If you're not sure which form of the pronoun to use, read the sentence with only the pronoun as the subject or the object. Your ear will tell you which form is correct.

When the pronoun *I, we, me,* or *us* is part of a compound subject or object, *I, we, me,* or *us* should come last. (It's simply courteous to name yourself or the group of which you are a part last.)

EXAMPLE Lee and **I** played some new tunes. **[not *I and Lee*]**

EXAMPLE Country music interests Lee and **me.** **[not *me and Lee*]**

In formal writing and speech, use a subject pronoun after a linking verb.

EXAMPLE The writer of this report was **she.**

EXAMPLE It is **I.**

A pronoun and a noun may be used together. The form of the pronoun depends on its use in the sentence.

EXAMPLE **We** students read the book. **[*We* is the subject.]**

EXAMPLE The book delighted **us** readers. **[*Us* is a direct object.]**

Some sentences make incomplete comparisons. The form of the pronoun can affect the meaning of such sentences. In any incomplete comparison, use the form of the pronoun that would be correct if the comparison were complete.

EXAMPLE You like pizza better than **I** [like pizza].

EXAMPLE You like pizza better than [you like] **me.**

PRACTICE Using Subject and Object Pronouns

Write the correct word or phrase from the choices in parentheses.

1. The seventh-graders and (we, us) will provide the information.
2. The teacher gave (we, us) students free passes for the film.
3. Dad prepared Jeremy and (they, them) a spaghetti dinner.

GRAMMAR / USAGE / MECHANICS

4. The manager told (Chris and I, I and Chris, Chris and me, me and Chris) to stock the shelves.
5. Johanna offers (him and me, me and him, he and I, I and him) a ride every morning.
6. Three of them and (us, we) qualified for the finals in gymnastics.
7. Ms. Sciarrone brought (he and I, I and he, me and him, him and me) a list of supplies.
8. The last two contestants in the spelling bee were Mai and (I, me).
9. (Dan and I, I and Dan, Me and Dan, Dan and me) walked to the store.
10. The program amazed (we, us) viewers.

GRAMMAR / USAGE / MECHANICS

4.3 PRONOUNS AND ANTECEDENTS CCSS L.6.1d

Read the following sentences. Can you tell to whom the pronoun *She* refers?

EXAMPLE Louisa May Alcott wrote a novel about a young woman. **She** had three sisters.

The sentence is not clear because the word *She* could refer to either *Louisa May Alcott* or *a young woman.* Sometimes you must repeat a noun or rewrite a sentence to avoid confusion.

EXAMPLE Louisa May Alcott wrote a novel about a young woman. **The young woman** had three sisters.

The word a pronoun refers to is called its **antecedent.** The word *antecedent* means "going before."

EXAMPLE **Jo March** is the main character in *Little Women.* **She** writes stories. **[*Jo March* is the antecedent of the pronoun *She.*]**

EXAMPLE **Meg, Beth,** and **Amy** are Jo's sisters. Jo writes **them** stories. **[*Meg, Beth,* and *Amy* are the antecedents of *them.*]**

When you use a pronoun, be sure it refers to its antecedent clearly. Be especially careful when you use the pronoun *they.* Read the following sentence.

EXAMPLE **They** have five books by Alcott at the school library.

The meaning of *They* is unclear. The sentence can be improved by rewriting it in the following way.

EXAMPLE The school library has five books by Alcott.

When you use pronouns, be sure they agree with their antecedents in **number** (singular or plural) and **gender.** The gender of a noun may be masculine (male), feminine (female), or neuter (referring to things).

EXAMPLE The Marches must face a death in the family. **They** face **it** with courage.

They is plural; it agrees with the plural antecedent *Marches. It* is singular and agrees with the singular antecedent *death.*

PRACTICE Identifying Pronouns and Antecedents

Write each personal pronoun and its antecedent. If a pronoun doesn't have a clear antecedent, rewrite the numbered item to make the meaning clear.

1. Deborah is reading about Charles Dickens. He is a famous British author.

2. Deborah's friends are also reading about Dickens. They are going to write a report.

3. Charles Dickens was the son of John Dickens, a clerk. He was born on February 7, 1812.

4. Charles's father was in debt. He was put in prison because he could not pay the debt.

5. Charles had to go to work. He worked in a shoe polish factory.

6. Dickens became a reporter. He wrote about social problems and debates in Parliament.

7. Sometimes they passed laws to stop the scandals that Dickens wrote about.

8. Some schools were closed after Dickens wrote the book *Nicholas Nickelby.* They had been unfair to children.

9. Thomas read *Oliver Twist,* a novel by Dickens about a poor boy. He enjoyed the story.

10. When Dickens died in 1870, he had not finished the novel *The Mystery of Edwin Drood*.

4.4 POSSESSIVE PRONOUNS CCSS L.6.1a, c

You often use personal pronouns to replace nouns that are subjects or objects in sentences. You can use pronouns in place of possessive nouns, too.

A **possessive pronoun** is a pronoun that shows who or what has something. A possessive pronoun may take the place of a possessive noun.

Read the following sentences. Notice the possessive nouns and the possessive pronouns that replace them.

EXAMPLE Lisa's class put on a play. **Her** class put on a play.

EXAMPLE The idea was Lisa's. The idea was **hers.**

Possessive pronouns have two forms. One form is used before a noun. The other form is used alone.

POSSESSIVE PRONOUNS

	SINGULAR	PLURAL
Used Before Nouns	my your her, his, its	our your their
Used Alone	mine yours hers, his, its	ours yours theirs

Possessive pronouns are not written with apostrophes. Don't confuse the possessive pronoun *its* with the word *it's*. *It's* is a contraction, or shortened form, of *it is* or *it has*.

EXAMPLE **Its** popularity is growing. **[possessive pronoun]**

EXAMPLE **It's** popular with many students. **[contraction of *It is*]**

EXAMPLE **It's** succeeded on the stage. **[contraction of *It has*]**

PRACTICE Identifying Possessive Pronouns

Write the possessive pronouns.

1. Shall we meet at your house or mine?
2. Our classroom is larger than yours.
3. Their report is longer than ours.
4. Was it his idea?
5. The table has lost its shine.
6. Their team has won more games than ours.
7. My dog is staying at their kennel.
8. Is the watch yours or his?
9. Where are your hockey sticks?
10. It was an honor to attend their graduation.

GRAMMAR / USAGE / MECHANICS

4.5 INDEFINITE PRONOUNS CCSS L.6.1c, d

An **indefinite pronoun** is a pronoun that does not refer to a particular person, place, or thing.

EXAMPLE **Everybody** thinks about the plot.

Some indefinite pronouns are always singular. Others are always plural. A few may be either singular or plural.

SOME INDEFINITE PRONOUNS

ALWAYS SINGULAR			ALWAYS PLURAL
another	everybody	no one	both
anybody	everyone	nothing	few
anyone	everything	one	many
anything	much	somebody	others
each	neither	someone	several
either	nobody	something	

The indefinite pronouns *all, any, most, none,* and *some* may be singular or plural, depending on the phrase that follows them.

When an indefinite pronoun is used as the subject of a sentence, the verb must agree with it in number.

EXAMPLE **Everyone reads** part of the novel. [singular]

EXAMPLE **Several enjoy** it very much. [plural]

EXAMPLE **Most** of the story **happens** in England. [singular]

EXAMPLE **Most** of the characters **seem** real. [plural]

Possessive pronouns often have indefinite pronouns as their antecedents. In such cases, the pronouns must agree in number. Note that in the first example below the words that come between the subject and the verb don't affect the agreement.

EXAMPLE **Each** of the actors memorizes **his** or **her** lines.

EXAMPLE **Many** are enjoying **their** roles in the play.

GRAMMAR / USAGE / MECHANICS

PRACTICE Using Indefinite Pronouns

Write the indefinite pronouns and the correct words from the choices in parentheses.

1. All of us (is, are) enjoying the trip to Chicago.
2. Several (have, has) visited the art museum.
3. Some (have, has) read about the city's neighborhoods.
4. One of the tour guides (explain, explains) about why the Old Water Tower is famous.
5. Many (is, are) interested in the story about the Great Chicago Fire of 1871.
6. Each of us (carry, carries) a street map of the city.
7. Everyone (want, wants) to visit Lincoln Park.
8. No one (have, has) to say good-bye to the city.
9. Everybody plans to spend all of (his or her, their) time touring.
10. Several missed (his or her, their) bus stop.

4.6 REFLEXIVE AND INTENSIVE PRONOUNS

CCSS L.6.1b, c

A **reflexive pronoun** ends with *-self* or *-selves* and refers to the subject of a sentence. In a sentence with a reflexive pronoun, the action of the verb returns to the subject.

EXAMPLE Yolanda bought **herself** a book on engine repair.

Reflexive Pronoun

Don't use a reflexive pronoun in place of a personal pronoun.

EXAMPLE Yolanda asked Pat and **me** for help. **[not *Pat and myself*]**

EXAMPLE Yolanda and **I** read the book. **[not *Yolanda and myself*]**

An **intensive pronoun** ends with *-self* or *-selves* and is used to draw special attention to a noun or a pronoun already named.

EXAMPLE Yolanda **herself** repaired the engine.

Intensive Pronoun

EXAMPLE Yolanda repaired the engine **herself.**

Intensive Pronoun

Reflexive and intensive pronouns are formed by adding *-self* or *-selves* to certain personal and possessive pronouns.

REFLEXIVE AND INTENSIVE PRONOUNS

SINGULAR	PLURAL
myself	ourselves
yourself	yourselves
himself, herself, itself	themselves

Don't use *hisself* or *theirselves* in place of *himself* and *themselves.*

GRAMMAR / USAGE / MECHANICS

PRACTICE Using Reflexive and Intensive Pronouns

Write the correct word from the choices in parentheses. Then write personal, reflexive, *or* intensive *to identify the word you chose.*

1. I gave (me, myself) a present for my birthday.
2. The teacher made the tape (himself, hisself).
3. We found (ourselves, us) on the wrong trail.
4. The children (themselves, they) cleaned and decorated the classroom.
5. Mom told Maureen and (me, myself) the message.
6. My friends and (myself, I) planned the party.
7. Bill and Sheila wrote the program (themselves, they).
8. The coach asked Jared and (herself, her) to lead the practice.
9. The children congratulated (themselves, yourselves) after the program.
10. Responsibility offers (ourselves, us) opportunities for trust.

4.7 INTERROGATIVE AND DEMONSTRATIVE PRONOUNS CCSS L.6.1a, c

An **interrogative pronoun** is a pronoun used to introduce an interrogative sentence.

The interrogative pronouns *who* and *whom* refer to people. *Who* is used when the interrogative pronoun is the subject of the sentence. *Whom* is used when the interrogative pronoun is an object.

EXAMPLE **Who** borrowed the book? **[subject]**

EXAMPLE **Whom** did the librarian call? **[direct object]**

Which and *what* refer to things and ideas.

EXAMPLES **Which** is it? **What** interests you?

Whose shows possession.

EXAMPLE I found a copy of the play. **Whose** is it?

Don't confuse *whose* with *who's*. *Who's* is a contraction of *who is* or *who has*.

A **demonstrative pronoun** is a pronoun that points out something.

The demonstrative pronouns are *this*, *that*, *these*, and *those*. *This* (singular) and *these* (plural) refer to things nearby. *That* (singular) and *those* (plural) refer to things at a distance.

EXAMPLE **This** is an interesting book. **[singular, nearby]**

EXAMPLE **These** are interesting books. **[plural, nearby]**

EXAMPLE **That** was a good movie. **[singular, at a distance]**

EXAMPLE **Those** were good movies. **[plural, at a distance]**

PRACTICE Using Interrogative and Demonstrative Pronouns

Write the correct word from the choices in parentheses.

1. (Whom, Who) was the first speaker to address the student assembly?
2. (Who's, Whose) coming at 8:00 A.M.?
3. Is (that, those) the last seat on the bus?
4. (Whose, Who's) jacket is on the floor?
5. (Which, What) of these two computer brands do you like better?
6. (Who, Whom) saw the game last night?
7. (This, These) glasses are dirty.
8. (That, Those) birds have made nests.
9. (Which, What) is in the picnic basket?
10. (Who, Whom) did the teacher ask to carry the flag?

PRACTICE Proofreading

Rewrite the following passage, correcting errors in spelling, capitalization, grammar, and usage. Add any missing punctuation. Write legibly to be sure one letter is not mistaken for another. There are ten mistakes.

Edmond Halley

[1]In science class, us students are reading about Edmond Halley. [2]Whom was Halley? [3]He were a famous English astronomer of the late 1600s and early 1700s.

[4]Halley received support from his father to study the stars in the Southern Hemisphere. [5]He then helped create a catalog of many of those stars. [6]These was the first catalog giving accurate locations.

[7]Halley saw a great comet sweep the sky in 1682. [8]He showed that its orbit was much like the orbits of comits seen in 1531 and 1607.

[9]Halley thought to him, "Could this be the same comet?" [10]He believed that it were. [11]He predicted it's return in 1758. [12]He was correct. [13]Halley's Comet is named after himself.

POSTTEST Personal Pronouns

Write each personal pronoun. Then write one of the following phrases to identify the pronoun: subject pronoun as subject, subject pronoun as predicate pronoun, object pronoun as direct object, object pronoun as indirect object.

1. You are making too many plans for one day.
2. They met him and me at the game.
3. The signers of the article were they.
4. She and I did homework together this afternoon.
5. She asked us about the movie.

POSTTEST Using Pronouns

Write the correct word or phrase from the choices in parentheses.

6. The game excited (we, us) fans.
7. Before the game, the ushers gave (they, them) the programs.
8. The most frightened climbers were (he and I, he and me, him and me, him and I).
9. Mr. Santi and (we, us) campers pitched the tents and stored our gear.
10. (I and you, You and I, Me and you, You and me) are reading the same book.
11. Mrs. Haskell helps (he and I, I and he, him and me, me and him) sort the cans for recycling.
12. Laurie and (her, she) picked tomatoes and other vegetables from the garden.
13. The guide showed (she and he, she and him, her and he, her and him) the new art exhibit.
14. (They, Them) spent the afternoon looking at the paintings.
15. The last ones to leave were (he and I, I and he, him and me, me and him).

POSTTEST Pronouns and Antecedents

Write each personal pronoun and its antecedent. If a pronoun doesn't have a clear antecedent, rewrite the numbered item to make the meaning clear.

16. Some animals are endangered. They need protection.
17. Giant pandas are endangered. They live in China.
18. Tory has a book about endangered animals. She read about the giant pandas.
19. Alphonse and Kim Su have to write about people helping endangered animals. They should read the book.
20. People sometimes use the land where animals live. Then they must find new places to live or die.

POSTTEST Identifying Pronouns

Write each pronoun. Then write possessive, indefinite, reflexive, intensive, interrogative, *or* demonstrative *to identify it.*

21. The magazine can still be read even though its cover and some of its pages are torn.
22. Who is Alvin Ailey?
23. The dancer himself founded a dance company.
24. His was a life of dedication to dancing and to the company.
25. Which of the following dances are difficult to learn and perform?
26. The young girl bought herself two books about dancing and three CDs of dance music.
27. The dancers make most of their costumes themselves.
28. Those were some of Angelina's goals in dancing.
29. Whom did Jessie ask for directions to the concert hall in the city?
30. Both want to learn how to dance, but neither has signed up for lessons.

POSTTEST Indefinite Pronouns

Write the subjects and the correct words from the choices in parentheses.

31. No one completely (understand, understands) the problem.
32. (Is, Are) either of the candidates speaking tonight?
33. Most of the planets in the solar system (have, has) moons.
34. Everybody in my family (like, likes) to cook.
35. Some of Earth's land features (include, includes) mountains, plains, and valleys.
36. Much of the program (was, were) unrehearsed.
37. Many of Earth's volcanoes (ring, rings) the Pacific Ocean.
38. (Is, Are) either of your parents coming to tonight's school board meeting?
39. (Do, Does) any of the experiment results support your hypothesis?
40. Some of Kristen's friends shop at retail stores, but others (buy, buys) clothes at resale shops.

POSTTEST Personal, Reflexive, Intensive, Interrogative, and Demonstrative Pronouns

Write the correct word from the choices in parentheses.

41. Do you know (whose, who's) pencils and notebooks these are?
42. The coach told (me, myself) about the extra practice scheduled after school this week.
43. (Who, Whom) did you talk to at the desk?
44. Are (those, that) Nancy's gloves?
45. (Whose, Who's) making your costume for you?
46. (That, Those) was a good idea.

47. The child gave Bjorn and (me, myself) a big smile when we waved at her.
48. The parents (theirselves, themselves) made the prizes.
49. Everyone (brings, bring) a sleeping bag.
50. (Who, Whom) made the list?

Chapter 5

Adjectives

PRETEST Identifying Adjectives

Write each adjective. Beside the adjective, write the noun it modifies.

1. On hot summer afternoons, the old dog loved to lie under the cooling spray of a lawn sprinkler.
2. The floor was littered with broken dishes, rotting vegetables, and overturned bottles.
3. In the old days, cola bottles were thick glass and had a greenish color.
4. The California peaches will spoil if you don't store them in a cool place.
5. Ian enjoyed watching the amazed faces when he performed astonishing acts.
6. Some people don't like board games.
7. Imagine yourself on a Hawaiian beach with a cool drink and a good book in early summer.
8. After Kristen ran through the muddy streets, her black and shiny leather shoes were filthy.

9. I have studied for seven long years, but I will never become fluent in the French language.
10. The colorful invitation asked us to attend a neighborhood pool party in two weeks.

PRETEST Articles and Demonstratives

Write the correct word or phrase from the choices in parentheses.

11. (A, The) man in the black cap is my father.
12. (These, Those) people over there have to be at the airport in (a, an) hour.
13. Babe Ruth signed (this, this here) baseball.
14. We will hike on (these, those) hills rather than (these, those) across the valley.
15. Neil Armstrong was (a, the) first person on the Moon.
16. That's (a, an) good idea for (a, an) interesting story.
17. Beth is (this, that) girl in the far corner.
18. Hand me (that, that there) hammer, please.
19. (This, These) scissors are blunt.
20. Get (them, those) dogs out of (this, this here) house.

PRETEST Comparative and Superlative Adjectives

Write the correct comparative or superlative form of the adjective in parentheses.

21. He always orders the (expensive) item on the menu.
22. Nothing is (elegant) than a plain gold ring.
23. Daniela always orders the (large) soft drink.
24. May is (cool) than July.
25. Please choose the (attractive) of the two carpets.
26. That is the (silly) film I've ever seen.
27. Few performers have been (successful) than Barbra Streisand.

28. Because Jenny practiced so hard, she has become the (accomplished) swimmer on the team.
29. The ads for that detergent claim that it will wash clothes (clean) than any other brand.
30. What makes spiders (scary) than kittens?

PRETEST Irregular Comparative and Superlative Adjectives

Write the correct word or phrase from the choices in parentheses.

31. That was by far the (worse, worst) movie that I have ever seen.
32. He is not a good fielder, but he is the (best, better) hitter on the team.
33. Amy complained that she was allowed to watch (less, more little) television than her friends.
34. How could any dog behave (worse, worst) than this one?
35. My sister's driving is a lot (more well, better) than my father's.
36. (More, Most) people watched the Super Bowl than any other show that day.
37. If you talked (littler, less), you would get more done.
38. Some of the (baddest, worst) times are when my friends are away.
39. Of the three friends, Jim had the (least, less) money.
40. Which planet has the (more, most) moons?

5.1 ADJECTIVES

The words we use to describe people, places, and things are called adjectives.

An **adjective** is a word that describes, or modifies, a noun or a pronoun.

Adjectives modify nouns in three ways.

	HOW ADJECTIVES MODIFY NOUNS
WHAT KIND?	We studied **ancient** history.
HOW MANY?	I read **four** chapters.
WHICH ONE?	**That** invention changed history.

Most adjectives come before the nouns they modify. Some adjectives follow linking verbs and modify the noun or pronoun that is the subject of the sentence.

EXAMPLE **Some** architects are **skillful** and **imaginative.**

The adjective *some* comes before the noun *architects.* The adjectives *skillful* and *imaginative* follow the linking verb, *are,* and modify the subject, *architects.* They are called predicate adjectives.

A **predicate adjective** follows a linking verb and modifies the subject of a sentence.

Two verb forms are often used as adjectives and predicate adjectives. They are the present participle and the past participle.

EXAMPLE The architect drew a **surprising** design. **[present participle]**

EXAMPLE Visitors seem **impressed**. **[past participle]**

Some adjectives are formed from proper nouns and begin with a capital letter. They are called proper adjectives.

Proper adjectives are adjectives formed from proper nouns.

Some proper adjectives have the same form as the noun. Others are formed by adding an ending to the noun form.

FORMING PROPER ADJECTIVES

PROPER NOUN	PROPER ADJECTIVE
oranges from **Florida**	**Florida** oranges
the history of **America**	**American** history

More than one adjective may modify the same noun.

EXAMPLE **These new frozen** *dinners* are **tasty** and **nutritious.**

These, new, frozen, tasty, and *nutritious* all modify *dinners.*

NOTE Many words that are usually nouns can also be used as adjectives: ***stone** wall, **band** uniform, **baseball** game.*

GRAMMAR / USAGE / MECHANICS

PRACTICE Identifying Adjectives

Write each adjective. Beside the adjective, write the noun it modifies.

1. Old movies are sometimes funny.
2. The star of this movie is a famous English comedian.
3. In one hilarious scene, he falls into a huge vat of wet cement.
4. That broken red seat is uncomfortable.
5. With amazing luck, we got the winning number!
6. Geese are grazing on the soccer field.
7. "The Laughing Policeman" is a silly song.
8. Here's a hard question: Why is the sky blue?
9. The long wait made some people look irritated.
10. The canceled flights were for European cities.

5.2 ARTICLES AND DEMONSTRATIVES

The words *a, an,* and *the* make up a special group of adjectives called **articles.**

A and *an* are called **indefinite articles** because they refer to one of a general group of people, places, things, or ideas. *A* is used before words beginning with a consonant sound. *An* is used before words beginning with a vowel sound. Don't confuse sounds with spellings. In speaking, you would say *a university* but *an uncle, a hospital* but *an honor.*

EXAMPLES **a** union **a** picture **an** hour **an** easel

The is called the **definite article** because it identifies specific people, places, things, or ideas.

EXAMPLE **The** picture beside **the** fireplace is **the** best one.

The words *this, that, these,* and *those* are called **demonstrative adjectives.** They are used to point out something.

DEMONSTRATIVE ADJECTIVES	
Take **this** umbrella with you.	**That** store is closed.
Take **these** boots too.	**Those** clouds are lovely.

Demonstrative adjectives point out something and modify nouns by answering the question *which one?* or *which ones?*

Use *this* and *that* with singular nouns. Use *these* and *those* with plural nouns. Use *this* and *these* to point out something close to you. Use *that* and *those* to point out something at a distance.

DEMONSTRATIVES

	SINGULAR	PLURAL
NEAR	this	these
FAR	that	those

GRAMMAR / USAGE / MECHANICS

Demonstratives can be used with nouns or without them. When they're used without nouns, they're called **demonstrative pronouns.**

DEMONSTRATIVE PRONOUNS	
This is mine.	**These** are his.
That is hers.	**Those** are yours.

The words *here* and *there* should not be used with demonstrative adjectives or demonstrative pronouns. The words *this, these, that,* and *those* already point out the locations *here* and *there.*

EXAMPLE Look at **this** photograph. [not *this here photograph*]

Don't use the object pronoun *them* in place of the demonstrative adjective *those.*

EXAMPLE I took a photo of **those** buildings. [not *them buildings*]

GRAMMAR / USAGE / MECHANICS

PRACTICE Using Articles and Demonstratives

Write the correct word from the choices in parentheses.

1. (Those, Those there) people are calling to us.
2. The medal was (a, an) honor she richly deserved.
3. (A, The) Louvre Museum is one of (a, the) world's largest museums.
4. (This, This here) is (a, an) intelligent young man.
5. Adding (a, an) onion livens up (a, the) salad.
6. Are you enjoying (this, these) summer days?
7. The Wright Brothers flew in (a, an) airplane like (those, them) double-winged models over there.
8. (This, That) ball is over (a, the) fence for (a, an) home run.
9. Dogs are (an, the) animal I love the best.
10. (This, That) bird is too far away to identify.

5.3 COMPARATIVE AND SUPERLATIVE ADJECTIVES

The **comparative form** of an adjective compares one person or thing with another.

The **superlative form** of an adjective compares one person or thing with several others.

For most adjectives with one syllable and for some with two syllables, add *-er* to form the comparative and *-est* to form the superlative.

EXAMPLE Is Venezuela **larger** than Peru?

EXAMPLE Is Brazil the **richest** country in South America?

For most adjectives with two or more syllables, form the comparative by using *more* before the adjective. Form the superlative by using *most* before the adjective.

EXAMPLE Is Chile **more mountainous** than Bolivia?

EXAMPLE Was Simón Bolívar South America's **most successful** general?

GRAMMAR / USAGE / MECHANICS

COMPARATIVE AND SUPERLATIVE FORMS

BASE FORM	COMPARATIVE	SUPERLATIVE
small	small**er**	small**est**
big	big**ger**	big**gest**
pretty	pretti**er**	pretti**est**
fabulous	**more** fabulous	**most** fabulous

The words *less* and *least* are used before both short and long adjectives to form the negative comparative and superlative.

NEGATIVE COMPARATIVE AND SUPERLATIVE FORMS	
BASE FORM	The first dancer was **graceful.**
COMPARATIVE	The second dancer was **less graceful** than the first.
SUPERLATIVE	The third dancer was the **least graceful** one.

Don't use *more, most, less,* or *least* before adjectives that already end with *-er* or *-est.* This is called a double comparison.

PRACTICE Using Comparative and Superlative Adjectives I

Write the correct comparative or superlative form of the adjective in parentheses.

1. Our new car is (fast) than our old one.
2. A Great Dane is (powerful) than a cocker spaniel.
3. That is the (lovely) sunset I have ever seen.
4. He won a prize for raising the (fat) pig.
5. These are the (valuable) stamps in my collection.
6. She is (generous) than her sister.
7. This chair is (cozy) than that one.
8. He wants to be (famous) than the president.
9. Sam is the (intelligent) boy I know.
10. These are the (hot) peppers I have ever tasted.

PRACTICE Using Comparative and Superlative Adjectives II

Write the correct word or phrase from the choices in parentheses.

1. Day by day, the puppy grew (activer, more active).
2. The book Miwako chose was the (less difficult, least difficult) of any on the list.
3. This has been the (happier, happiest) day of my life.

4. Buy the (cheerfuler, more cheerful) of the two photos.
5. Your garden is (drier, most dry) than mine.
6. The teacher was (less satisfied, least satisfied) with these papers than with the first ones.
7. Ours is the (higher scoring, highest scoring) team in the whole league.
8. That's the (sensiblest, most sensible) idea I've heard all week.
9. Every movie she stars in is (unusualer, more unusual) than the last one.
10. I can't think of a (less enjoyable, least enjoyable) field trip than the one we took last year.

5.4 IRREGULAR COMPARATIVE AND SUPERLATIVE ADJECTIVES

The comparative and superlative forms of some adjectives are not formed in the regular way.

EXAMPLE Harriet Tubman believed in a **good** cause.

EXAMPLE She knew that freedom was **better** than slavery.

EXAMPLE The Underground Railroad was the **best** route to freedom.

Better is the comparative form of the adjective *good.* *Best* is the superlative form of *good.*

IRREGULAR COMPARATIVE AND SUPERLATIVE FORMS

BASE FORM	COMPARATIVE	SUPERLATIVE
good, well	better	best
bad	worse	worst
many, much	more	most
little	less	least

Don't use *more* or *most* before irregular adjectives that are already in the comparative or superlative form.

EXAMPLE Tubman felt **better** at the end of the day. **[not *more better*]**

PRACTICE Using Irregular Adjectives

Write the correct word or phrase from the choices in parentheses.

1. Surely Michael can do (better, more well) than that.
2. We had (less, least) snow this year than last year.
3. Kim went on (many, more) rides than anyone else.
4. The storms on those mountains are among the (baddest, worst) in the world.
5. I've just read the (best, most best) book.
6. Brian always manages to do the (less, least) amount of work possible.
7. By putting out (littler, less) food for the birds, you won't attract so many squirrels.
8. Of the twins, Amy was the (more, most) chatty.
9. Who in this class is (better, best) at spelling?
10. During a thunderstorm, one of the (worse, worst) places to be is under an isolated tall tree.

PRACTICE Proofreading

Rewrite the following passage, correcting errors in spelling, capitalization, grammar, and usage. Add any missing punctuation. Write legibly to be sure one letter is not mistaken for another. There are ten mistakes.

Thomas Jefferson

[1]Thomas Jefferson was the third president of the United States. [2]He is most best known today as the author of the Declaration of Independence. [3]He was also a expert in architecture and farming.

[4]Jefferson held many jobs before becoming president. [5]As a young man, he was an lawyer in Virginia. [6]When the American colonies rebelled against the British, he wrote the Declaration of Independence. [7]He later became governor of Virginia, minister to France, and secretary of state.

[8]As President, Jefferson is remembered for the louisiana Purchase. [9]In 1803, he bought land from France, doubling a country's size. [10]Jefferson served as president for two terms.

[11]As well as being a politician, Jefferson was one of the famousest architects in the country. [12]He designed Monticello, his beatiful home in Virginia. [13]Today these thirty-five-room mansion is a major tourist attraction.

[14]Jefferson loved to farm. [15]In retirement at Monticello, he experimented with the latest seeds. [16]His aim was to grow more better vegetables and flowers. [17]He also owned over six thousand books. [18]He was one of this here country's most brilliant citizens.

POSTTEST Identifying Adjectives

Write each adjective. Beside the adjective, write the noun it modifies.

1. Under an orange moon, the children sang folk songs.
2. Seventeen students are going on the New York trip.
3. The favorite soup in the school cafeteria is creamy tomato soup.
4. The blue suit makes you look mature.
5. To the European settlers, the great prairie appeared to be an endless sea of waving grass.
6. These flies are so tiny that they can get in through the screen windows of the new tent.
7. Don't be afraid.
8. Babysitters generally avoid reading scary bedtime stories to little children.

9. Senta laughed at the astonished expressions of people when they got off the new roller coaster.
10. Haroun chose to do the high jump at the track meet on Sunday.

POSTTEST Articles and Demonstratives

Write the correct word or phrase from the choices in parentheses.

11. (A, The) automobile had not been invented in (these, those) days.
12. After a day of searching, we found (a, the) hamster and returned it to (a, the) cage.
13. They measured time with (a, an) hourglass.
14. (This, These) baseball season seems to go on and on.
15. (Them, Those) school books are in bad repair.
16. (A, The) driver of (that, that there) car swerved to avoid (a, an) opossum.
17. Do you prefer (these, those) apples I am holding or (these, those) in the orchard?
18. He was driving in (a, the) wrong direction on (a, an) one-way street.
19. Andrew was (a, an, the) only person wearing (a, the) jacket and tie at the ball game.
20. Give (these, these here) flowers to the people setting the tables.

POSTTEST Comparative and Superlative Adjectives

Write the correct comparative or superlative form of the adjective in parentheses.

21. That's the (weird) book I've ever read.
22. Can I make you (comfortable)?
23. He has a (charming) manner than his brother.

24. The lake is (muddy) than the river.
25. Bill made the (useful) remark at our meeting.
26. From the (tall) of those two towers, you can see the White Mountains.
27. The (old) puppy in the pet shop looked at us sadly through the window.
28. That movie was (terrifying) than I had expected.
29. The cheetah can run (fast) than any other mammal.
30. The (dramatic) episode of the series made me cry.

POSTTEST Irregular Comparative and Superlative Adjectives

Write the correct word or phrase from the choices in parentheses.

31. Carlos knows a (better, more better) way of getting home than you do.
32. That's the (more, most) points Luisa has ever scored.
33. As she grew weaker, there was (more little, less) the doctor could do to help.
34. This trip will take the (less, least) amount of time to complete.
35. The (worse, worst) storm of the century struck in December of last year.
36. His golf game went from bad to (worse, worser).
37. Noriko buys the (much, most) expensive clothes.
38. In the old western movies, the (worst, baddest) outlaw was punished for his or her crimes.
39. I don't think many people can do (more well, better) than that.
40. Summer is the season in which I have the (most, mostest) fun.

Chapter 6

Adverbs

PRETEST Identifying Adverbs

Write each adverb and the word it modifies. Then write whether the modified word is a verb, *an* adjective, *or an* adverb.

1. Knock gently on the green door.
2. Come to my office immediately.
3. Do you often go to the movies?
4. Americans will forever remember the nation's first president, George Washington.
5. We looked for a very long time but could find her ring nowhere.
6. Proceed extremely cautiously along the snowy road.
7. Jim emerged suddenly from the icy water with a rather wild look in his eyes.
8. The cat leapt gracefully onto the wall and licked its fur quietly in the sun.
9. She plays the piano skillfully but is just brilliant on the violin.
10. When it is raining extremely hard, people generally drive slowly.

PRETEST Comparative and Superlative Adverbs

Write the correct word or phrase from the choices in parentheses.

11. I think the second movie was (better, more better) than the first, but I fell asleep halfway through the first one.
12. Jack lives (farther, farthest) from the school than Juanita does.
13. He plays (worse, worst) than I do.
14. The tiger returned to its cage (quietlier, more quietly, most quietly) than we had expected.
15. She was playing the (better, best) of all the girls on the field.
16. Of the five boys, Miko swims (less, least) confidently.
17. I follow lots of sports but enjoy football the (more, most).
18. The (oftener, more often, oftenest) you practice, the better you will become.
19. Of all the birds, the chickadee visits our feeder the (more frequently, most frequently).
20. When grades came out, Jeff learned that he was doing (more better, better, best) than he had thought.

PRETEST Using Adjectives and Adverbs

Write the correct word from the choices in parentheses.

21. That's a (real, really) bad bruise she has on her leg.
22. People like Fred are (good, well) to have with you in emergencies.
23. Kristin can (sure, surely) skate well.
24. Don't feel (bad, badly) about breaking the vase.
25. I (most, almost) always fall asleep while reading books with small print.
26. Coming out of the hospital, he said he felt (good, well).
27. You can be (sure, surely) that there will be snow next month.

28. He wanted the tickets so (bad, badly) that he slept on the sidewalk outside the office.
29. It was (real, really) clever of you to recall her name by using a memory device.
30. A bear may look (slow, slowly), but it can run fast.

PRETEST Correcting Double Negatives

Rewrite each sentence so it correctly expresses a negative idea.

31. He didn't hardly know what to say.
32. Don't never go into those woods again.
33. I'm beginning to think that there isn't no way out this building.
34. During the day the traffic was loud, but after dark there wasn't barely a sound.
35. The suspect swore he hadn't done nothing.
36. She didn't see no one suspicious when she entered the house that evening.
37. You aren't going nowhere dressed like that.
38. When he first left home, Jessie used to hear from him, but now he scarcely never phones her.
39. There isn't nothing left to paint.
40. In the old days, horse-drawn vehicles were the chief means of transport, but now there are hardly none left.

6.1 ADVERBS THAT MODIFY VERBS

Adjectives are words that modify nouns and pronouns. Adverbs are another type of modifier. They modify verbs, adjectives, and other adverbs.

An **adverb** is a word that modifies a verb, an adjective, or another adverb.

WHAT ADVERBS MODIFY	
VERBS	People *handle* old violins **carefully.**
ADJECTIVES	**Very** *old* violins are valuable.
ADVERBS	Orchestras **almost** *always* include violins.

An adverb may tell *how* or *in what manner* an action is done. It may tell *when* or *how often* an action is done. It may also tell *where* or *in what direction* an action is done.

WAYS ADVERBS MODIFY VERBS

ADVERBS TELL	EXAMPLES
HOW	grandly, easily, completely, neatly, gratefully, sadly
WHEN	soon, now, immediately, often, never, usually, early
WHERE	here, there, everywhere, inside, downstairs, above, far

When an adverb modifies an adjective or another adverb, the adverb usually comes before the word it modifies. When an adverb modifies a verb, the adverb can occupy different positions in a sentence.

POSITION OF ADVERBS MODIFYING VERBS	
BEFORE THE VERB	Guests **often** dine at the White House.
AFTER THE VERB	Guests dine **often** at the White House.
AT THE BEGINNING	**often** guests dine at the White House.
AT THE END	Guests dine at the White House **often.**

Many adverbs are formed by adding *-ly* to adjectives. However, not all words that end in *-ly* are adverbs. The words *friendly, lively, kindly, lovely,* and *lonely* are usually adjectives. On the other hand, not all adverbs end in *-ly.*

SOME ADVERBS NOT ENDING IN *-LY*			
afterward	everywhere	near	short
already	fast	never	sometimes
always	forever	not	somewhere
anywhere	hard	now	soon
away	here	nowhere	straight
below	home	often	then
even	late	outside	there
ever	long	seldom	well

PRACTICE Identifying Adverbs I

Write each adverb. Beside the adverb, write the verb it modifies.

1. Lying silently on a wide branch, the leopard intently watched its prey.
2. The glacier crept gradually toward the sea.
3. Step outside for a minute and have a look at the fantastic sunset.
4. We have been walking for miles, but I am sorry to say that we are getting nowhere.
5. Everywhere you travel, you will meet people who are curious to learn about life in the United Sates.
6. Go straight along Main Street.
7. Some people seldom appear unhappy.
8. Shake the orange juice well before serving it.
9. The mountaineer often described the terror he had felt when the volcano erupted.
10. Never had the castaway been as happy as when he saw a tiny sail on the horizon.

6.2 ADVERBS THAT MODIFY ADJECTIVES AND OTHER ADVERBS

Adverbs are often used to modify adjectives and other adverbs. Notice how adverbs affect the meaning of the adjectives in the following sentences. Most often they tell *how* or *to what extent.*

EXAMPLE Harry Truman used **extremely** direct language.

EXAMPLE He became a **very** popular president.

In the first sentence, the adverb *extremely* modifies the adjective *direct. Extremely* tells to what extent Truman's language was direct. In the second sentence, the adverb *very* modifies the adjective *popular. Very* tells to what extent Truman was popular.

In the following sentences, adverbs modify other adverbs.

EXAMPLE Truman entered politics **unusually** late in life.

EXAMPLE He moved through the political ranks **quite** quickly.

In the first sentence, the adverb *unusually* modifies the adverb *late. Unusually* tells how late Truman entered politics. In the second sentence, the adverb *quite* modifies the adverb *quickly. Quite* tells how quickly Truman moved through the ranks.

When an adverb modifies an adjective or another adverb, the adverb almost always comes directly before the word it modifies. On the following page is a list of some adverbs that are often used to modify adjectives and other adverbs.

ADVERBS OFTEN USED TO MODIFY ADJECTIVES AND OTHER ADVERBS			
almost	just	rather	too
barely	nearly	really	totally
extremely	partly	so	unusually
hardly	quite	somewhat	very

PRACTICE Identifying Adverbs II

Write each adverb and the word it modifies. Then write whether the modified word is a verb, *an* adjective, *or an* adverb.

1. She sang quite beautifully at the concert.
2. You have to be an awfully good shot to hit the bull's eye from this distance.
3. The dog looked perfectly happy lying in the sun.
4. Thelma's voice was just audible to those who could not get into the auditorium.
5. Corey returned from summer camp very reluctantly.
6. Brooke skated so quickly that the rink attendant gave her a warning.
7. Sal and his sister almost never go on vacations.
8. Chips and soda is a totally unhealthful lunch.
9. Today will be partly cloudy and rather cool.
10. He spoke really sternly to the boys.

6.3 COMPARATIVE AND SUPERLATIVE ADVERBS

The **comparative form** of an adverb compares one action with another.

The **superlative form** of an adverb compares one action with several others.

Most short adverbs add *-er* to form the comparative and *-est* to form the superlative.

COMPARING ADVERBS WITH *-ER* AND *-EST*	
COMPARATIVE	The pianist arrived **earlier** than the violinist.
SUPERLATIVE	The drummer arrived **earliest** of all the players.

Long adverbs and a few short ones require the use of *more* or *most.*

COMPARING ADVERBS WITH *MORE* AND *MOST*	
COMPARATIVE	The violinist plays **more often** than the harpist.
SUPERLATIVE	Which musicians play **most often?**

Some adverbs have irregular comparative and superlative forms.

IRREGULAR COMPARATIVE AND SUPERLATIVE FORMS

BASE FORM	COMPARATIVE	SUPERLATIVE
well	better	best
badly	worse	worst
little	less	least
far (distance)	farther	farthest
far (degree)	further	furthest

The words *less* and *least* are used before adverbs to form the negative comparative and superlative.

EXAMPLES I play **less well.** I play **least accurately.**

Don't use *more, most, less,* or *least* before adverbs that already end in *-er* or *-est.*

GRAMMAR / USAGE / MECHANICS

PRACTICE Using Comparative and Superlative Adverbs

Write the correct word or phrase from the choices in parentheses.

1. The dog cleans up under the table (more, most) successfully with its tongue than Rafael does with a broom.
2. That is the (less, least) likely story I've ever heard.
3. He goes to the ball game (oftener, more often, most often) than I do.
4. I wish you'd got here (sooner, more sooner).
5. If you study math (further, furthest), you will find that it is a very rewarding subject.
6. Jaime throws the ball (farther, more farther, farthest) than anyone else on the team.
7. The mockingbird sings (sweetlier, more sweetly, more sweetlier) than the crow.
8. Bill enjoys history class (better, more better) than Jesse does.
9. Who plays soccer (better, best)–Fernando, Michael, or Abel?
10. Ours is the (worse, worst) prepared team in the school.

6.4 USING ADJECTIVES AND ADVERBS

Sometimes it's hard to decide whether a sentence needs an adjective or an adverb. Think carefully about how the word is used.

EXAMPLE He was (**careful, carefully**) with the antique clock.

EXAMPLE He worked (**careful, carefully**) on the antique clock.

In the first sentence, the missing word follows a linking verb and modifies the subject, *He.* Therefore, an adjective is needed. *Careful* is the correct choice. In the second sentence, the missing word modifies the verb, *worked.* Thus, an adverb is needed, and *carefully* is the correct choice.

The words *good* and *well* and the words *bad* and *badly* are sometimes confused. *Good* and *bad* are adjectives. Use them before nouns and after linking verbs. *Well* and *badly* are adverbs. Use them to modify verbs. *Well* may also be used as an adjective to mean "healthy": *You look well today.*

TELLING ADJECTIVES FROM ADVERBS

ADJECTIVE	ADVERB
The band sounds **good.**	The band plays **well.**
The band sounds **bad.**	The band plays **badly.**
The soloist is **well.**	The soloist sings **well.**

Use these modifiers correctly: *real* and *really, sure* and *surely, most* and *almost. Real* and *sure* are adjectives. *Really, surely,* and *almost* are adverbs. *Most* can be an adjective or an adverb.

TELLING ADJECTIVES FROM ADVERBS

ADJECTIVE	ADVERB
Music is a **real** art.	This music is **really** popular.
A pianist needs **sure** hands.	Piano music is **surely** popular.
Most pianos have eighty-eight keys.	Piano strings **almost** never break.

PRACTICE Using Adjectives and Adverbs

Write the correct word from the choices in parentheses.

1. I feel so (good, well) to have finished that book.
2. Getting on the team is not a (sure, surely) thing for me.

3. It was (sure, surely) lucky that a police officer was nearby.
4. She looked (bad, badly) after hearing the news.
5. Debbie studied so (good, well) that she had no trouble on the test.
6. There are some (real, really) nice kids in this club.
7. The teacher detected (real, really) ability in Juan.
8. (Most, Almost) all the students had seen the movie.
9. The bear looked at me (angry, angrily).
10. I hope I did not do as (bad, badly) as I think I did.

6.5 CORRECTING DOUBLE NEGATIVES

The adverb *not* is a **negative word,** expressing the idea of "no." *Not* often appears in a short form as part of a contraction. When *not* is part of a contraction, as in the words in the chart below, *n't* is an adverb.

CONTRACTIONS WITH *NOT*		
are not = aren't	does not = doesn't	should not = shouldn't
cannot = can't	had not = hadn't	was not = wasn't
could not = couldn't	has not = hasn't	were not = weren't
did not = didn't	have not = haven't	will not = won't
do not = don't	is not = isn't	would not = wouldn't

In all but two of these words, the apostrophe replaces the *o* in *not.* In *can't* both an *n* and the *o* are omitted. *Will not* becomes *won't.*

Other negative words are listed in the following chart. Each negative word has several opposites. These are **affirmative words,** or words that show the idea of "yes."

SOME NEGATIVE AND AFFIRMATIVE WORDS	
NEGATIVE	**AFFIRMATIVE**
never, scarcely, hardly, barely	always, ever
nobody	anybody, everybody, somebody
no, none	all, any, one, some
no one	anyone, everyone, one, someone
nothing	anything, something
nowhere	anywhere, somewhere

GRAMMAR / USAGE / MECHANICS

Don't use two negative words to express the same idea. This is called a **double negative.** Only one negative word is necessary to express a negative idea. You can correct a double negative by removing one of the negative words or by replacing one of the negative words with an affirmative word.

EXAMPLE **INCORRECT** I **don't** have **no** homework.

EXAMPLE **CORRECT** I have **no** homework.

EXAMPLE **CORRECT** I **don't** have **any** homework.

PRACTICE Expressing Negative Ideas

Rewrite each sentence so it correctly expresses a negative idea.

1. The doctor said there wasn't nothing wrong with Joel.
2. If we keep on polluting the water, there won't be nowhere left to swim.
3. Imo wasn't hardly talking during the movie.
4. Isn't there none of that lemonade left?
5. This little snake couldn't do no harm.

6. Why didn't nobody tell Frank about the party?
7. You haven't barely eaten a thing all day.
8. There's never nothing to do in this town.
9. You shouldn't tell no one about this.
10. Sally is afraid she won't get no birthday presents.

PRACTICE Proofreading

Rewrite the following passage, correcting errors in spelling, capitalization, grammar, and usage. Add any missing punctuation. Write legibly to be sure one letter is not mistaken for another. There are ten mistakes.

Galileo

[1]Galileo Galilei was born in Pisa, Italy, in 1564. [2]All his life, he hardly never stopped trying to understand the universe. [3]He is remembered today as a real famous scientist.

[4]Galileo did not invent the telescope, but he observed the skies carefullier than others had done. [5]He was the first to see that the Moon was mountainous. [6]He also looked more deeper into space than anyone else. [7]The planet Jupiter, he observed, had moons that circled it. [8]This led him to an amazing discovery. [9]Before his time, people had thought that the Earth was the most important planet. [10]They said it was in the center of the universe and didn't never move. [11]Galileo's observations proved that the Earth sure was in motion.

[12]The Church leaders in Rome did not approve of Galileo's findings. [13]They angriley put him on trial. [14]After that he talked least about the planets than he had before. [15]But people today know that Galileo was most always right. [16]He had advanced the study of astronomy more further than anyone before him.

POSTTEST Identifying Adverbs

Write each adverb and the word it modifies. Then write whether the modified word is a verb, *an* adjective, *or an* adverb.

1. I will be forever grateful to the person who returns my wallet.
2. Speak very softly in a library.
3. As she left, Branka shut the door unnecessarily loudly.
4. A really accurate shot will win the competition.
5. Too many politicians do not take the public seriously.
6. "Trick or treat," whispered the little ghost timidly.
7. Jeff was badly hurt during the game.
8. Soon you will understand what I am talking about.
9. So many people turned up for the game that it was nearly impossible to get a really good seat.
10. We all thought that he behaved extremely rudely.

GRAMMAR / USAGE / MECHANICS

POSTTEST Comparative and Superlative Adverbs

Write the correct word or phrase from the choices in parentheses.

11. Juan played (more, most) in that one game than he did all last season.
12. I would like to travel (oftener, more often), but I don't have the time or the money.
13. Of all her siblings, Ashley tries (harder, more harder, hardest) to excel.
14. We extended our search for the missing dog (farther, more farther) into the woods.
15. In our class, Bonny was voted (more, most) likely to become a movie star.
16. Of all my subjects, I do (less, least) well in music.
17. He addressed us (more seriously, seriouslier) than he ever had previously.

18. The rhinoceros charges (more fiercely, most fiercely) than the armadillo!
19. He plays (better, best) of all when he is rested.
20. Of the three brothers, Eugene behaved (worse, worst) on the camping trip.

POSTTEST Using Adjectives and Adverbs

Write the correct word from the choices in parentheses.

21. I can't explain how (bad, badly) I want the trophy.
22. If you are feeling (good, well) enough to play football, you can go to school.
23. "Summer is (almost, most) over," he groaned.
24. The cat looks (fierce, fiercely) when it is hunting mice.
25. You cleaned up that car (real, really) (nice, nicely).
26. I can't believe how (quick, quickly) she ran.
27. We are (sure, surely) to win the game now.
28. It is (good, well) to get plenty of sleep.
29. The chances of getting out alive looked (bad, badly).
30. Here's a (real, really) opportunity to earn some money.

GRAMMAR / USAGE / MECHANICS

POSTTEST Correcting Double Negatives

Rewrite each sentence so it correctly expresses a negative idea.

31. You shouldn't never swim out so far that you can't easily swim back
32. Don't write nothing until I tell you to start.
33. Haven't you got nowhere to go after school?
34. Kalisha can't remember nothing about first grade.
35. When Renzo first arrived in this country, he couldn't speak hardly any English.
36. Don't tell nobody that I know this.
37. At that distance, we could hear barely nothing.
38. Jules wanted a soda, but there weren't none left.
39. I can't understand why Sandra hasn't got no friends.
40. As far as I could see, nobody did nothing.

Chapter 7

Prepositions, Conjunctions, and Interjections

PRETEST Prepositions and Prepositional Phrases

Write each prepositional phrase. Underline the preposition and circle the object of the preposition. Then write the word the prepositional phrase modifies. Finally, write adjective *or* adverb *to tell how the prepositional phrase is used.*

1. It was a beautiful day for a baseball game.
2. Two small clouds floated above the field.
3. The rest of the sky was clear and bright blue.
4. The people at the game seemed happy.
5. They ate hot dogs and peanuts during the game.
6. The home team was ahead by the second inning.
7. In the fourth inning, the visitors tied the game.
8. However, the home team won by two runs.

9. The home team got one run in the fifth inning.
10. The last run came at the end of the ninth, so it was a very exciting game!

PRETEST Pronouns as Objects of Prepositions

Write the correct word or phrase from the choices in parentheses.

11. Please get tickets for Susan, Tony, and (I, me) in the second section, if possible.
12. We want to sit near Sam's brother and (he, him).
13. Our seats are above Jim and (they, them).
14. We are across from Mr. Benedict and (she, her).
15. Our old friends are sitting near (we, us).
16. Sandy sat by (she, her) and Judy.
17. She talked to (he, him) last night.
18. From (who, whom) did you receive the letter you told me about yesterday?
19. Please give copies of the letter to (I, me) and to Mr. Johnson in the front office.
20. We sent birthday presents to our cousin Fred, the boys, and (she, her).

PRETEST Conjunctions

Write each conjunction. Then write compound subject, compound object, compound predicate, *or* compound sentence *to tell what parts the conjunction joins.*

21. The Eagles or the Orioles will probably win the baseball championship.
22. They both have good hitters, but the Orioles have a better pitching staff.
23. Amy Anderson can pitch and hit well.
24. The Eagles won the game and a place in the tournament.

25. The Orioles' two best pitchers were injured or sick.
26. Weather can be very interesting to study, but it is also very complicated.
27. Sunny weather and rainy days are easy to observe.
28. The forecaster neither expected nor predicted the storm.
29. Not only does a forecaster consider wind direction, but he or she looks also at weather in other places.
30. Meteorologists and forecasters work hard.

PRETEST Making Compound Subjects and Verbs Agree

Write the correct word from the choices in parentheses.

31. Mr. Lopez and his class (is, are) going on a field trip.
32. Neither the teacher nor the students (has, have) been to Washington, D.C., before.
33. The students or their parents (pay, pays) for the trip.
34. Seth, Amanda, and Nick (work, works) after school.
35. Not only they but also other students (go, goes) to work too.
36. Either Tim's father or his mother (plan, plans) to chaperone the trip with Mr. Lopez.
37. A bus ticket and a hotel room (cost, costs) a lot.
38. Neither the boys nor the girls (want, wants) to be in a hotel room alone.
39. The chaperones or the teacher (stay, stays) in a suite.
40. (Do, Does) the boys or the girls have more luggage?

PRETEST Conjunctive Adverbs

Write each sentence. Underline the conjunctive adverb. Add appropriate punctuation.

41. School starts early this year however there will be a longer spring vacation than usual.

42. There are eleven holidays still students want more.
43. Teachers think students have enough time off from school moreover many think school should be all year round.
44. In times past, students had to help on the farm in the summer thus they needed to have summers off.
45. Most students no longer work on farms nevertheless many have jobs in the summer.

7.1 PREPOSITIONS AND PREPOSITIONAL PHRASES

A **preposition** is a word that relates a noun or a pronoun to another word in a sentence.

EXAMPLE The boy **near** the window is French.

The word *near* is a preposition. It shows the relationship between the noun *window* and the word *boy.*

COMMON PREPOSITIONS				
aboard	at	down	off	to
about	before	during	on	toward
above	behind	except	onto	under
across	below	for	opposite	underneath
after	beneath	from	out	until
against	beside	in	outside	up
along	besides	inside	over	upon
among	between	into	past	with
around	beyond	like	since	within
as	but (except)	near	through	without
	by	of	throughout	

A preposition may consist of more than one word.

EXAMPLE Yasmin will visit Trinidad **instead of** Jamaica.

SOME PREPOSITIONS OF MORE THAN ONE WORD			
according to	aside from	in front of	instead of
across from	because of	in place of	on account of
along with	except for	in spite of	on top of

A **prepositional phrase** is a group of words that begins with a preposition and ends with a noun or a pronoun, which is called the **object of the preposition.**

EXAMPLE Hang the painting **outside the new auditorium.**

A preposition may have a compound object.

EXAMPLE Between the **chair** and the **table** was a window.

GRAMMAR / USAGE / MECHANICS

PRACTICE Identifying Prepositional Phrases

Write each prepositional phrase. Underline the preposition and draw a circle around the object of the preposition.

1. The map of Africa is on the last page of the sixth-grade geography book.
2. Africa is the second largest of the seven continents in the world.
3. Africa has many countries with many kinds of people and governments.
4. In earlier times, many people of Africa were taken away from their homes and enslaved.
5. Now people from countries around the world visit large animal preserves in Kenya and other African nations.
6. People must stay inside their cars when they are driving through an animal preserve.

7. People who have been there say that countries throughout the whole continent of Africa are beautiful.
8. The Nile River, in northern Africa, runs through Egypt from south to north.
9. Many large museums have displays of objects from ancient Egypt.
10. The pyramids of ancient Egypt still stand, and camels still gallop past them.

7.2 PRONOUNS AS OBJECTS OF PREPOSITIONS CCSS L.6.1a

When a pronoun is the object of a preposition, use an object pronoun, not a subject pronoun.

EXAMPLE Dan handed the tickets to Natalie.

EXAMPLE Dan handed the tickets to **her.**

In the example, the object pronoun *her* replaces *Natalie* as the object of the preposition *to.*

A preposition may have a compound object: two or more nouns, two or more pronouns, or a combination of nouns and pronouns. Use object pronouns in compound objects.

EXAMPLE I borrowed the suitcase from Ivan and Vera.

EXAMPLE I borrowed the suitcase from Ivan and **her.**

EXAMPLE I borrowed the suitcase from **him** and Vera.

EXAMPLE I borrowed the suitcase from **him** and **her.**

Object pronouns are used in the second, third, and fourth sentences. In the second sentence, *Ivan and her* is the compound object of the preposition *from.* In the third sentence, *him and Vera* is the compound object of the preposition *from.* In the fourth sentence, *him and her* is the compound object of the preposition *from.*

If you're not sure whether to use a subject pronoun or an object pronoun, read the sentence aloud with only the pronoun.

EXAMPLE I borrowed the suitcase from **her.**

EXAMPLE I borrowed the suitcase from **him.**

Who is a subject pronoun. *Whom* is an object pronoun.

EXAMPLE **Who** lent you the suitcase?

EXAMPLE From **whom** did you borrow the suitcase?

PRACTICE Using Pronouns as Objects of Prepositions

Write the correct word or phrase from the choices in parentheses.

1. Between you and (I, me), I think we should have less homework.
2. Math is easy for me but difficult for Niko and (she, her).
3. According to (them, they), they need help to complete their math homework.
4. As a result, Sarah and Niko depend on (I, me) to complete the work.
5. At times I forget with (who, whom) I am working.
6. Then I work too fast for (he and she, him and her).
7. Sometimes my mother brings drinks to (we, us) as we work on our homework.
8. I get help from (he and she, him and she, him and her, he and her) in geography.
9. They move the maps toward (me, I).
10. The three of (we, us) are a team.

7.3 PREPOSITIONAL PHRASES AS ADJECTIVES AND ADVERBS

A prepositional phrase is an **adjective phrase** when it modifies, or describes, a noun or a pronoun.

EXAMPLE The servers **at the new restaurant** are courteous.

EXAMPLE The atmosphere includes photographs **from old movies.**

In the first sentence, the prepositional phrase *at the new restaurant* modifies the subject of the sentence, *servers.* In the second sentence, the prepositional phrase *from old movies* modifies the direct object, *photographs.*

Notice that, unlike most adjectives, an adjective phrase usually comes after the word it modifies.

A prepositional phrase is an **adverb phrase** when it modifies a verb, an adjective, or another adverb.

ADVERB PHRASES

USE	EXAMPLES
Modifies a Verb	The servers *dress* **like movie characters.**
Modifies an Adjective	The restaurant is *popular* **with young people.**
Modifies an Adverb	The restaurant opens *early* **in the morning.**

Most adverb phrases tell *when, where,* or *how* an action takes place. More than one prepositional phrase may modify the same word.

HOW ADVERB PHRASES MODIFY VERBS

WHEN?	Many people eat a light meal **during the lunch hour.**
WHERE?	Some eat lunch **on the covered patio.**
HOW?	Others eat their meals **in a hurry.**

PRACTICE Identifying Adjective and Adverb Phrases

Write each prepositional phrase. Then write the word it modifies. Finally, write adjective *or* adverb *to tell how it's used.*

1. Sometimes there are good programs on television.
2. Sports programs are preferred by many people.
3. They want football without commercials.
4. Ten ads may air within one break, though.
5. Other people like shows about nature.
6. They are often scheduled on public television.
7. News shows are popular with many people.
8. People can learn about presidential candidates.
9. Voters can choose among candidates.
10. Debates between candidates are held during a campaign.

GRAMMAR / USAGE / MECHANICS

7.4 TELLING PREPOSITIONS AND ADVERBS APART

Sometimes it can be difficult to tell whether a particular word is being used as a preposition or as an adverb. Both prepositions and adverbs can answer the questions *where?* and *when?* The chart below shows fifteen words that can be used as either prepositions or adverbs. Whether any one of these words is a preposition or an adverb depends on its use in a particular sentence.

SOME WORDS THAT CAN BE USED AS PREPOSITIONS OR ADVERBS		
about	below	out
above	down	outside
around	in	over
before	inside	through
behind	near	up

If you have trouble deciding whether a word is being used as a preposition or as an adverb, look at the other words in the sentence. If the word is followed closely by a noun or a pronoun, the word is probably a preposition, and the noun or pronoun is the object of the preposition.

EXAMPLE We ate our lunch **outside** the **library.**

EXAMPLE We walked **around** the **park** for an hour.

In the first example, *outside* is followed closely by the noun *library. Outside* is a preposition, and *library* is the object of the preposition. In the second example, *around* is a preposition, and *park* is the object of the preposition.

If the word is not followed closely by a noun or a pronoun, the word is probably an adverb.

EXAMPLE We ate our lunch **outside.**

EXAMPLE We walked **around** for an hour.

In the first sentence, *outside* answers the question *where?* but is not followed by a noun or a pronoun. In this sentence, *outside* is an adverb. In the second sentence, *around* is an adverb. *For an hour* is a prepositional phrase.

PRACTICE Identifying Prepositions and Adverbs

Write preposition *or* adverb *to identify each underlined word.*

1. Go up the stairs to the second floor.
2. The kite flew up quickly.
3. The book you want is on the shelf above that one.
4. Look for the one above.
5. It's too cold today to play outside.
6. The sidewalk is broken outside the building.
7. Look out below!
8. Write this down on your paper.
9. Let's go over to Sue's house.
10. Put that cover over the chair.

7.5 CONJUNCTIONS

A **coordinating conjunction** is a word used to connect compound parts of a sentence. *And, but, or, nor,* and *for* are coordinating conjunctions. *So* and *yet* are also sometimes used as coordinating conjunctions.

USING COORDINATING CONJUNCTIONS TO FORM COMPOUNDS	
COMPOUND SUBJECT	Allison **and** Rosita have lived in Mexico City.
COMPOUND OBJECTS	Give your suitcases **and** packages to Ben **or** Bill.
COMPOUND PREDICATE	Tourists shop **or** relax on the beaches.
COMPOUND SENTENCE	Tillie shopped every day, **but** we toured the city.

To make the relationship between words or groups of words especially strong, use correlative conjunctions.

Correlative conjunctions are pairs of words used to connect compound parts of a sentence. Correlative conjunctions include *both . . . and, either . . . or, neither . . . nor,* and *not only . . . but also.*

EXAMPLE Examples of great architecture exist in **both** New York **and** Paris.

EXAMPLE **Neither** Luis **nor** I have visited those cities.

When a compound subject is joined by *and,* the subject is usually plural. The verb must agree with the plural subject.

EXAMPLE Winnie **and** Sumi **are** in Madrid this week.

When a compound subject is joined by *or* or *nor,* the verb must agree with the nearer subject.

EXAMPLE **Neither** Rhondelle **nor** the twins **speak** Spanish.

EXAMPLE **Neither** the twins **nor** Rhondelle **speaks** Spanish.

PRACTICE Identifying Conjunctions and Compounds

Write each conjunction. Then write compound subject, compound object, compound predicate, *or* compound sentence *to tell what parts the conjunction joins.*

1. All sixth-graders play either soccer or softball.
2. Luis likes soccer best, but Kristina and Karen enjoy both soccer and softball.
3. When playing softball, Kristina plays center field, and Karen plays at first base.
4. Luis and Ginger take turns being goalie in soccer.
5. Neither Luis nor Ginger has scored in the last three games, but they made two saves.
6. Either Karen or Kristina got two hits in the last game, but neither girl scored a run or struck out.
7. Usually both Karen and Kristina hit and field well.
8. Not only are they good players, but they and the whole team have also been even better than usual this season.
9. The whole soccer team sometimes attends softball games, but few softball players go to soccer games.
10. Either the soccer players just like baseball, or they are fans of Kristina and Karen.

PRACTICE Making Compound Subjects and Verbs Agree

Write the correct word from the choices in parentheses.

1. Both Patrick and Patricia (babysit, babysits) for the family next door.
2. Kevin and Kathy (behave, behaves) best for Patrick, even though they like Patricia too.
3. Neither Kathy nor the twins (like, likes) the playground at the school.
4. But the twins and Kathy (like, likes) the park.

5. Neither the park nor the playground (has, have) swings, but there are slides at both places.
6. Either Kevin and Kathy's mother or the twins (provide, provides) a snack.
7. Patrick and Patricia always (watch, watches) the children carefully.
8. Sports drinks or juice (is, are) available at the park.
9. The children and their babysitter also (enjoy, enjoys) cracker snacks.
10. Ducks and geese (think, thinks) the crackers taste good too!

GRAMMAR / USAGE / MECHANICS

7.6 CONJUNCTIVE ADVERBS

You can use a special kind of adverb instead of a conjunction to join the simple sentences in a compound sentence. This special kind of adverb is called a **conjunctive adverb.**

EXAMPLE Many Asians use chopsticks, but some use forks.

EXAMPLE Many Asians use chopsticks; **however,** some use forks.

A conjunctive adverb, such as *however,* is usually stronger and more exact than a coordinating conjunction like *and* or *but.*

USING CONJUNCTIVE ADVERBS	
TO REPLACE *AND*	besides, furthermore, moreover
TO REPLACE *BUT*	however, nevertheless, still
TO STATE A RESULT	consequently, therefore, thus
TO STATE EQUALITY	equally, likewise, similarly

A **conjunctive adverb** may be used to join the simple sentences in a compound sentence.

When two simple sentences are joined with a conjunctive adverb, use a semicolon at the end of the first sentence. Place a comma after a conjunctive adverb that begins the second part of a compound sentence. If a conjunctive adverb is used in the middle of a simple sentence, set it off with commas.

EXAMPLE The school cafeteria sometimes serves casseroles; **however,** these meals are not very tasty.

EXAMPLE The school cafeteria sometimes serves casseroles; these meals, **however,** are not very tasty.

GRAMMAR / USAGE / MECHANICS

PRACTICE Identifying Conjunctive Adverbs

Write each sentence. Underline the conjunctive adverb. Add appropriate punctuation.

1. At Washington School, most students eat in the cafeteria however some go home for lunch.
2. Sometimes the food is better at home besides it's fun to watch TV for a few minutes.
3. Some students would rather eat at school therefore they bring their lunches.
4. Snacks are sold at school soccer games nevertheless, some people would rather bring their own.
5. As a result, the people running the snack bar have fewer customers consequently they make less money.
6. The snack-bar managers have complained to the school moreover they have raised their prices.
7. They are even considering shutting down completely thus no snacks would be on sale in the gym.
8. This might inconvenience some students still most bring their own snacks.
9. The cafeteria might run the snack bar some parents likewise might take it over.
10. A school club might choose the snack bar as a project however the students would need adult supervision.

7.7 INTERJECTIONS

You can express emotions in short exclamations that aren't complete sentences. These exclamations are called interjections.

An **interjection** is a word or group of words that expresses emotion. It has no grammatical connection to other words in a sentence.

Interjections are used to express emotion, such as surprise or disbelief. They're also used to attract attention.

SOME COMMON INTERJECTIONS			
aha	great	my	ouch
alas	ha	no	well
gee	hey	oh	wow
good grief	hooray	oops	yes

An interjection that expresses strong emotion may stand alone. It begins with a capital letter and ends with an exclamation point.

EXAMPLE **Good grief!** My favorite restaurant has closed.

When an interjection expresses mild feeling, it is written as part of the sentence. In that case, the interjection is set off with commas.

EXAMPLE **Oh, well,** I'll just eat at home.

NOTE Most words may be more than one part of speech. A word's part of speech depends on its use in a sentence.

EXAMPLE A duck has soft **down** on its body. [noun]

EXAMPLE The hungry boy **downed** the hamburger in three bites. [verb]

EXAMPLE Libby felt **down** all day. [adjective]

GRAMMAR / USAGE / MECHANICS

EXAMPLE The baby often falls **down.** **[adverb]**

EXAMPLE A car drove **down** the street. **[preposition]**

EXAMPLE **"Down!"** I shouted to the dog. **[interjection]**

PRACTICE Writing Sentences with Interjections

Write ten sentences, using a different interjection with each. Punctuate correctly.

PRACTICE Proofreading

Rewrite the following passage, correcting errors in spelling, capitalization, grammar, and usage. Add any missing punctuation. Write legibly to be sure one letter is not mistaken for another. There are ten mistakes.

Ilya Anopolsky

[1]At age twelve, Ilya Anopolsky won an award for the best business plan for a web-design company. [2]A year later, he started his own design company, called Devotion, Inc. [3]He had worked on more than fifty Web sites by the time he was thirteen imagine that

[4]Many of his friends and his teachers seems to expect Ilya to fix their computers. [5]Well since he wired up the computer room at his school, perhaps that is not so surpriseing.

[6]Ilya and his mother moved to brooklyn New York, from Ukraine when he was two-years-old. [7]His mother worries about him now because he works so hard besides his job makes life difficult for she and him. [8]She worries that the pressure from people who need help is too much for him. [9]She also worries that he works too hard. [10]Sometimes she gets up at 3:00 A.M. and finds that Ilya has fallen asleep at the computer.

[11]Ilya is a specialist in programming languages [12]He knows HTML, DHTML, and JavaScript. [13]He designs many Web sites, including some for on-line dealers in different kinds of merchandise.

POSTTEST Prepositions and Prepositional Phrases

Write each prepositional phrase. Underline the preposition and circle the object of the preposition. Then write the word the prepositional phrase modifies. Finally, write adjective *or* adverb *to tell how the prepositional phrase is used.*

1. Most sixth-graders already know about computers.
2. They use computers for written reports and research on the Internet.
3. You can go to the Web site of an encyclopedia for information.
4. Also, you can usually locate through a popular search engine more information about your topic.
5. You can also find a calculator on your computer.
6. The calculator can help you with your math homework.
7. The calculator on the computer is not part of the Internet.
8. That means the time you spend on the calculator is not charged to an Internet account.
9. The time you spend on the Internet is charged to an account paid for by your family or by the school.
10. A computer is a useful tool for many people.

GRAMMAR / USAGE / MECHANICS

POSTTEST Pronouns as Objects of Prepositions

Write the correct word from the choices in parentheses.

11. We heard about the neighborhood from (she, her).
12. We will live next to (she, her) and her family.
13. I hope we like (she and they, her and them, she and them, her and they).
14. Her daughter and son called my brother and (I, me).
15. They suggested some neighborhood places for (him and I, I and he, him and me, he and me) to visit.
16. I wondered to (who, whom) I was speaking.
17. They want to meet all of (we, us) soon.
18. It was very nice of (they, them) to call.

19. They asked whether we had questions for (he and she, him and her, him and she, he and her).
20. According to (she, her), we will like the town.

POSTTEST Conjunctions

Write each conjunction. Then write compound subject, compound object, compound predicate, *or* compound sentence *to tell what parts the conjunction joins.*

21. Many cities and towns have summertime farmers' markets.
22. People can buy vegetables and flowers there.
23. Both the farmers and the shoppers often get an early start.
24. Some shoppers go early to get the freshest produce, but they go back later in the day to get bargains on produce that has not sold.
25. The vegetables and fruit are so beautiful that some people like just to look at them.
26. Neither the shoppers nor the farmers, however, ever forget about how delicious the vegetables are.
27. Most shoppers browse and choose carefully.
28. Sometimes cooks and chefs shop at the market, or they send their assistants.
29. Chefs want the freshest vegetables and fruit.
30. They pick and choose carefully.

POSTTEST Making Compound Subjects and Verbs Agree

Write the correct word from the choices in parentheses.

31. Many kids and their families (go, goes) on vacations at some time during the school year.
32. Neither Lisa nor her sister (want, wants) to leave home this summer, though.

33. The girls and their neighbor Josh (skateboard, skateboards) in the park almost every day.

34. Skateboarding and bike riding (is, are) their favorite things to do.

35. The girls' father and mother (think, thinks) the family should visit their grandparents.

36. Either their mother or grandmother (do, does) a lot of baking when they visit.

37. The girls or Grandmother (look, looks) for recipes.

38. Lisa and Jen (leave, leaves) the bicycles at home.

39. Mom and Dad (allow, allows) them to take their skateboards, however.

40. Now both Lisa and Jen (seem, seems) happy.

POSTTEST Conjunctive Adverbs

Write each sentence. Underline the conjunctive adverb. Add appropriate punctuation.

41. There are seven continents on Earth however some are smaller than others.

42. Africa and South America could fit together like puzzle pieces therefore scientists think they probably once were connected.

43. Alaska and Russia could also fit together thus they too might have been connected.

44. Other clues suggest the origin of continents from one big landmass consequently some scientists find this a fascinating subject to study.

45. I firmly support the theory that all the continents were once part of one large landmass moreover the evidence should be compelling to all thoughtful people.

Chapter 8

Clauses and Complex Sentences

PRETEST Simple, Compound, and Complex Sentences

Write simple, compound, *or* complex *to identify each sentence.*

1. Houses are usually built of brick, wood, concrete, or a combination of these materials.
2. When builders start a house, they start with the foundation.
3. Small apartment buildings are constructed like houses; however, they often have features such as elevators.
4. Skyscraper construction is different; skyscrapers often have steel supporting beams.
5. New York and Chicago were homes to the first skyscrapers that were ever constructed.
6. Today New York and Chicago still have some of the world's tallest buildings.

7. Chicago's Willis Tower (formerly Sears Tower) has 110 stories; New York's Empire State Building has 102 stories.

8. Louis Sullivan, who is known as the founder of the Chicago school of architecture, built skyscrapers.

9. Sullivan designed many well-known buildings, and he wrote about his design ideas in books and articles.

10. In 1889 his firm finished building the Auditorium Theater in Chicago, which became well-known for its quality of sound.

GRAMMAR / USAGE / MECHANICS

PRETEST Adjective, Adverb, and Noun Clauses

Identify each italicized clause by writing adjective, adverb, *or* noun.

11. Last night we saw a show *that we really enjoyed.*

12. The show featured performers *who were acrobats.*

13. *How some of them performed their acts* was amazing.

14. I held my breath *while one acrobat twirled on a trapeze.*

15. *Whatever he did* seemed impossible.

16. In another act, two acrobats caught each other *as they jumped from one trapeze to another.*

17. Another act *that thrilled us* was the tightrope walkers.

18. One rode a bicycle on the high wire *as another performer balanced on his shoulders.*

19. *Whoever performs on the high wire* must train and rehearse for hours every day.

20. High-wire acts are among those *that are seen at circuses.*

21. In years past, tents were *where circuses were held.*

22. *Although some small circuses still use tents,* today most large circuses are held in big-city arenas.

23. *Since I was a child,* I have enjoyed circus acrobatics.

24. Last night's acts were among the best *that I have ever seen.*

25. You may want to go to the show *if tickets are available.*

8.1 SENTENCES AND CLAUSES

A **sentence** is a group of words that has a subject and a predicate and expresses a complete thought.

A **simple sentence** has one complete subject and one complete predicate.

The **complete subject** names whom or what the sentence is about. The **complete predicate** tells what the subject does or has. Sometimes the complete predicate tells what the subject is or is like. The complete subject or the complete predicate or both may be compound.

COMPLETE SUBJECT	COMPLETE PREDICATE
People	travel.
Neither automobiles nor airplanes	are completely safe.
Travelers	meet new people and see new sights.
Trains and buses	carry passengers and transport goods.

A **compound sentence** contains two or more simple sentences. Each simple sentence is called a main clause.

A **main clause** has a subject and a predicate and can stand alone as a sentence.

Main clauses can be connected by a comma and a conjunction, by a semicolon, or by a semicolon and a conjunctive adverb. The conjunctive adverb is followed by a comma. In the following examples, each main clause is in black. The connecting elements are in blue type.

EXAMPLE Many people live in cities, **but** others build houses in the suburbs. **[comma and coordinating conjunction]**

EXAMPLE Most people travel to their jobs; others work at home. **[semicolon]**

EXAMPLE Companies relocate to the suburbs; **therefore,** more people leave the city. **[semicolon and conjunctive adverb]**

GRAMMAR / USAGE / MECHANICS

PRACTICE Identifying and Punctuating Simple and Compound Sentences

Write each sentence. Underline each main clause. Add commas or semicolons where they're needed. Write simple *or* compound *to identify the sentence.*

1. Most students in sixth grade become interested in new things.
2. Many students really like sports but others like playing musical instruments.
3. Of course, some do both consequently all their time after school is filled up with practice.
4. Most students in sixth grade have learned something about computers many even have computers at home.
5. For some students, computers are just a tool for others, computers are fascinating avenues to new worlds.
6. Some want to know how computers and programs work.
7. Others like to explore the Internet and spend as much time as possible on it.
8. Some become very good at using computers a few even start computer companies.
9. Students like that are rare, though.
10. Do you know anyone like that?

GRAMMAR / USAGE / MECHANICS

8.2 COMPLEX SENTENCES

A **main clause** has a subject and a predicate and can stand alone as a sentence. Some sentences have a main clause and a subordinate clause.

A **subordinate clause** is a group of words that has a subject and a predicate but does not express a complete thought and cannot stand alone as a sentence. A subordinate clause is always combined with a main clause in a sentence.

A **complex sentence** has one main clause and one or more subordinate clauses.

In each complex sentence that follows, the subordinate clause is in blue type.

EXAMPLE Mariah, **who moved here from Montana,** is very popular.

EXAMPLE **Since Mariah moved to Springfield,** she has made many new friends.

EXAMPLE Everyone says **that Mariah is friendly.**

Subordinate clauses can function in three ways: as adjectives, as adverbs, or as nouns. In the examples, the first sentence has an adjective clause that modifies the noun *Mariah.* The second sentence has an adverb clause that modifies the verb *has made.* The third sentence has a noun clause that is the direct object of the verb *says.* Adjective, adverb, and noun clauses are used in the same ways one-word adjectives, adverbs, and nouns are used.

NOTE A **compound-complex sentence** has two or more main clauses and one or more subordinate clauses.

PRACTICE Identifying Simple and Complex Sentences

Write each sentence. Underline each main clause once and each subordinate clause twice. Write simple *or* complex *to identify the sentence.*

1. In a social studies class, sometimes students explore the areas where their ancestors lived.
2. Most people in the United States are the descendants of people who moved here long ago.
3. However, many families have arrived here recently.
4. Their reasons for coming to this country are different.
5. Some came to earn a better living wherever they could.
6. Others are here because a family member came to attend college.
7. Most need to learn English so that they can get along.

8. Children usually learn English when they go to school.
9. Sometimes the parents take longer to learn a new language.
10. Children find learning a language easier than adults do.

8.3 ADJECTIVE CLAUSES

An **adjective clause** is a subordinate clause that modifies a noun or a pronoun in the main clause of a complex sentence.

EXAMPLE The Aqua-Lung, **which divers strap on,** holds oxygen.

EXAMPLE The divers breathe through a tube **that attaches to the tank.**

Each subordinate clause in blue type is an adjective clause that adds information about a noun in the main clause. An adjective clause is usually introduced by a relative pronoun. The relative pronoun *that* may refer to people or things. *Which* refers only to things.

RELATIVE PRONOUNS				
that	which	who	whom	whose

An adjective clause can also begin with *where* or *when.*

EXAMPLE Divers search for reefs **where much sea life exists.**

EXAMPLE Herb remembers the day **when he had his first diving experience.**

A relative pronoun that begins an adjective clause is often the subject of the clause.

EXAMPLE Some divers prefer equipment **that is lightweight.**

EXAMPLE Willa is a new diver **who is taking lessons.**

In the first sentence, *that* is the subject of the adjective clause. In the second sentence, *who* is the subject of the adjective clause.

PRACTICE Identifying Adjective Clauses

Write each adjective clause. Underline the subject of the adjective clause. Then write the word the adjective clause modifies.

1. Harry Potter, who is a fictional character, nevertheless is extremely popular today.

2. Several of the Harry Potter books, which center around Harry and his adventures, are set in the Hogwarts School somewhere in Great Britain.

3. It is at Hogwarts where most of the action takes place.

4. Some people don't like books that are about magic.

5. People who don't like magic should stay away from the books about Harry Potter.

6. The Harry Potter books have stories that are imaginative and adventurous.

7. In the first book, Harry is shocked at the idea that he can go to the Hogwarts School.

8. In each book after that, he is a boy who is a year older.

9. Harry enjoys the days when he can play quidditch.

10. He is a student whose talent for quidditch is amazing.

8.4 ESSENTIAL AND NONESSENTIAL CLAUSES CCSS L.6.2a

Read the example sentence. Is the adjective clause in blue type needed to make the meaning of the sentence clear?

EXAMPLE The girl **who is standing beside the coach** is our best swimmer.

The adjective clause in blue type is essential to the meaning of the sentence. The clause tells *which* girl is the best swimmer.

An **essential clause** is a clause that is necessary to make the meaning of a sentence clear. Don't use commas to set off essential clauses.

Now look at the adjective clause in this sentence.

EXAMPLE Janice, **who is standing beside the coach,** is our best swimmer.

In the example, the adjective clause is set off with commas. The clause is nonessential, or not necessary to identify which swimmer the writer means. The clause simply gives additional information about the noun it modifies.

A **nonessential clause** is a clause that is not necessary to make the meaning of a sentence clear. Use commas to set off nonessential clauses.

In this book, adjective clauses that begin with *that* are always essential, and adjective clauses that begin with *which* are always nonessential.

EXAMPLE Were you at the meet **that** our team won yesterday? [essential]

EXAMPLE That meet, **which** began late, ended after dark. [nonessential]

GRAMMAR / USAGE / MECHANICS

GRAMMAR / USAGE / MECHANICS

PRACTICE Identifying and Punctuating Adjective Clauses

Write each sentence. Underline the adjective clause. Add commas where they're needed. Write essential *or* non-essential *to identify each adjective clause.*

1. Many people like pizza that is covered with vegetables such as mushrooms, onions, and green peppers.
2. This pizza which also includes pepperoni is truly delicious.
3. The person who delivered the pizza looked familiar.
4. He was the older brother of a friend whom we had not seen for months.
5. We tipped him for the pizza that we had ordered.
6. Once my family went to a restaurant where we ordered pizza.
7. My friend's brother who had delivered the pizza waited on us there.
8. We ordered a different kind of pizza which we did not like so well.
9. We did not like the pizza which had spinach and tomatoes on it.
10. Next time, we will order the kind that we like best.

8.5 ADVERB CLAUSES

An **adverb clause** is a subordinate clause that often modifies the verb in the main clause of a complex sentence.

An adverb clause tells *how, when, where, why,* or *under what conditions* the action occurs.

EXAMPLE **After we won the meet,** we shook hands with our opponents.

EXAMPLE We won the meet **because we practiced hard.**

In the first sentence, the adverb clause *After we won the meet* modifies the verb *shook.* The adverb clause tells *when* we shook hands. In the second sentence, the adverb clause *because we practiced hard* modifies the verb *won.* The adverb clause tells *why* we won the meet.

An adverb clause is introduced by a subordinating conjunction. A subordinating conjunction signals that a clause is a subordinate clause and cannot stand alone.

SUBORDINATING CONJUNCTIONS			
after	because	though	whenever
although	before	till	where
as	if	unless	whereas
as if	since	until	wherever
as though	than	when	while

Use a comma after an adverb clause that begins a sentence. You usually don't use a comma before an adverb clause that comes at the end of a sentence.

NOTE Adverb clauses can also modify adjectives and adverbs.

PRACTICE Identifying Adverb Clauses

Write each adverb clause. Underline the subordinating conjunction. Then write the verb the adverb clause modifies.

1. Many people visit large cities because the cities have so much to offer.
2. When you go to a big city, you will usually see something very interesting.
3. If you visit Chicago, for example, you will find the lakefront especially fascinating and enjoyable.
4. Don't miss Navy Pier when you visit the lakefront.

5. When you're there, be sure to ride the Ferris wheel.
6. You will feel as if you are on an airplane!
7. However, you might avoid it if you're afraid of heights.
8. Some people ride it although they feel a little frightened.
9. You may also enjoy a boat ride on the lake unless you get seasick.
10. You can see Chicago's skyline while you ride the boat.

GRAMMAR / USAGE / MECHANICS

8.6 NOUN CLAUSES

A **noun clause** is a subordinate clause used as a noun.

Notice how the subject in blue type in the following sentence can be replaced by a clause.

EXAMPLE **A hockey player** wears protective equipment.

EXAMPLE **Whoever plays hockey** wears protective equipment.

The clause in blue type, like the words it replaces, is the subject of the sentence. Because this kind of clause acts as a noun, it's called a noun clause.

You can use a noun clause in the same ways you use a noun—as a subject, a direct object, an indirect object, an object of a preposition, and a predicate noun. In most sentences containing noun clauses, you can replace the noun clause with the word *it,* and the sentence will still make sense.

HOW NOUN CLAUSES ARE USED	
SUBJECT	**Whoever plays hockey** wears protective equipment.
DIRECT OBJECT	Suzi knows **that ice hockey is a rough game.**
INDIRECT OBJECT	She tells **whoever will listen** her opinions.
OBJECT OF A PREPOSITION	Victory goes to **whoever makes more goals.**
PREDICATE NOUN	This rink is **where the teams play.**

Here are some words that can introduce noun clauses.

WORDS THAT INTRODUCE NOUN CLAUSES		
how, however	when	who, whom
if	where	whoever, whomever
that	whether	whose
what, whatever	which, whichever	why

EXAMPLE **Whichever you choose** will look fine.

EXAMPLE **What I wonder** is **why she said that.**

EXAMPLE I don't know **who left this package here.**

EXAMPLE Ask the teacher **if this is the right answer.**

EXAMPLE Promise **whoever calls first** a special bonus.

EXAMPLE He worried about **what he had done.**

GRAMMAR / USAGE / MECHANICS

PRACTICE Identifying Noun Clauses

Write each noun clause. Then write subject, direct object, indirect object, object of a preposition, *or* predicate noun *to tell how the noun clause is used.*

1. Please tell me why you did that.
2. How you do the job is not my concern.
3. I don't know when we are leaving.
4. Give the package to whoever opens the door.
5. On the first day of school, Jim did not know where he should go.
6. Ask the principal whose locker this is.
7. Do you care whether I go to the game or not?
8. Wherever we go is all right with me.
9. The next president will be whoever wins the most electoral votes.
10. Come to the party in whatever costume you can make from objects around the house.

PRACTICE Proofreading

Rewrite the following passage, correcting errors in spelling, capitalization, grammar, and usage. Add any missing punctuation. Write legibly to be sure one letter is not mistaken for another. There are ten mistakes.

Madeleine Albright

[1]Madeleine Albright was the first woman to became the Secretary of State in the United states. [2]She was born in Czechoslovakia in 1937, she and her family moved to the United States in 1948. [3]She graduated from Wellesley College with a bachelor's degree and she received both master's and doctorate degrees from Columbia University. [4]She worked for sevreal nonprofit organizations besides she was a professor of international affairs at Georgetown University in Washington, D.C. [5]In 1993 she was named ambassador to the United Nations where she served before becoming Secretary of State in 1997. [6]The Senate unanimously confirmed her appointment to the position. [7]She had a reputation which was gained by her hard work as a tough supporter of American intrests. [8]As she served in the United Nations, she suggested how to accomplish foreign policy goals through political and military means.

POSTTEST Simple, Compound, and Complex Sentences

Write simple, compound, *or* complex *to identify each sentence.*

1. You have seen many books, but have you ever looked closely at them?

2. The number of pages in books is always a multiple of four; however, larger books are made in multiples of 16, 32, and even 64.

3. In most books, every right-hand page has an odd number and every left-hand page has an even number.
4. In one mystery story, the villain insisted that he placed a key piece of paper between pages 47 and 48 of a book.
5. Since this was impossible, the detective knew the villain was guilty!
6. Some people think that computers will someday replace books.
7. However, people will probably always want to have books.
8. For one thing, books are easy for people to carry and pack.
9. Some artists specialize in designing type faces that are used in books, magazines, and newspapers.
10. Word-processing programs on computers now use many of those same typefaces, and artists often use computers to design new ones.

GRAMMAR / USAGE / MECHANICS

POSTTEST Adjective, Adverb, and Noun Clauses

Identify each italicized clause by writing adjective, adverb, *or* noun.

11. People *who live in different parts of the world* usually dress to reflect the climate.
12. *Since the weather in most areas near the Equator is warm*, people there do not need heavy clothes.
13. Similarly, *whoever lives near the Arctic Circle* could not use clothes suitable for the beach.
14. Choosing clothes can be a problem for people in places *that have seasonal changes.*
15. Appropriate clothes depend on *whatever the weather is during a particular season.*
16. One day you may need a sweater *because temperatures are in the 60s.*
17. *If the next day is warmer,* you may not need a sweater.

18. *When they travel,* some people always take an umbrella and a sweater or jacket.

19. They believe *that it is best to be prepared for any kind of weather.*

20. *Before you go outside*, be sure to check the temperature.

21. A coat or jacket *that has a warm lining* is important clothing for the cold winters of the Northeast.

22. *Whatever kind of coat you have* should be warm enough for the coldest weather.

23. You'll probably need boots, *which you might want to make waterproof.*

24. Some organizations give *whomever needs one* a warm coat.

25. *Whenever it is cold*, people should wear heavy coats, hats, and gloves.

Chapter 9

Subject-Verb Agreement

PRETEST Subject-Verb Agreement

Write the correct verb from the choices in parentheses.

1. Anna (wants, want) a babysitting job for the summer.
2. The owner of the puppies (seems, seem) interested in finding them good homes.
3. There (was, were) an accident on the highway near my home.
4. My teacher explained that physics (is, are) the study of energy, matter, and motion.
5. All of Remy's work (looks, look) neat and organized.
6. Either my mom or your parents (drive, drives) the car pool this week.
7. On the shelf in my office (is, are) pictures of my dog.
8. Keanu Reeves (plays, play) many roles in movies.
9. Each of the authors (writes, write) great novels.
10. Queen Victoria (was, were) eighteen years old when she became queen in 1837.
11. The teacher (needs, need) our project by Monday.
12. The members of the team (runs, run) in the race.

13. Both Plato and Aristotle (was, were) Greek philosophers and writers.
14. Sometimes lightning (causes, cause) forest fires.
15. Several (wants, want) to go to the zoo tomorrow.
16. She (like, likes) all of Jules Verne's novels.
17. Some stories by Edgar Allan Poe (is, are) detective stories set in Paris.
18. (Has, Have) the jeans been patched yet?
19. The poet and novelist who wrote *The Hunchback of Notre Dame* (was, were) Victor Hugo.
20. There (is, are) enough seats for everyone.
21. Everybody on the rides (seems, seem) excited.
22. None of my sisters (has, have) birthdays during the winter months.
23. The Red Cross (brings, bring) help to those in need.
24. All of the music (was, were) classical.
25. The student or his teachers (wants, want) to change the appointment.

9.1 MAKING SUBJECTS AND VERBS AGREE

CCSS L.6.1c

The basic idea of subject-verb agreement is a simple one: A singular subject requires a singular verb, and a plural subject requires a plural verb. The subject and its verb are said to *agree in number.*

Notice that in the present tense the singular form of the verb usually ends in *-s* or *-es.*

SUBJECT-VERB AGREEMENT WITH NOUNS AS SUBJECTS	
SINGULAR	**PLURAL**
A **botanist studies** plant life.	**Botanists study** plant life.
A **plant requires** care.	**Plants require** care.

A verb must also agree with a subject that is a pronoun. Look at the chart that follows. Notice how the verb changes. In the present tense, the *-s* ending is used with the subject pronouns *he*, *she*, and *it.*

SUBJECT-VERB AGREEMENT WITH PRONOUNS AS SUBJECTS

SINGULAR	PLURAL
I **work.**	We **work.**
You **work.**	You **work.**
He, she, *or* it **works.**	They **work.**

The irregular verbs *be*, *have*, and *do* can be main verbs or helping verbs. These verbs must agree with the subject whether they're main verbs or helping verbs.

EXAMPLES I **am** a botanist. He **is** a botanist. They **are** botanists. **[main verbs]**

EXAMPLES She **is** working. You **are** studying. **[helping verbs]**

EXAMPLES I **have** a job. She **has** a career. **[main verbs]**

EXAMPLES He **has** planted a tree. They **have** planted trees. **[helping verbs]**

EXAMPLES He **does** well. They **do** the job. **[main verbs]**

EXAMPLES It **does** sound good. We **do** work hard. **[helping verbs]**

PRACTICE Making Subjects and Verbs Agree I

Write the subject. Then write the correct verb from the choices in parentheses.

1. Many important inventions (is, are) credited to Thomas Alva Edison.

2. Germaine (agrees, agree) with the answer.

GRAMMAR / USAGE / MECHANICS

3. The baby (smiles, smile) at her father.
4. It (is, are) a story about space travel.
5. We (says, say) the Pledge of Allegiance in class.
6. The soldier (gets, get) a letter from home.
7. Greek fables (has, have) a moral at the end.
8. Wynton Marsalis (has, have) recorded many jazz tunes.
9. He (does, do) enjoy listening to various melodies.
10. The doors (closes, close) behind you as you leave.

9.2 PROBLEMS IN LOCATING THE SUBJECT

Making a verb agree with its subject is easy when the verb directly follows the subject. Sometimes, however, a prepositional phrase comes between the subject and the verb.

EXAMPLE This **book** of Mark Twain's stories **appeals** to people of all ages.

EXAMPLE **Stories** by Washington Irving **are** also popular.

In the first sentence, *of Mark Twain's stories* is a prepositional phrase. The singular verb *appeals* agrees with the singular subject, *book,* not with the plural noun *stories,* which is the object of the preposition *of.* In the second sentence, *by Washington Irving* is a prepositional phrase. The plural verb *are* agrees with the plural subject, *Stories,* not with the singular noun *Washington Irving,* which is the object of the preposition *by.*

An **inverted sentence** is a sentence in which the subject follows the verb.

Inverted sentences often begin with a prepositional phrase. Don't mistake the object of the preposition for the subject of the sentence.

EXAMPLE Across the ocean **sail millions** of immigrants.

In inverted sentences beginning with *Here* or *There*, look for the subject after the verb. *Here* or *there* is never the subject of a sentence.

EXAMPLE Here **is** a **picture** of my grandparents.

EXAMPLE There **are** many **immigrants** among my ancestors.

By rearranging the sentence so the subject comes first, you can see the agreement between the subject and the verb.

EXAMPLE **Millions** of immigrants **sail** across the ocean.

EXAMPLE A **picture** of my grandparents **is** here.

EXAMPLE Many **immigrants are** there among my ancestors.

In some interrogative sentences, a helping verb comes before the subject. Look for the subject between the helping verb and the main verb.

EXAMPLE **Do** these **stories interest** you?

You can check the subject-verb agreement by making the sentence declarative.

EXAMPLE These **stories do interest** you.

GRAMMAR / USAGE / MECHANICS

PRACTICE Making Subjects and Verbs Agree II

Write the subject. Then write the correct verb from the choices in parentheses.

1. Inside my building (is, are) four apartments.
2. There (was, were) too much work for me to finish.
3. The chapters in the book (looks, look) interesting.
4. Here (is, are) the answers to the problems.
5. (Does, Do) you know Picasso's complete name or the names of some of his paintings?
6. Museums in Paris (display, displays) many of Rodin's sculptures.
7. (Was, Were) Abraham Lincoln the sixteenth president of the United States?

8. Near the palace (marches, march) the queen's guards.
9. On the shelf (is, are) many maps of the Miami area.
10. Listeners of that station (hear, hears) the latest news.

9.3 COLLECTIVE NOUNS AND OTHER SPECIAL SUBJECTS

A **collective noun** names a group.

Collective nouns follow special agreement rules. A collective noun has a singular meaning when it names a group that acts as a unit. A collective noun has a plural meaning when it refers to the members of the group acting as individuals. The meaning helps you decide whether to use the singular or plural form of the verb.

EXAMPLE The **audience sits** in silence. **[a unit, singular]**

EXAMPLE The **audience sit** on chairs and pillows. **[individuals, plural]**

Certain nouns, such as *news* and *mathematics,* end in *s* but require singular verbs. Other nouns that end in *s* and name one thing, such as *scissors* and *binoculars,* require plural verbs.

EXAMPLE **News is** important to everyone. **[singular]**

EXAMPLE The **scissors are** in the top drawer. **[plural]**

SPECIAL NOUNS THAT END IN *S*

SINGULAR		PLURAL	
civics	physics	binoculars	scissors
Los Angeles	United Nations	jeans	sunglasses
mathematics	United States	pants	trousers
news		pliers	tweezers

A subject that refers to an amount as a single unit is singular. A subject that refers to a number of individual units is plural.

EXAMPLE **Ten years seems** a long time. **[single unit]**

EXAMPLE **Ten years pass** quickly. **[individual units]**

EXAMPLE **Three dollars is** the admission price. **[single unit]**

EXAMPLE **Three dollars are** on the table. **[individual units]**

The title of a book or a work of art is always singular, even if a noun in the title is plural.

EXAMPLE ***Snow White and the Seven Dwarfs*** **is** a good Disney movie.

EXAMPLE ***The Last of the Mohicans*** **was** written by James Fenimore Cooper.

GRAMMAR / USAGE / MECHANICS

PRACTICE Making Subjects and Verbs Agree III

Write the subject. Then write the correct verb from the choices in parentheses.

1. *The Pickwick Papers* (is, are) a novel by Charles Dickens, an English writer.
2. Six dollars (was, were) too much to pay.
3. The scissors (seems, seem) sharp.
4. Physics (is are) a difficult subject for some students.
5. The class (give, gives) their written reports to the teacher on Mondays.
6. Three dollars (is, are) scattered on the floor.
7. The group (plans, plan) to go downtown.
8. The collection (is, are) on display at the modern art museum.
9. *Gulliver's Travels* (was, were) written by Jonathan Swift.
10. Three days (is, are) enough time to practice.

9.4 INDEFINITE PRONOUNS AS SUBJECTS

CCSS L.6.1c

An **indefinite pronoun** is a pronoun that does not refer to a particular person, place, or thing.

Some indefinite pronouns are singular. Others are plural. When an indefinite pronoun is used as a subject, the verb must agree in number with the pronoun.

SOME INDEFINITE PRONOUNS

SINGULAR			PLURAL
another	everybody	no one	both
anybody	everyone	nothing	few
anyone	everything	one	many
anything	much	somebody	others
each	neither	someone	several
either	nobody	something	

The indefinite pronouns *all, any, most, none,* and *some* may be singular or plural, depending on the phrase that follows.

EXAMPLE **Most** of the forest **lies** to the east. **[singular]**

EXAMPLE **Most** of these scientists **study** forest growth. **[plural]**

Often a prepositional phrase follows an indefinite pronoun that can be either singular or plural. To decide whether the pronoun is singular or plural, look at the object of the preposition. In the first sentence, *most* refers to *forest.* Because *forest* is singular, *most* must be considered as a single unit. In the second sentence, *most* refers to *scientists.* Because *scientists* is plural, *most* should be considered as individual units.

PRACTICE Making Subjects and Verbs Agree IV

Write the subject. Then write the correct verb from the choices in parentheses.

1. Anyone at the desk (takes, take) the money.
2. Most of the books (sell, sells) at discount.
3. Few (finds, find) the subject interesting.
4. All of his work (remains, remain) lost.
5. Either of the choices (is, are) fine.
6. Some of the states (holds, hold) primary elections on the same day.
7. All of the cheering (is, are) making the hall noisy.
8. Everything (comes, come) to those who wait.
9. No one (wants, want) to be the villain in the play.
10. Most of the senators (leave, leaves) Washington before the Labor Day weekend.

9.5 AGREEMENT WITH COMPOUND SUBJECTS

A **compound subject** contains two or more simple subjects that have the same verb.

Compound subjects may require a singular or a plural verb, depending on how the subjects are joined. When two or more subjects are joined by *and* or by the correlative conjunction *both . . . and*, the plural form of the verb should be used.

EXAMPLE New York, Denver, **and** London **have** smog.

EXAMPLE **Both** automobiles **and** factories **contribute** to smog.

Sometimes *and* is used to join two words that are part of one unit or refer to a single person or thing. In these cases, the subject is singular. In the following example, *captain* and *leader* refer to the same person. Therefore, the singular form of the verb is used.

EXAMPLE The captain **and** leader of the team **is** Ms. Cho.

When two or more subjects are joined by *or* or by the correlative conjunction *either . . . or* or *neither . . . nor*, the verb agrees with the subject that is closer to it.

EXAMPLE The cities **or** the state **responds** to pollution complaints.

EXAMPLE **Either** smoke **or** gases **cause** the smog.

In the first sentence, *responds* is singular because the closer subject, *state*, is singular. In the second sentence, *gases* is the closer subject. The verb is plural because the closer subject is plural.

PRACTICE Making Subjects and Verbs Agree V

Write the complete subject. Then write the correct verb from the choices in parentheses.

1. Thomas Edison and Joseph Swan (shares, share) the credit for inventing the light bulb.
2. Both plants and animals (has, have) scientific names that indicate the group to which they belong.
3. Neither my grandparents nor my aunt (calls, call) me by my nickname.
4. The outlaws or Robin Hood (was, were) sure to win the Sheriff of Nottingham's archery contest.
5. Either Dimitri or his sisters (gets, get) to fly to Greece to visit the family.
6. My favorite teacher and tutor (was, were) Ms. Hidaka.
7. Porthos, Athos, and Aramis (is, are) the names of the Three Musketeers.
8. Either the sandwiches or the chef's salad (provides, provide) a good nutritional meal.
9. Zosha and her friends (brings, bring) stuffed animals to all of the sleepovers.
10. Neither the Beatles nor Elvis Presley (has, have) lost popularity with young listeners.

PRACTICE Proofreading

Rewrite the following passage, correcting errors in spelling, capitalization, grammar, and usage. Add any missing punctuation. Write legibly to be sure one letter is not mistaken for another. There are 10 mistakes.

Eldrick Woods

[1]Does the name Eldrick Woods sound familiar [2]If not, perhaps his nickname Tiger ring a bell. [3]Tiger Woods are the first golfer of African American descent to win the Masters Tournament. [4]It remain one of the most important golf events.

[5]tiger, born in 1975, is the son of Earl and Kultida Woods. [6]By the age of fifteen, he was the yungest winner of the U.S. Junior Amateur Championship. [7]Woods have become the first golfer in over two decades to win eight PGA tournaments in a year. [8]Ben Hogan's streak of six consecutive wins were tied by Woods. [9]Six million dollars are the amount Woods has earned in a season. [10]Because of him, more young people has tried golf.

GRAMMAR / USAGE / MECHANICS

POSTTEST Subject-Verb Agreement

Write the correct verb from the choices in parentheses.

1. Raheem, Gita, and Nina (discusses, discuss) the problems in their native countries.
2. She (looks, look) for clues to the puzzle.
3. All stories by Hans Christian Andersen (is, are) children's stories written in the nineteenth century.
4. A famous leader of civil rights (was, were) Martin Luther King Jr.
5. The flock (flies, fly) south for the winter.
6. Both David Livingstone and Henry Morton Stanley (is, are) known as great explorers.
7. Six days (seems, seem) like a long time to be sick.
8. Each of the meals (has, have) been wrapped in foil.

9. Los Angeles (seems, seem) like an interesting city.
10. Somebody (calls, call) my house every morning and wakes me up.
11. My slacks (looks, look) fashionable.
12. Neither the flute nor the violins (was, were) played in the big band.
13. One kind of painting (is, are) called a fresco.
14. Facial expressions or gestures (helps, help) a mime create a silent play.
15. The family (does, do) ride in the same car.
16. Several of the tourists (visits, visit) the Art Institute of Chicago.
17. *Twenty Thousand Leagues Under the Sea* (is, are) one of the first science fiction stories.
18. In the exhibit at the zoo (rests, rest) the aged lion.
19. (Does, Do) detective stories appeal to you?
20. All of Edgar Allan Poe's work (was, were) written in the 1800s.
21. Most of his stories (features, feature) frightening or mysterious scenes.
22. There (is, are) five parts in a pentathlon: riding, fencing, running, swimming, and shooting.
23. She (tries, try) to warm up before each event.
24. Many (pulls, pull) muscles during a sporting event.
25. Either the music teacher or his students (tunes, tune) the instruments for the concert.

Chapter 10

Diagraming Sentences

PRETEST Diagraming Sentences

Diagram each sentence.

1. Raindrops fell.
2. Class has started.
3. Run!
4. May I go?
5. Set the table.
6. Mrs. Alvarez showed us a map.
7. The singer gave her fan an autograph.
8. The little white dog rolled in the thick mud.
9. Sometimes a very funny actor performs here.

10. The author of the book competed in the Olympics.
11. Scooters have suddenly become very popular.
12. Winston Churchill was Prime Minister of Britain.
13. Buses and taxis crowded the streets of the city.
14. Many birds whistled and chirped.
15. Robert Peary explored the Arctic, and Robert Scott explored Antarctica.
16. Dan rarely writes letters, but he sends e-mail every day.
17. Spiders that live in the rain forest often grow huge.
18. Since Tyra fell asleep, she missed her favorite show.
19. What he said was a fact.
20. President Kennedy hoped that Americans would land on the Moon.

10.1 DIAGRAMING SIMPLE SUBJECTS AND SIMPLE PREDICATES

The basic parts of a sentence are the subject and the predicate. To diagram a sentence, first draw a horizontal line. Then draw a vertical line that crosses the horizontal line.

To the left of the vertical line, write the simple subject. To the right of the vertical line, write the simple predicate. Use capital letters as they appear in the sentence, but don't include punctuation.

EXAMPLE **People are working.**

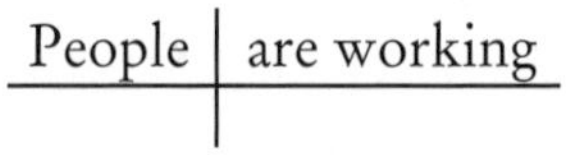

In a diagram, the positions of the subject and the predicate always remain the same.

EXAMPLE **Caravans rumbled** across the prairie.

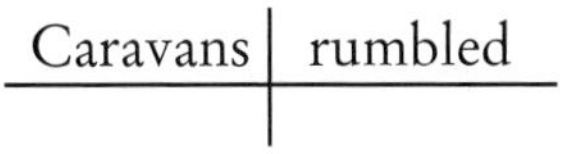

EXAMPLE Across the prairie **rumbled caravans.**

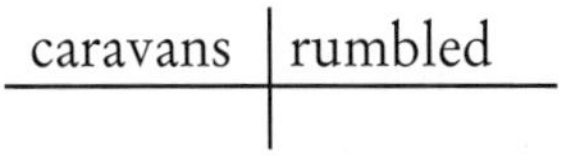

PRACTICE Diagraming Simple Subjects and Simple Predicates

Diagram the simple subject and the simple predicate.

1. People change.
2. The sauce smells spicy.
3. First came the marching band.
4. Jefferson had been Washington's secretary of state.
5. The neighbors are having a cookout.
6. Over the prairie galloped the wild horses.
7. Planes landed frequently.
8. Into the ballroom walked the beautiful princess.
9. The air is so fresh near the ocean.
10. The scientists had been searching for dinosaur bones.

10.2 DIAGRAMING THE FOUR KINDS OF SENTENCES

Study the diagrams of the simple subject and the simple predicate for the four kinds of sentences. Recall that in an interrogative sentence the subject often comes between the two parts of a verb phrase. In an imperative sentence, the simple subject is the understood *you.*

Notice that the positions of the simple subject and the simple predicate in a sentence diagram are always the same, regardless of the word order in the original sentence.

DECLARATIVE

EXAMPLE **People write** letters.

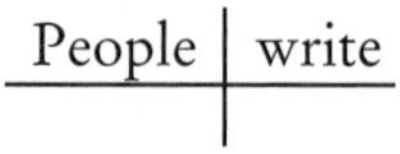

INTERROGATIVE

EXAMPLE **Do** many **people write** letters?

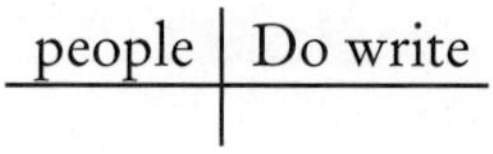

IMPERATIVE

EXAMPLE **Write** a letter.

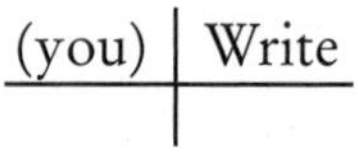

EXCLAMATORY

EXAMPLE What interesting letters **you write!**

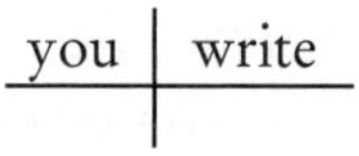

PRACTICE Diagraming the Four Kinds of Sentences

Diagram the simple subject and the simple predicate.

1. Call me at home tonight.
2. What a sad movie I saw!
3. Many reptiles live in the desert.
4. Forget about your problems.
5. Did Neil Armstrong make a second trip to the Moon?
6. How bold General Washington was!
7. Shall we go fishing?
8. Add these numbers.
9. The city is quiet tonight.
10. Have the tulips bloomed yet?

10.3 DIAGRAMING DIRECT AND INDIRECT OBJECTS

A direct object is part of the predicate. In a sentence diagram, write the direct object to the right of the verb. Draw a vertical line to separate the verb from the direct object. This vertical line, however, does *not* cross the horizontal line.

EXAMPLE People invent **machines.**

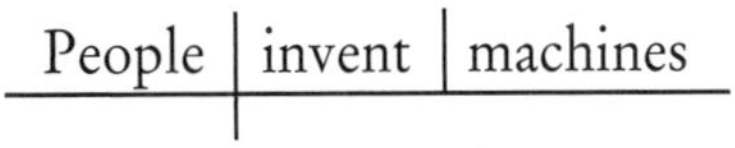

EXAMPLE Students use **computers.**

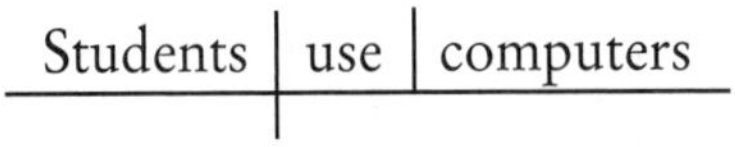

An indirect object is also part of the predicate. It usually tells to whom or for whom the action of a verb is done. An indirect object always comes before a direct object in a sentence. In a sentence diagram, write an indirect object on a horizontal line below and to the right of the verb. Join it to the verb with a slanted line.

EXAMPLE Rosa gave the **dog** a bone.

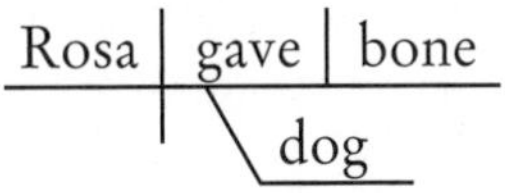

PRACTICE Diagraming Direct and Indirect Objects

Diagram the simple subject, the simple predicate, and the direct object. Diagram the indirect object if the sentence has one.

1. Hurricane Hugo struck South Carolina.
2. The waiter was serving the family dessert.
3. The settlers planted crops.
4. Mozart wrote over forty symphonies.
5. Canadian Indians invented the game of lacrosse.

6. The sun gave me a headache.
7. A watchdog protected the house.
8. The French gave Americans the Statue of Liberty.
9. Louis Armstrong played the trumpet.
10. Mom wrote the company a letter.

10.4 DIAGRAMING ADJECTIVES, ADVERBS, AND PREPOSITIONAL PHRASES

In a diagram, write adjectives and adverbs on slanted lines beneath the words they modify.

EXAMPLE **Elena's strange** dream faded **quickly.**

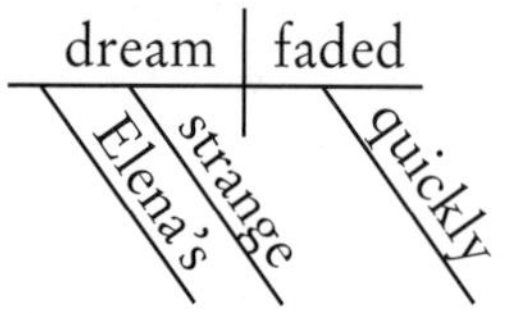

EXAMPLE **The very old** tree produced **incredibly delicious** apples **rather slowly.**

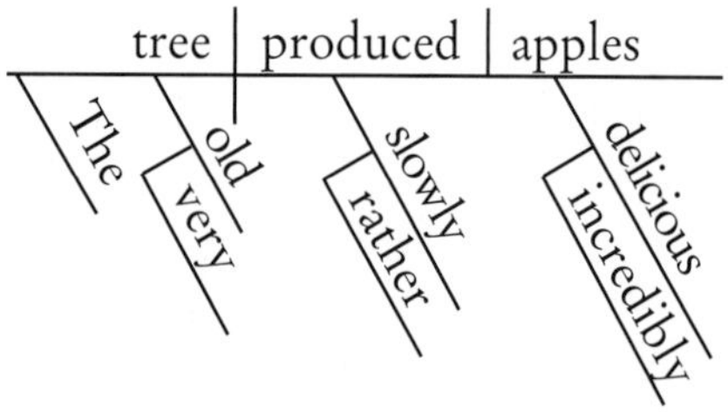

A prepositional phrase can be either an adjective phrase or an adverb phrase. Study the diagram for prepositional phrases.

EXAMPLE A woman **in a pink hat** was sitting **beside me.**

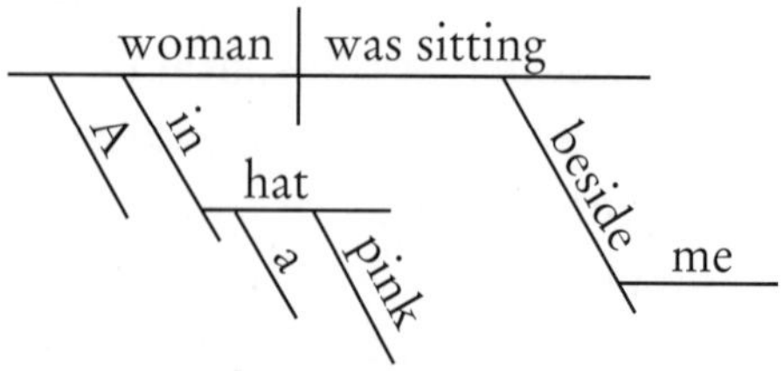

PRACTICE **Diagraming Adjectives, Adverbs, and Prepositional Phrases**

Diagram each sentence.

1. A bad winter storm destroyed the huge oak tree.
2. A tiny baby was born to the panda at the city zoo.
3. The race car driver went around the last curve too fast.
4. The very first buses were pulled by horses.
5. In 1965 Martin Luther King Jr. led a march for civil rights in Alabama.
6. A British scientist discovered penicillin in 1928.
7. The huge ocean liner makes several trips across the Atlantic each year.
8. The girls always had a delicious snack at the bakery on the corner.
9. Charles Schulz drew his popular comic strip for nearly fifty years.
10. The ship sailed around the southern coast of Africa on its way to India.

10.5 DIAGRAMING PREDICATE NOUNS AND PREDICATE ADJECTIVES

In a sentence diagram, a direct object follows the verb.

EXAMPLE People use telephones.

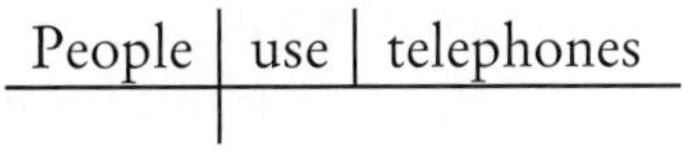

To diagram a sentence with a predicate noun, write the predicate noun to the right of the linking verb. Draw a slanted line to separate the verb from the predicate noun.

EXAMPLE Telephones are useful **instruments.**

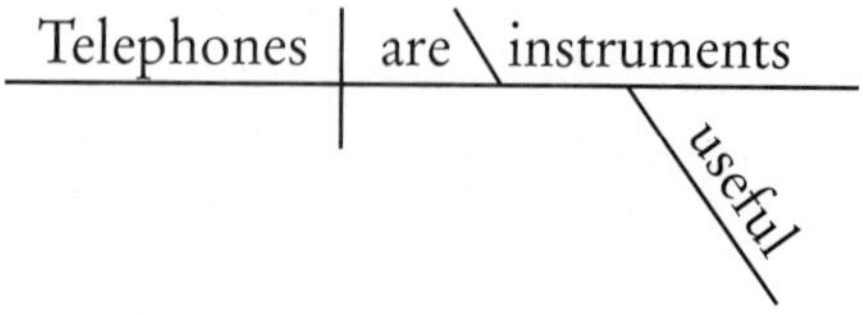

Diagram a predicate adjective in the same way.

EXAMPLE Telephones are **useful.**

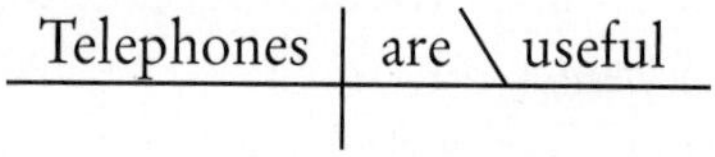

PRACTICE Diagraming Predicate Nouns and Predicate Adjectives

Diagram each sentence.

1. The sky is clear today.
2. Elizabeth II became Queen of Great Britain in 1952.
3. The bridge seemed sturdy enough.
4. I felt rather sad on the last day of school.
5. The first assignment was a play by Shakespeare.
6. The unripe plums tasted sour.
7. Franklin Roosevelt was president for twelve years.
8. The Model T Ford was a popular car.
9. Bald eagles look quite powerful.
10. One important Roman invention was concrete.

10.6 DIAGRAMING COMPOUND SENTENCE PARTS

Coordinating conjunctions such as *and, but,* and *or* are used to join compound parts: words, phrases, or sentences. To diagram compound parts of a sentence, write the second part of the compound below the first. Write the coordinating conjunction on a dotted line connecting the two parts.

COMPOUND SUBJECT

EXAMPLE **Gas and oil** heat homes.

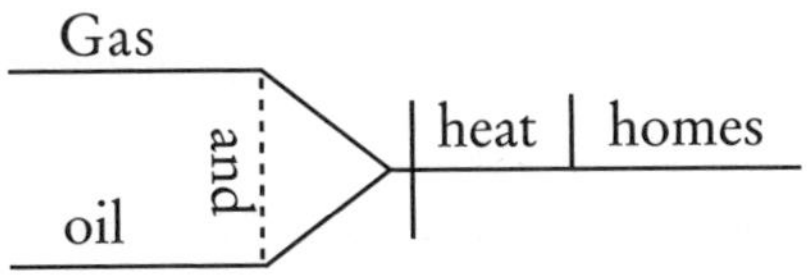

COMPOUND PREDICATE

EXAMPLE Babies **eat and sleep.**

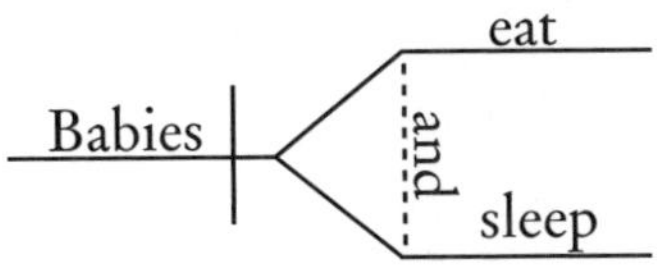

COMPOUND DIRECT OBJECT

EXAMPLE The bakery serves **sandwiches and beverages.**

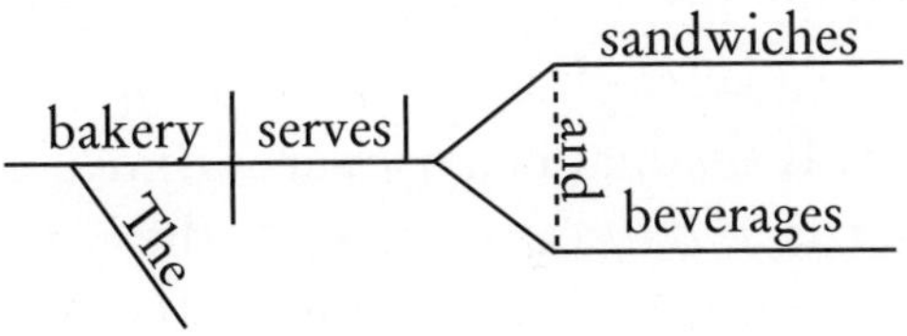

COMPOUND PREDICATE NOUN OR PREDICATE ADJECTIVE

EXAMPLE Dogs are **loyal and friendly.**

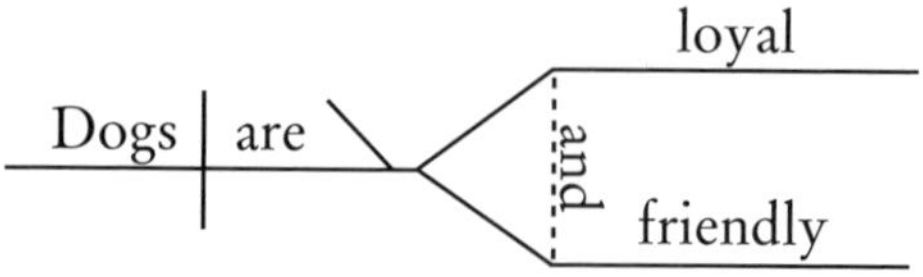

PRACTICE Diagraming Compound Sentence Parts

Diagram each sentence.

1. Lewis and Clark explored the Pacific coast.
2. Fishers in Maine catch lobsters and crabs.
3. The campers sail or swim.
4. Lions and tigers are larger than leopards.
5. Summers in Arizona are hot and dry.
6. Tomatoes and peppers grew in the garden.
7. His friends became bankers and lawyers.
8. The tacos were tasty but hot.
9. The Bering Strait separates Alaska and Siberia.
10. The children shouted and laughed.

10.7 DIAGRAMING COMPOUND SENTENCES

To diagram a compound sentence, diagram each main clause separately. If the main clauses are connected by a semicolon, use a vertical dotted line to connect the verbs of the clauses. If the main clauses are connected by a conjunction such as *and, but,* or *or,* write the conjunction on a solid horizontal line and connect it to the verb in each clause with a dotted line.

EXAMPLE James practices football after school, **and** on Saturdays he helps his parents at their restaurant.

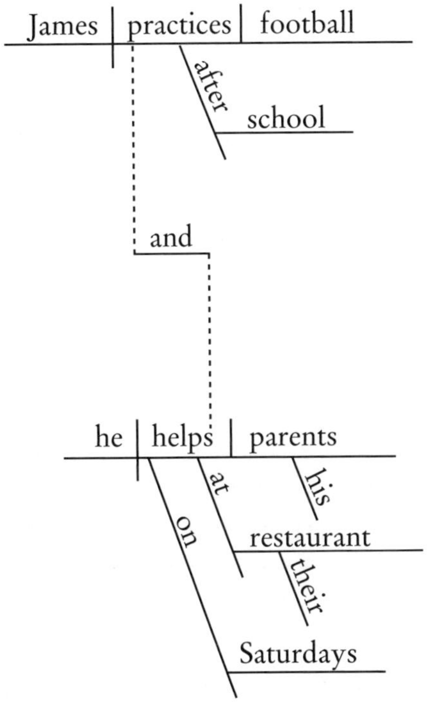

GRAMMAR / USAGE / MECHANICS

PRACTICE Diagraming Compound Sentences

Diagram each sentence.

1. The day had been hot, yet the evening was chilly.
2. A Siamese cat has short hair, and a Persian cat has long fluffy fur.
3. You can eat in the cafeteria, or you can take your lunch outside.
4. The Empire State Building is in New York City, and the Willis Tower is in Chicago.
5. We looked for a meteor, but we never saw one.
6. The first automobiles had engines in the rear; later models had engines in the front.
7. The garlic smelled strong, but it tasted delicious in the stew.

8. The first batter got a single; he stole second base.
9. The castle's moat kept enemies out, and its drawbridge let friends in.
10. The winter days were warm, but it often rained.

10.8 DIAGRAMING COMPLEX SENTENCES WITH ADJECTIVE AND ADVERB CLAUSES

To diagram a sentence with an adjective clause, write the adjective clause below the main clause. Draw a dotted line between the relative pronoun in the adjective clause and the word the adjective clause modifies in the main clause. Position the relative pronoun according to its use in its own clause. In the first example, *who* is the subject of the verb *complete.* In the second example, *that* is the direct object of the verb *watched.*

GRAMMAR / USAGE / MECHANICS

ADJECTIVE CLAUSE

EXAMPLE Students **who complete their assignments** will surely succeed.

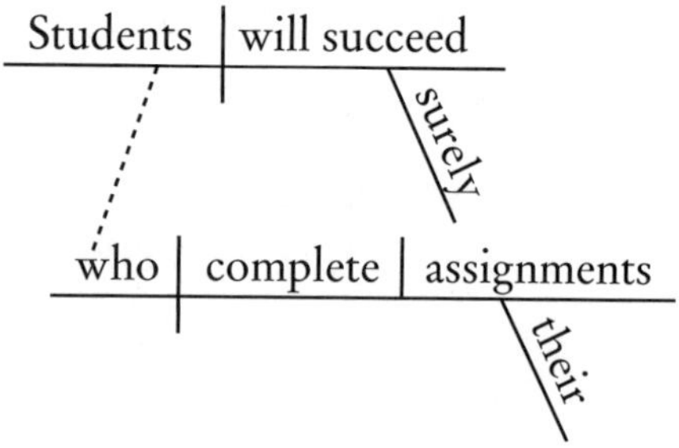

EXAMPLE The movie **that we watched** was very funny.

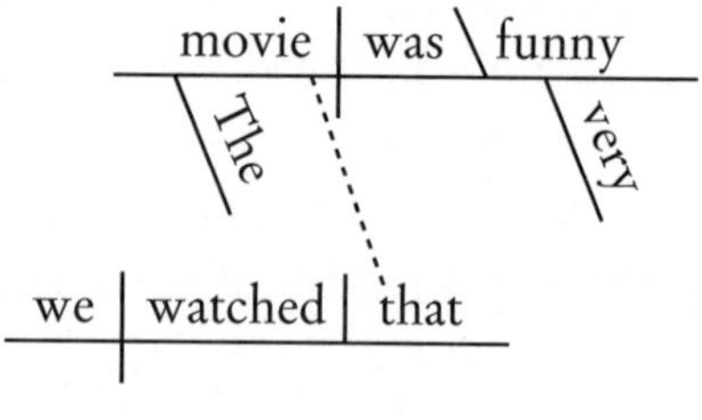

Diagram an adverb clause below the main clause. Draw a dotted line between the verb in the adverb clause and the word the adverb clause modifies in the main clause. Then write the subordinating conjunction on the dotted connecting line.

ADVERB CLAUSE

EXAMPLE **If you complete your assignments,** you will surely succeed.

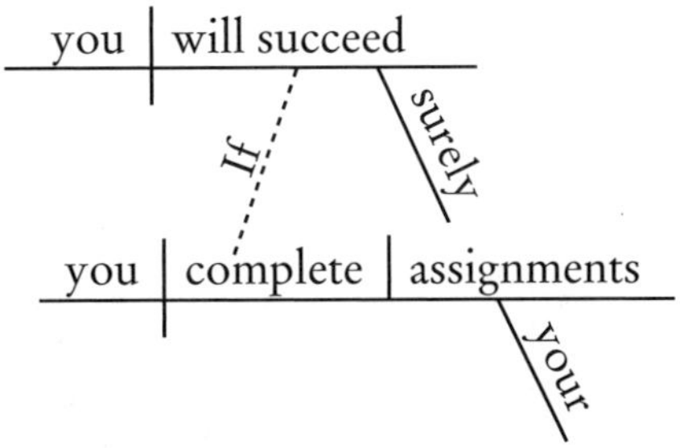

PRACTICE Diagraming Complex Sentences with Adjective and Adverb Clauses

Diagram each sentence.

1. Everyone left town when the nearby volcano erupted.
2. Sally Ride, whom I admire, flew on the space shuttle.
3. Before you play a tennis match, you must practice.
4. The tornado that struck Oklahoma did much damage.
5. Tim must work very hard if he makes the team.
6. Because the water is rough, people rarely swim across the English Channel.
7. Paul McCartney wrote many songs after the Beatles broke up.
8. The book that I liked best was *Jane Eyre*.
9. The person who wrote it was Charlotte Brontë.
10. We played outside until the sun set.

10.9 DIAGRAMING NOUN CLAUSES

Noun clauses can be used in sentences as subjects, direct objects, indirect objects, objects of prepositions, and predicate nouns. In the following example, the noun clause is the subject.

NOUN CLAUSE AS SUBJECT

EXAMPLE **What she told us** was the simple truth.

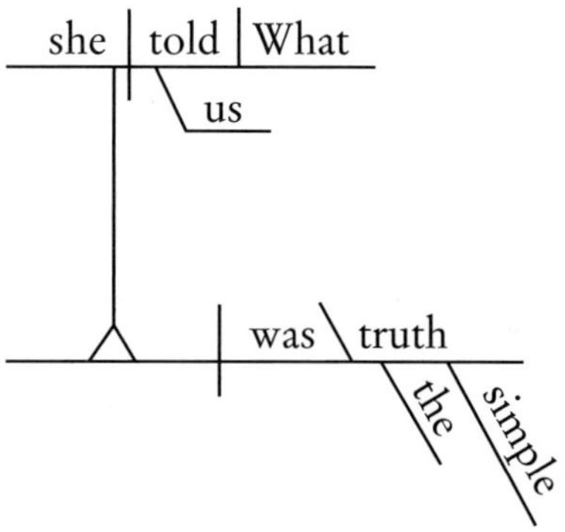

Notice that the clause is written on a "stilt" placed on the base line where the subject usually appears. The word that introduces a noun clause is diagramed according to its use within its own clause. In the noun clause in the example, the word *What* is the direct object. If the word that introduces the noun clause isn't really part of either the noun clause or the main clause, write the word on its own line.

NOUN CLAUSE AS DIRECT OBJECT

EXAMPLE Terry knows **that good grades are important.**

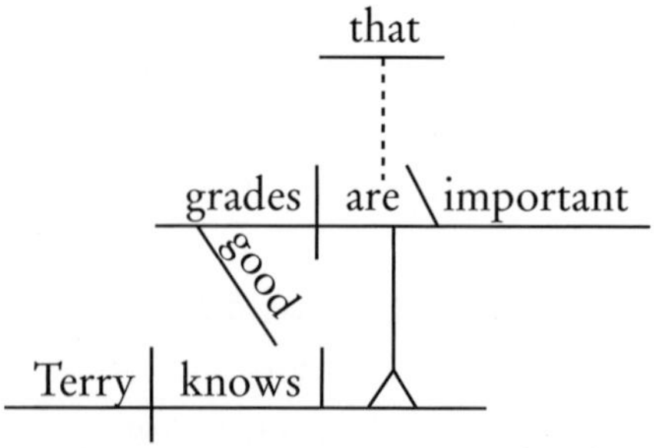

NOUN CLAUSE AS INDIRECT OBJECT

EXAMPLE Tell **whomever you see** the news.

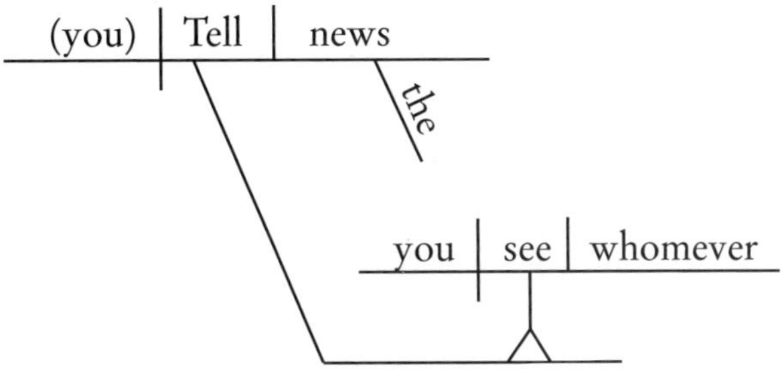

NOUN CLAUSE AS OBJECT OF A PREPOSITION

EXAMPLE This is an example of **what I mean.**

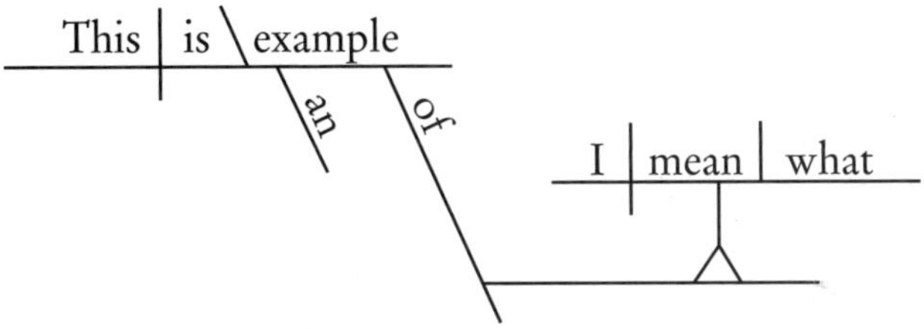

NOUN CLAUSE AS PREDICATE NOUN

EXAMPLE The result was **that nobody believed me.**

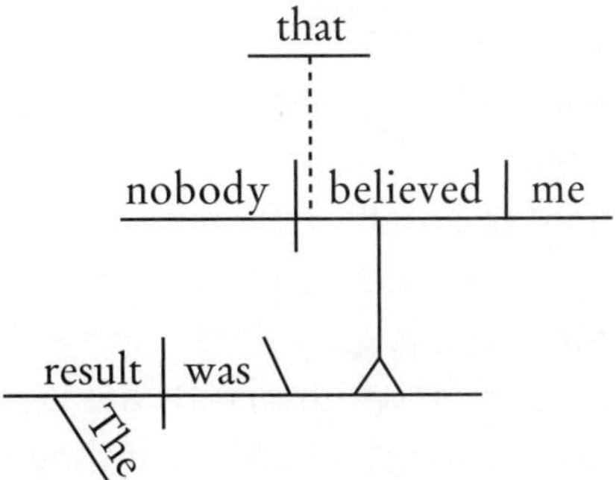

PRACTICE Diagraming Noun Clauses

Diagram each sentence.

1. The class sang a song for whoever had a birthday.
2. The ending of the movie was what surprised me.
3. On Saturdays, Josh does whatever he wants.
4. Why Amelia Earhart disappeared remains a mystery.
5. Whatever happens can be blamed on the weather.
6. Give whoever shows up your extra ticket.
7. It appears that the Mets will be in the World Series.
8. Scientists have learned what causes Lyme disease.
9. General Eisenhower decided when D-Day would occur.
10. You can use the money for whatever you choose.

POSTTEST Diagraming Sentences

Diagram each sentence.

1. Dogs barked.
2. Everyone was writing.
3. Has Sharon called?
4. Beware!
5. Read this article.
6. J. K. Rowling gave her readers another Harry Potter book.
7. The coach handed the team captains new uniforms.
8. The young boy sang beautifully in many concerts.
9. Robert Frost wrote poems about the interesting landscape of New England.
10. The very first Scottish golf ball consisted of feathers with a leather cover.
11. The herb garden smells very fresh.
12. Our country is a democracy.
13. Jen's favorite outfit is gray slacks and a pink shirt.
14. St. Bernards and Newfoundlands are rescue dogs.
15. Venice's canals look delightful, but they cause many problems.

16. Calcium is found in milk, and it is also added to other food products.
17. That singer, whom we saw in concert, has a new CD.
18. If you like modern art, you should visit the new museum in London.
19. Why dinosaurs died out is unknown.
20. Some experts think that the earth became too cold.

Chapter 11

Capitalization

PRETEST Capitalization

Write each sentence. Use capital letters correctly.

1. did you know that the movie *titanic* won the Oscar for best picture in 1997?

2. When i visited Cape Canaveral, i saw the space shuttle *columbia*.

3. *oklahoma*! was a musical that premiered on broadway in 1943.

4. My Father is a member of the city council who ran on the Green Party ticket.

5. Do You live on River road or daisy Lane?

6. I visited the National Women's hall of fame, which is located in Seneca falls, New york.

7. Maryland was named for queen Henrietta Maria, who was married to king charles I of England.

8. The author of the article is the well-known children's doctor Kenneth Baker, m.d.

9. After president Richard Milhous Nixon resigned on August 9, 1974, Vice President gerald r. Ford became President.
10. Elaine's Uncle took her Brother and younger sister to see the film.
11. Zak said, "i want to visit washington, D.C., in the spring when the cherry trees are blooming."
12. Lily mentioned that She wanted to visit the grand canyon.
13. Has anyone in the class read the Book *The diary of Anne Frank*?
14. Aunt Jody lives in Northern Minnesota, but her sister lives in southern California.
15. Mr. and mrs. lopez moved from the Southwest to new England.
16. The humber River bridge in England is one of the longest Bridges in the world.
17. The book *A Drop of Water: A Book of science and Wonder* was written by Walter Wick.
18. The cleveland Museum of Art has a new Exhibit in its main hall.
19. Beginning in december, Mr. Brady will teach Language Arts.
20. When I wash up after gardening, i use Mother earth soap.
21. The Wives of Presidents have made important contributions to our nation.
22. Mrs. Johnson began a campaign to clean up the highways of the united states.
23. We met dr. Kramer and his family at a japanese restaurant downtown.
24. did you see the article about the declaration of Independence and the beginning of the American Revolution in Sunday's *Boston globe*?
25. In her report, Telma said, "camels and rattlesnakes can live in the Desert."

11.1 CAPITALIZING SENTENCES, QUOTATIONS, AND LETTER PARTS

CCSS L.6.2

A capital letter marks the beginning of a sentence. A capital letter also marks the beginning of a direct quotation and the salutation and the closing of a letter.

RULE 1 Capitalize the first word of every sentence.

EXAMPLE **M**any people worked for the independence of the colonies.

RULE 2 Capitalize the first word of a direct quotation that is a complete sentence. A direct quotation gives a speaker's exact words.

EXAMPLE Travis said, "**O**ne of those people was Paul Revere."

RULE 3 When a direct quotation is interrupted by explanatory words, such as *she said,* don't begin the second part of the direct quotation with a capital letter.

EXAMPLE "I read a famous poem," said Kim, "**a**bout Paul Revere."

When the second part of a direct quotation is a new sentence, put a period after the explanatory words and begin the second part of the quotation with a capital letter.

EXAMPLE "I know that poem," said Sarah. "**M**y class read it last week."

RULE 4 Don't capitalize an indirect quotation. An indirect quotation does not repeat a person's exact words and should not be enclosed in quotation marks. An indirect quotation is often introduced by the word *that.*

EXAMPLE The teacher said **t**he poem was written by Longfellow.

EXAMPLE The teacher said **that t**he poem was written by Longfellow.

RULE 5 Capitalize the first word in the salutation and the closing of a letter. Capitalize the title and the name of the person addressed.

EXAMPLES **D**ear **M**rs. **A**damson, **S**incerely yours,

EXAMPLES **M**y dear **A**bigail, **W**ith love,

NOTE Usually, the first word in each line of a poem is capitalized, but many modern poets don't follow this style. When you copy a poem, use the style of the original version.

GRAMMAR / USAGE / MECHANICS

PRACTICE Capitalizing Sentences, Quotations, and Letter Parts

Write each sentence. Use capital letters correctly. If a sentence is already correct, write correct.

1. colds are common illnesses that many people experience once or twice a year.
2. chris asked, "how do you catch a cold?"
3. "I think," said Maura, "that you catch a cold by going outside without a coat."
4. "That is incorrect," said Patrick. "colds are caused by viruses, and the best way to avoid a cold is to wash your hands."
5. There is no cure for a Cold.
6. some vitamins can make you feel better.
7. Donna said, "a cold lasts for about one or two weeks."
8. Jason said That he had many colds last year.
9. this year he will eat well and get enough sleep.
10. *Rewrite each salutation and closing correctly.*
    a. dear Dr. kwan,
    b. My dear marcela,
    c. yours sincerely,
    d. your Friend always,

11.2 CAPITALIZING NAMES AND TITLES OF PEOPLE CCSS L.6.2

RULE 1 Capitalize the names of people and the initials that stand for their names.

EXAMPLES **C**lark **K**ent **S**usan **B**. **A**nthony **E**. **C**. **S**tanton

RULE 2 Capitalize a title or an abbreviation of a title when it comes before a person's name.

EXAMPLES **P**resident Wilson **D**r. Martin Luther King **M**s. Ruiz

Capitalize a title when it's used instead of a name.

EXAMPLE "Has the enemy surrendered, **G**eneral?" asked the colonel.

Don't capitalize a title that follows a name or one that is used as a common noun.

EXAMPLE Woodrow Wilson, **p**resident of the United States during World War I, supported cooperation among nations.

EXAMPLE Who was Wilson's **v**ice **p**resident?

RULE 3 Capitalize the names and abbreviations of academic degrees that follow a name. Capitalize *Jr.* and *Sr.*

EXAMPLES M. Katayama, **M.D.** Janis Stein, **P**h.**D**. Otis Ames **J**r.

RULE 4 Capitalize words that show family relationships when they're used as titles or as substitutes for names.

EXAMPLE Last year **F**ather and **A**unt Beth traveled to several western states.

Don't capitalize words that show family relationships when they follow possessive nouns or pronouns.

EXAMPLE Jo's **u**ncle took photographs. My **a**unt Mary framed them.

RULE 5 Always capitalize the pronoun *I*.

EXAMPLE American history is the subject **I** like best.

PRACTICE Capitalizing Names and Titles of People

Write each sentence. Use capital letters correctly. If a sentence is already correct, write correct.

1. Johannes gutenberg changed how books were made.
2. My Uncle Ed said that we could visit aunt beverly and him any time.
3. Will i be invited to ms. Simpson's play?
4. In the story by r. l. Stevenson, dr. Jekyll and mr. hyde were two sides of the same person.
5. The new first-grade teacher is p. sami lin, who is Su Lin's Uncle.
6. Antonio Galves jr. helped campaign for his father.
7. My father and my uncle Lewis always go on a fishing trip to Canada in the summer.
8. President John q. Adams was the son of the second President, John Adams.
9. Bill Cosby, ed.d., is a popular comic, actor, and author.
10. Last week I saw the letters that the General wrote.

11.3 CAPITALIZING NAMES OF PLACES

CCSS L.6.2

The names of specific places are proper nouns and should be capitalized. Don't capitalize articles and short prepositions that are part of geographical names.

RULE 1 Capitalize the names of cities, counties, states, countries, and continents.

EXAMPLES	**S**an **D**iego	**C**ook **C**ounty	**N**orth **C**arolina
	Japan	**M**exico	**E**urope

RULE 2 Capitalize the names of bodies of water and other geographical features.

EXAMPLES Lake Michigan Gulf of Mexico Pacific Ocean
Mojave Desert Napa Valley Rocky Mountains

RULE 3 Capitalize the names of sections of a country.

EXAMPLES the Sun Belt New England the Great Plains

RULE 4 Capitalize direction words when they name a particular section of a country.

EXAMPLES the South the West Coast the Northeast

Don't capitalize direction words used in other ways.

EXAMPLES southern California northerly winds
Kansas is west of Missouri.

RULE 5 Capitalize the names of streets and highways.

EXAMPLES Main Street Route 66 Pennsylvania Turnpike

RULE 6 Capitalize the names of particular buildings, bridges, monuments, and other structures.

EXAMPLES the White House Golden Gate Bridge
Lincoln Memorial the Rose Bowl

GRAMMAR / USAGE / MECHANICS

PRACTICE Capitalizing Names of Places

Write each sentence. Use capital letters correctly.

1. Springfield, not chicago, is the capital of illinois.
2. Dad visited japan last year.
3. Africa's nile river, which flows North into the mediterranean sea, is the world's longest river.
4. The Pacific ocean is much larger than the atlantic.
5. Boston is Northeast of New york.
6. We will mainly travel on interstate 95.

7. Huge dust storms covered much of the great plains in the 1930s.
8. The Grand canyon is located in the southwest.
9. We stopped in cleveland on our way to buffalo.
10. Did you know that california is called the Golden State?

11.4 CAPITALIZING OTHER PROPER NOUNS AND ADJECTIVES CCSS L.6.2

Many nouns besides the names of people and places are proper nouns and should be capitalized. Adjectives formed from proper nouns are called proper adjectives and should also be capitalized.

RULE 1 Capitalize all important words in the names of clubs, organizations, businesses, institutions, and political parties.

EXAMPLES		
	Girl Scouts of America	American Red Cross
	Microsoft Corporation	Smithsonian Institution
	University of Nebraska	Republican Party

RULE 2 Capitalize brand names but not the nouns following them.

EXAMPLES Downhome soup Lull-a-bye diapers Kruncho crackers

RULE 3 Capitalize all important words in the names of particular historical events, time periods, and documents.

EXAMPLES Revolutionary War Iron Age Gettysburg Address

RULE 4 Capitalize the names of days of the week, months of the year, and holidays. Don't capitalize the names of the seasons.

EXAMPLES Sunday April Thanksgiving Day spring

GRAMMAR / USAGE / MECHANICS

RULE 5 Capitalize the first word and the last word in the titles of books, chapters, plays, short stories, poems, essays, articles, movies, television series and programs, songs, magazines, and newspapers. Capitalize all other words except articles, coordinating conjunctions, and prepositions of fewer than five letters. Don't capitalize the word *the* before the title of a magazine or newspaper.

EXAMPLES *A Wrinkle in Time* "Mammals and Their Young"
"The Lady or the Tiger?" "The Truth About Dragons"
"Over the Rainbow" *Seventeen*

RULE 6 Capitalize the names of languages, nationalities, and ethnic groups.

EXAMPLES English Japanese Native Americans

RULE 7 Capitalize proper adjectives. A proper adjective is an adjective formed from a proper noun.

EXAMPLES African American voters Mexican art
a Broadway musical Appalachian families

NOTE Capitalize the names of religions and the people who practice them. Capitalize the names of holy days, sacred writings, and deities.

EXAMPLES Islam Muslims Easter the Bible Allah

NOTE Capitalize the names of trains, ships, airplanes, and spacecraft.

EXAMPLES the Orient Express *Titanic*
Spirit of St. Louis *Voyager 2*

NOTE Don't capitalize the names of school subjects, except for proper nouns and adjectives and course names followed by a number.

EXAMPLES language arts geography earth science
American history French Algebra 1

PRACTICE Capitalizing Other Proper Nouns and Adjectives

Write each sentence. Use capital letters correctly.

1. In August 1807, Robert Fulton's steamboat *clermont* traveled up the Hudson River for the first time.
2. Next year I will take Algebra, spanish, english, and world history 1.
3. The koran is the holy book of muslims, and the bible is the holy book of christians.
4. The chinese chefs teach cooking lessons at the college of Lake County.
5. Read the chapter that is titled "types of insects."
6. The united way raises funds for many organizations.
7. The movie explained the background of the civil War.
8. This year, thanksgiving day will be on thursday, november 24.
9. Paul Simon, an american songwriter, produced the album *graceland* with south african musicians.
10. Mom bought High-Rise biscuits for sunday brunch.

GRAMMAR / USAGE / MECHANICS

PRACTICE Proofreading

Rewrite the following letter, correcting errors in spelling, capitalization, grammar, and usage. Add any missing punctuation. Write legibly to be sure one letter is not mistaken for another. There are ten mistakes.

Elvis Presley

[1]dear Jenny,

[2]I am enjoying my vacation in memphis, Tennessee. [3]did you know that this is where Elvis presley lived? [4]For a long time, he was the most popular American singer in the world. [5]I saw his home, Graceland.

[6]Elvis was born in 1935 in mississippi. [7]When he was a tean, Elvis paid to make a record for his Mother's birthday. [8]The owner of the studio offered him a job. [9]His first hit record was "That's all Right, mama." [10]By the time he died in the Summer of 1977, he had recorded more than forty gold albums.

[11]Best Wishes,
[12]Colin

POSTTEST Capitalization

Write each sentence. Use capital letters correctly.

1. Melinda asked, "where do you live?
2. "We just moved to a small town in Southern wisconsin," i answered.
3. Are you a Chicago White sox, Chicago cubs, or milwaukee Brewers fan?
4. Do you know how many Vice Presidents have become president?
5. *Charlotte's web*, by e. b. White, is a well-known Children's book.
6. my chores include cleaning my room on fridays and doing the dishes every other Day.
7. Do you and your family gather with other relatives for the thanksgiving holiday?
8. Last Month we sang " this land is your land" for the assembly.
9. In december many jewish families celebrate Chanukah, the Festival of Lights.
10. Johann sebastian Bach came from a musical family.
11. Bob dylan is a famous folk Singer.
12. From venice, italy, Marco Polo and his father traveled to asia.
13. Coal is mined in many countries, including the united states and china.

14. The eiffel tower, built by Gustave Eiffel in the 1880s, is located in paris, france.

15. John Glenn was the first american astronaut to orbit Earth.

16. The Supermarket was giving away samples of Clean 'n' bright Detergent, a new laundry product.

17. In the 1600s, timbuktu was an important trading center of the mali empire.

18. Uncle Steven and his Father are planning a trip to australia in the Summer.

19. Bill Clinton was the american President from 1993 to 2001.

20. On her book tour, the Author dr. Jean Benson spoke about food issues.

21. The *queen elizabeth 2* is a huge passenger ship that can cross the atlantic ocean in less than a week.

22. Eric told me that He is training to be a lifeguard.

23. The *New York times* reporter spoke to our class about Careers.

24. "Call me after work this evening," said Judy. "i'll be home at 7:00."

25. The first olympics were held in athens, Greece.

Chapter 12

Punctuation

PRETEST Commas, Semicolons, Colons, and End Punctuation

Write each sentence. Add commas, semicolons, colons, and end punctuation where needed.

1. Wow I can't believe I got every answer right
2. No Michael you didn't miss the first team practice
3. "You must have forgotten to lock the door" said Meg.
4. In a bid for the presidency candidates campaign vigorously.
5. The vacation home was cozy and the view of the mountains was great
6. In the sky above the horizon a jet left a silver trail
7. Would you like something to drink while we wait

8. If you will buy the tickets I will pay the cab fare
9. Mr. Wu replied "The coyote too is a member of the wild dog family."
10. I mailed the request to Marsha Lewis M.D. 739 South Locust Street Van Nuys CA 91401
11. Holding their gear over their heads Brianna and Rob waded into the creek
12. You will need these supplies for art class drawing pencils charcoal and pastel chalk
13. Jane McCormick my regular dentist is on vacation however Dr. John Pelz is handling her patients' emergencies.
14. The contest began October 5 2000 and ran to the end of June 2001
15. My dog can sit up roll over and play dead he cannot seem to remember to stay off the couch

PRETEST Quotation Marks, Italics, and Apostrophes

Write each sentence. Add quotation marks, underlining (for italics), apostrophes, and other punctuation marks where they're needed. If the sentence is already correct, write correct.

16. You will find said Ms. Hohlman that Mark Twain was quite a humorist as well as a first-rate writer
17. Mark Twains real name was Samuel Langhorne Clemens she continued.
18. Didn't he take that name from a water-measuring term asked Marcus. He worked as a riverboat pilot too
19. The writers experiences on the river provided several stories worth of raw material added the teacher.
20. Arent The Adventures of Huckleberry Finn and The Adventures of Tom Sawyer set on the Mississippi?
21. Besss favorite short story is The Celebrated Jumping Frog of Calaveras County, which is printed in our literature book, Adventures in Appreciation.

22. Troy lost his book and wants to borrow hers or yours.
23. Did she say there will be a test on Twain tomorrow
24. The books humor and characters are its claim to fame.
25. What would you say if I told you I forgot to study for the test asked Malika.

PRETEST Hyphens, Dashes, Parentheses, and Numbers

Write each sentence. Add hyphens, dashes, and parentheses where they're needed. Use the correct form for each number. If the sentence is already correct, write correct.

26. Bogs lowland marshes full of underwater plants are the source of England's peat.
27. The much loved Chocolate Supreme sells best of all our twenty four kinds of pies.
28. Nine tenths of the population has little skill in decision making; if you can, learn decision making skills now.
29. My great uncle, a self made man, had three hundred sixty two employees working for him.
30. The biologist tagged the turtle on July sixth at one ten P.M.; it weighed eighty one pounds and was three feet, seven inches long.
31. The data tell us that 431 students approve of the new cafeteria food and fifty five do not.
32. On the 2nd day of June at exactly three fifteen P.M., I will be on vacation, headed for Magic Waters water park at Three Six Two Sudbury Lane.
33. Sly Stallone did I tell you we went to high school together? has been to my house three times.
34. 128 people live in the apartment complex at 604 South 4th Street.
35. In the mock election, the principal received seventy percent of the votes and the vice principal got thirty percent.

12.1 USING END PUNCTUATION CCSS L.6.2

RULE 1 Use a period at the end of a declarative sentence. A declarative sentence makes a statement.

EXAMPLE Tractors perform many jobs on a farm.

EXAMPLE I worked on a farm during the summer.

RULE 2 Use a period at the end of an imperative sentence. An imperative sentence gives a command or makes a request.

EXAMPLE Turn the key. **[command]**

EXAMPLE Please start the motor. **[request]**

RULE 3 Use a question mark at the end of an interrogative sentence. An interrogative sentence asks a question.

EXAMPLE Who built the first tractor?

EXAMPLE Did you know that?

RULE 4 Use an exclamation point at the end of an exclamatory sentence. An exclamatory sentence expresses strong feeling.

EXAMPLE How powerful your tractor is!

EXAMPLE What a loud noise it makes!

RULE 5 Use an exclamation point after a strong interjection. An interjection is a word or group of words that expresses emotion.

EXAMPLES				
	Wow!	Whew!	My goodness!	Ouch!
	Yippee!	Hi!	Hey!	Oops!

PRACTICE **Using End Punctuation**

Write each sentence. Add the correct end punctuation. Then write declarative, imperative, interrogative, exclamatory, *or* interjection *to show the reason for the end mark you chose.*

1. I have ridden my bike over a thousand miles this summer
2. Whew How much farther did you say we have to ride
3. Check your tire pressure and fill your water bottle
4. Yippee We're going to Disney World
5. Did Mom order the airline tickets and reserve our hotel rooms
6. What a great time we will have
7. Brent wondered whether he could ride on Space Mountain
8. Decide what to take and pack your bags
9. The flight was crowded, noisy, and rough
10. How many nights will you be staying with us

12.2 USING COMMAS I CCSS L.6.2, a

When you use commas to *separate* items, you place a comma between items. When you use commas to *set off* an item, you place a comma before and after the item. Of course, you never place a comma at the beginning or the end of a sentence.

RULE 1 Separate three or more words, phrases, or clauses in a series.

EXAMPLE Cars, buses, and trucks clog city streets. **[words]**

EXAMPLE Beside the fence, on the porch, or outside the back door is a good place for that potted plant. **[phrases]**

EXAMPLE Call me before you leave town, while you're in Florida, or after you return home. **[clauses]**

RULE 2 Set off an introductory word such as *yes, no,* or *well.*

EXAMPLE Yes, we enjoyed your performance in the play.

EXAMPLE No, you didn't sing off key.

RULE 3 Set off names used in direct address.

EXAMPLE Claire, have you ever traveled on a ship?

EXAMPLE I traveled to Alaska, Mr. Hess, on a cruise ship.

EXAMPLE Did you enjoy your trip down the Ohio River, Dale?

RULE 4 Set off two or more prepositional phrases at the beginning of a sentence. Set off a single long prepositional phrase at the beginning of a sentence.

EXAMPLE In the fall of 1998, Frank Jordan ran for mayor. **[two prepositional phrases–*In the fall* and *of 1998*]**

EXAMPLE Beneath a dozen fluttering red and blue banners, he made his campaign speech. **[one long prepositional phrase–*Beneath a dozen fluttering red and blue banners*]**

You need not set off a single short prepositional phrase, but it's not wrong to do so.

EXAMPLE In 1998 Frank Jordan ran for mayor. **[one short prepositional phrase–*In 1998*]**

RULE 5 Set off participles and participial phrases at the beginning of a sentence.

EXAMPLE Talking, we lost track of the time.

EXAMPLE Talking on the telephone, we lost track of the time.

Set off a participial phrase that is not essential to the meaning of a sentence.

EXAMPLE The band, marching in formation, moves down the field.

EXAMPLE Independence Day, celebrated on July 4, is a national holiday.

RULE 6 Set off words that interrupt the flow of thought in a sentence.

EXAMPLE Politicians, of course, sometimes forget their campaign promises after the election.

RULE 7 Use a comma after a conjunctive adverb, such as *however, moreover, furthermore, nevertheless,* or *therefore.*

EXAMPLE The school district is growing; therefore, taxes will rise.

RULE 8 Set off an appositive that is not essential to the meaning of a sentence.

EXAMPLE The *Titanic*, a luxury liner, sank on its first voyage. **[The appositive, *a luxury liner*, is not essential.]**

PRACTICE Using Commas I

Write the following sentences. Add commas where they're needed.

1. Listening to a CD Jennifer did not hear us bring in the groceries.
2. Thomas Jefferson our nation's third president disliked public life; nonetheless he served two terms in office.
3. Without too much detail Jim describe the room for us.
4. The rest of the grading period as you know has only two weeks in it.
5. Call us if you have car trouble run out of money or lose your way.
6. One lonely leaf tattered and shriveled by winter wind remained on the vine.
7. Tony will you remember to bring in the mail and the paper?
8. Well Marna you earned that B for paying attention in class doing your homework and studying hard.

9. With the hope of winning the tournament our soccer team practiced hard; however we were eliminated in the second round.
10. Long after the closing of stores offices and factories the popcorn vendor strolled the streets.

12.3 USING COMMAS II CCSS L.6.2, a

RULE 9 Use a comma before a coordinating conjunction (*and, but, or, nor,* or *for*) that connects the two parts of a compound sentence.

EXAMPLE Steve opened the door, and the dog ran out.

EXAMPLE Mari called her best friend, but no one answered.

EXAMPLE They will raise money, or they will donate their time.

RULE 10 Set off an adverb clause at the beginning of a sentence. An adverb clause begins with a subordinating conjunction, such as *after, although, as, because, before, if, since, though, unless, until, when, whenever, where, wherever,* or *while.*

EXAMPLE Whenever I feel afraid, I whistle a happy tune.

Usually, an adverb clause that falls at the end of a sentence is not set off.

EXAMPLE I whistle a happy tune whenever I feel afraid.

RULE 11 Set off a nonessential adjective clause. A nonessential adjective clause simply gives additional information and is not necessary to the meaning of a sentence. An adjective clause usually begins with a relative pronoun, such as *who, whom, whose, which,* or *that.*

EXAMPLE My house, which has green shutters, is at the corner of Elm and Maple.

Don't set off an essential adjective clause. An essential adjective clause is necessary to the meaning of a sentence.

EXAMPLE The house that has green shutters is at the corner of Elm and Maple.

PRACTICE Using Commas II

Write each sentence. Add commas where they're needed. If a sentence needs no commas, write correct.

1. Are you sure of your facts and is that your final answer?
2. Until you learn to take responsibility for your actions you will not be ready for independence.
3. The movie ended but no one moved a muscle.
4. Juanita who is only five feet tall is a fine gymnast.
5. The house that I grew up in was shabby and down-at-the-heels.
6. I will wait for you until the last bus arrives.
7. Because a donor gave $1,000 the charity met its goal.
8. I packed sandwiches and lemonade for I'd be gone all day.
9. Tyler offered us a ride but we wanted to walk home.
10. My brother Carl whom I think you know is sixteen today.

12.4 USING COMMAS III CCSS L.6.2

RULE 12 In a date, set off the year when it's used with both the month and the day. Don't use a comma if only the month and the year are given.

EXAMPLE The ship struck an iceberg on April 14, 1912, and sank early the next morning.

EXAMPLE The ship sank in April 1912 on its first voyage.

RULE 13 Set off the name of a state or a country when it's used after the name of a city. Set off the name of a city when it's used after a street address. Don't use a comma after the state if it's followed by a ZIP code.

EXAMPLE The ship was sailing from Southampton, England, to New York City.

EXAMPLE You can write to Leeza at 15 College Court, Stanford, CA 94305.

RULE 14 Set off an abbreviated title or degree following a person's name.

EXAMPLE Michelle Nakamura, Ph.D., will be the graduation speaker.

EXAMPLE Letisha Davis, M.D., is our family physician.

RULE 15 Set off *too* when it's used in the middle of a sentence and means "also." Don't set off *too* at the end of a sentence.

EXAMPLE Parents, too, will attend the ceremony.

EXAMPLE Parents will attend the ceremony too.

RULE 16 Set off a direct quotation.

EXAMPLE Mom asked, "Have you finished your homework?"

EXAMPLE "I did it," I replied, "in study hall."

EXAMPLE "Tell me what you learned," said Mom.

RULE 17 Use a comma after the salutation of a friendly letter and after the closing of both a friendly letter and a business letter.

EXAMPLES Dear Dad, Your loving daughter, Yours truly,

RULE 18 Use a comma to prevent misreading.

EXAMPLE Instead of two, five teachers made the trip.

EXAMPLE In the field below, the brook gurgled merrily.

GRAMMAR / USAGE / MECHANICS

PRACTICE Using Commas III

Write each sentence. Add commas where they're needed.

1. "The new furniture is coming" I informed her "all the way from Copenhagen Denmark."
2. The horses too are tired and hungry after the long ride.
3. The Declaration of Independence was actually signed by all the delegates in August 1776 in Philadelphia Pennsylvania.
4. "The Declaration is kept at the National Archives Exhibition Hall in Washington D.C." said Mr. Richoz.

5. The cattle were herded along the Chisholm Trail from San Antonio Texas to Abilene Kansas.
6. Lewis Thomas M.D. wrote books on the practice of medicine and his views of life.
7. Ryan reminded his cousins "My eleventh birthday will be April 11 2002; send cards to me at 3 Pine Court Salem IL 62881."
8. Ona left Charleston South Carolina when she was ten and did not return until October 18 2001.
9. Until the week before Dad's birthday shopping hadn't seemed like a priority.
10. *Write the following message, adding commas where needed.*

Dear Grandma Bernice

Thanks for writing me. I too enjoy getting "snail mail." Your letters are always fun to read.

Your loving granddaughter
Samantha

GRAMMAR / USAGE / MECHANICS

12.5 USING SEMICOLONS AND COLONS

CCSS L.6.2

RULE 1 Use a semicolon to join the main clauses of a compound sentence if they're not joined by a conjunction such as *and, but, or, nor,* or *for.*

EXAMPLE The electric car was once the most popular car in the United States**;** people liked electric cars because they were clean and quiet.

RULE 2 Use a semicolon to join the main clauses of a compound sentence if they're long and if they already contain commas. Use a semicolon even if the clauses are joined by a coordinating conjunction such as *and, but, or, nor,* or *for.*

EXAMPLE Before the invention of the automobile, people rode horses, bicycles, or streetcars for short distances**;** and they used horse-drawn carriages, trains, or boats for longer trips.

RULE 3 Use a semicolon to separate main clauses joined by a conjunctive adverb, such as *consequently, furthermore, however, moreover, nevertheless,* or *therefore.*

EXAMPLE I started my homework immediately after school**;** consequently, I finished before dinner.

RULE 4 Use a colon to introduce a list of items that ends a sentence. Use a word or a phrase such as *these, the following,* or *as follows* before the list.

EXAMPLE I'll need **these** supplies for my project**:** newspapers, flour, water, string, and paint.

EXAMPLE I participate in **the following** sports**:** softball, tennis, basketball, and swimming.

Don't use a colon immediately after a verb or a preposition.

EXAMPLE My subjects **include** reading, math, home economics, and language arts.

EXAMPLE I sent messages **to** Grandma, Aunt Rita, and Julie.

RULE 5 Use a colon to separate the hour and the minutes when you use numerals to write the time of day.

EXAMPLE The train left the station at 10**:**17 A.M. and arrived in the city at 12**:**33 P.M.

RULE 6 Use a colon after the salutation of a business letter.

EXAMPLES Dear Professor Sanchez**:** Dear Editor in Chief**:**

PRACTICE Using Semicolons and Colons

Write each sentence. Add semicolons and colons where they're needed. If a sentence is already correct, write correct.

1. Lightning streaked across the sky then thunder boomed.
2. I added these things to the time capsule a remote control, a Web address, and a AA battery.

GRAMMAR / USAGE / MECHANICS

3. A terrible earthquake occurred off the coast of Ecuador in 1906 it measured 8.9 on the Richter scale.
4. The tremors began at 257 A.M.
5. Big earthquakes have occurred in California, Alaska, and Mexico however, the worst quake in North America occurred in the Midwest along the New Madrid fault.
6. After a perfect day at the beach, no one wanted to leave for home so we sat on the sand, walked along the shore, listened to the waves crash, and watched the sun set and stars come out.
7. My teammates finished the five-mile race at these times Carlton, 1159 A.M., Jon, 1201 P.M., Smitty, 1202 P.M.
8. Her favorite fruits are peaches, bananas, and blueberries.
9. In the 1990s, Michael Jordan was the world's greatest basketball player, an advertising giant, and a public figure with huge appeal therefore, his decision to leave pro basketball, buy a team, and run it surprised many.
10. *Write the following business letter, adding necessary punctuation.*

    Dear Sir

    I am enclosing the following materials the rebate form for the *e*One computer, my sales receipt, and the proof of purchase.

    Yours truly,
    Christa Milner

12.6 USING QUOTATION MARKS AND ITALICS

CCSS L.6.2

RULE 1 Use quotation marks to enclose a direct quotation.

EXAMPLE "Please return these books to the library," said Ms. Chu.

RULE 2 Use quotation marks to enclose each part of an interrupted quotation.

EXAMPLE "Spiders," explained Sean, "have eight legs."

RULE 3 Use commas to set off an explanatory phrase, such as *he said,* from the quotation itself. Place commas inside closing quotation marks.

EXAMPLE "Spiders," explained Sean, "have eight legs."

RULE 4 Place a period inside closing quotation marks.

EXAMPLE Toby said, "My aunt Susan received her degree in June."

RULE 5 Place a question mark or an exclamation point inside closing quotation marks if it's part of the quotation.

EXAMPLE Yoko asked, "Have you ever visited Florida?"

Place a question mark or an exclamation point outside closing quotation marks if it's part of the entire sentence but not part of the quotation.

EXAMPLE Did Jerry say, "Spiders have ten legs"?

When both a sentence and the direct quotation at the end of the sentence are questions (or exclamations), use only one question mark (or exclamation point). Place the mark inside the closing quotation marks.

EXAMPLE Did Yoko ask, "Have you ever visited Florida?"

NOTE When you're writing conversation, begin a new paragraph each time the speaker changes.

EXAMPLE

"You're kidding!" I exclaimed. "That sounds unbelievable. Did she really say that?"

"Indeed she did," Kara insisted.

RULE 6 Enclose in quotation marks titles of short stories, essays, poems, songs, articles, book chapters, and single television shows that are part of a series.

EXAMPLES "Charles" [short story] "Jingle Bells" [song]

RULE 7 Use italics or underlining for titles of books, plays, movies, television series, magazines, newspapers, works of art, music albums, and long musical compositions. Also use italics or underlining for the names of ships, airplanes, and spacecraft. Don't italicize or underline the word *the* before the title of a magazine or newspaper.

EXAMPLE *The Adventures of Tom Sawyer* **[book]**

EXAMPLE The Monsters Are Due on Maple Street **[play]**

EXAMPLE *The Hunchback of Notre Dame* **[movie]**

EXAMPLE Sesame Street **[television series]**

EXAMPLE *Cricket* **[magazine]**

EXAMPLE the New York Times **[newspaper]**

EXAMPLE the *Mona Lisa* **[painting]**

EXAMPLE The Best of Reba McEntire **[music album]**

EXAMPLE *Rhapsody in Blue* **[long musical composition]**

EXAMPLE Titanic **[ship]**

EXAMPLE the *Spirit of St. Louis* **[airplane]**

EXAMPLE Friendship 7 **[spacecraft]**

PRACTICE Using Quotation Marks, Italics, and Other Punctuation

Write each sentence. Add quotation marks, underlining (for italics), and other punctuation marks where they're needed.

1. One of my favorite shows said Darrell is The West Wing, starring Martin Sheen as the president.
2. We read O. Henry's story The Gift of the Magi before the holiday vacation.
3. How I loved reading that story! Nora blurted out.
4. Did you read the article about children and the Internet in the New York Times, asked Perry.
5. It's my turn to use the computer Juju said.
6. The Princess Bride said Lee, is a great movie.
7. Mary added I have memorized some of the dialogue
8. Did someone ask Where's the popcorn
9. Chief Joseph said I will fight no more forever
10. This chapter of my mystery is called Murder in Mind

GRAMMAR / USAGE / MECHANICS

12.7 USING APOSTROPHES CCSS L.6.2

RULE 1 Use an apostrophe and *s ('s)* to form the possessive of a singular noun.

EXAMPLES girl + **'s** = girl**'s** James + **'s** = James**'s**

RULE 2 Use an apostrophe and *s ('s)* to form the possessive of a plural noun that does not end in *s*.

EXAMPLES men + **'s** = men**'s** geese + **'s** = geese**'s**

RULE 3 Use an apostrophe alone to form the possessive of a plural noun that ends in *s*.

EXAMPLES boys + **'** = boys**'** judges + **'** = judges**'**

RULE 4 Use an apostrophe and *s ('s)* to form the possessive of an indefinite pronoun, such as *everyone, everybody, anyone, no one*, or *nobody.*

EXAMPLES anybody + **'s** = anybody**'s** someone + **'s** = someone**'s**

Don't use an apostrophe in the possessive personal pronouns *ours, yours, his, hers, its,* and *theirs.*

EXAMPLES That car is **ours.** Is that cat **yours**?

The bird flapped **its** wings. These skates are **hers.**

RULE 5 Use an apostrophe to replace letters that are omitted in a contraction.

EXAMPLES it is = it's you are = you're

I will = I'll is not = isn't

GRAMMAR / USAGE / MECHANICS

PRACTICE Using Apostrophes

Write each sentence. Add apostrophes where they're needed. If the sentence is already correct, write correct.

1. Girls clothing is on the first floor, and womens wear is on the second floor.
2. Theyll never believe that Sandras dog ate her work.
3. Whether the pilots union will strike is anybodys guess.
4. The CD player is his, but the CDs are hers.
5. Ill make sure no ones order gets messed up.
6. The mices nest had been destroyed by the plough.
7. The boats motor isnt working.
8. Havent you ever wished you could fly?
9. Someones pencil, with its point broken, lay on the table.
10. Its important to try to see our parents point of view.

12.8 USING HYPHENS, DASHES, AND PARENTHESES CCSS L.6.2, a

RULE 1 Use a hyphen to divide a word at the end of a line. Divide words only between syllables.

EXAMPLE With her husband, Pierre, Marie Sklodowska Curie discovered radium and polonium.

RULE 2 Use a hyphen in compound numbers.

EXAMPLES **thirty-two** pianos **sixty-five** experiments

RULE 3 Use a hyphen in fractions expressed in words.

EXAMPLE Add **one-half** cup of butter or margarine.

EXAMPLE **Three-fourths** of the students sing in the chorus.

RULE 4 Use a hyphen or hyphens in certain compound nouns. Check a dictionary for the correct way to write a compound noun.

EXAMPLES great-aunt brother-in-law attorney-at-law editor in chief vice president

RULE 5 Use a hyphen in a compound modifier when it comes before the word it modifies.

EXAMPLES Fido is a **well-trained** dog. The dog is **well trained.**

RULE 6 Use a hyphen after the prefixes *all-*, *ex-*, and *self-*. Use a hyphen to separate any prefix from a word that begins with a capital letter.

EXAMPLES all-powerful ex-president self-educated trans-Atlantic

RULE 7 Use dashes to set off a sudden break or change in thought or speech.

EXAMPLE Billy Adams—he lives next door—is our team manager.

RULE 8 Use parentheses to set off words that define or explain a word.

EXAMPLE Simulators (devices that produce the conditions of space flight) are used in flight training for the space program.

PRACTICE Using Hyphens, Dashes, and Parentheses

Write each sentence. Add hyphens, dashes, and parentheses where they're needed.

1. Lois was proud that Wild Bill Hickok was her great uncle.
2. To pass, the bill needs two thirds of the votes.
3. Our new cat he's a long haired Persian drinks only ice water.
4. A case contains twenty four items, and a gross contains twelve dozen or a hundred forty four items.
5. Mae's father in law he's a college professor invited himself along on vacation.
6. The best laid plans don't always work out.
7. When you reach problem 20, you'll be four fifths of the way through the assignment.
8. If you are well prepared, the sixth grade achievement test will seem simple.
9. Agoraphobia fear of open or public places can keep people shut up in their homes for years.
10. For twenty five years, the firm's ex president will receive a pension equal to her salary.

GRAMMAR / USAGE / MECHANICS

12.9 USING ABBREVIATIONS CCSS L.6.2

RULE 1 Use the abbreviations *Mr., Mrs., Ms.,* and *Dr.* before a person's name. Abbreviate professional or academic degrees that follow a person's name. Abbreviate *Junior* as *Jr.* and *Senior* as *Sr.* when they follow a person's name.

EXAMPLES **Mr.** Ed Hall **Dr.** Ann Chu Juan Diaz, **Ph.D.**

Ava Danko, **D.D.S.** Amos Finley **Jr.**

RULE 2 Use capital letters and no periods for abbreviations that are pronounced letter by letter or as words. Exceptions are *U.S.* and Washington, *D.C.*, which should have periods.

EXAMPLES **MVP** most valuable player **EST** eastern standard time

NASA National Aeronautics and Space Administration

RULE 3 Use the abbreviations *A.M.* (*ante meridiem*, "before noon") and *P.M.* (*post meridiem*, "after noon") with times. For dates use *B.C.* (before Christ) and, sometimes, *A.D.* (*anno Domini*, "in the year of the Lord," after Christ).

EXAMPLES 6:22 **A.M.** 4:12 **P.M.** 33 **B.C.** **A.D.** 476

RULE 4 Abbreviate days and months only in charts and lists.

EXAMPLES **Mon.** **Wed.** **Thurs.** **Jan.** **Apr.** **Aug.** **Nov.**

RULE 5 In scientific writing, abbreviate units of measure. Use periods with abbreviations of U.S. units but not with abbreviations of metric units.

EXAMPLES inch(es) **in.** foot (feet) **ft.** gram(s) **g** liter(s) **l**

RULE 6 In addressing envelopes, abbreviate words that refer to streets. Spell out these words everywhere else.

EXAMPLES **St.** (Street) **Ave.** (Avenue) **Rd.** (Road)

I live at the corner of Elm **Street** and Maple **Road.**

RULE 7 In addressing envelopes, use the two-letter postal abbreviations for states. Spell out state names everywhere else.

EXAMPLES Texas **TX** Florida **FL** California **CA**

My cousin lives in Chicago, **Illinois.**

RULE 8 When an abbreviation with a period falls at the end of a sentence, don't add another period. Add a question mark if the sentence is interrogative; add an exclamation point if the sentence is exclamatory.

EXAMPLE I just met Francis X. Colavito Jr.

EXAMPLE Have you met Francis X. Colavito Jr.?

For more information about abbreviations, see pages 56–61 in Part One, Ready Reference.

PRACTICE Using Abbreviations

Write the abbreviation for each item described.

1. liters
2. the month after February
3. twenty-seven minutes past five in the morning
4. the title used with the name of a dentist
5. District of Columbia
6. the state of Arizona in an address on an envelope
7. Parent Teacher Organization
8. the phrase *anno Domini* when used with a date
9. the day after Wednesday
10. the title used after the name of a person who has a doctor of philosophy degree

12.10 WRITING NUMBERS CCSS L.6.2

In charts and tables, always write numbers as figures. In ordinary sentences, you sometimes spell out numbers and sometimes write them as numerals.

RULE 1 Spell out numbers you can write in one or two words. If the number is greater than 999,999, see Rule 4.

EXAMPLE There are **twenty-six** students in the class.

EXAMPLE The arena holds **fifty-five hundred** people.

RULE 2 Use numerals for numbers of more than two words.

EXAMPLE The distance between the two cities is **150** miles.

RULE 3 Spell out any number that begins a sentence or reword the sentence so it doesn't begin with a number.

EXAMPLE **Four thousand two hundred eighty-three** fans attended the game.

EXAMPLE Attendance at the game was **4,283.**

RULE 4 Use figures for numbers greater than 999,999, followed by the word *million, billion*, and so on, even if the number could be written in two words.

EXAMPLES **1 million** **280 billion** **3.2 trillion**

RULE 5 Numbers of the same kind should be written in the same way. If one number must be written as a numeral, write all the numbers as numerals.

EXAMPLE On September 8, **383** students voted for the new rule, and **50** students voted against it.

RULE 6 Spell out ordinal numbers (*first, second, third*, and so on) under one hundred.

EXAMPLE The **ninth** of June will be the couple's **twenty-fourth** wedding anniversary.

RULE 7 Use words to write the time of day unless you are using *A.M.* or *P.M.*

EXAMPLE I usually go for a walk at **four o'clock** in the afternoon. I return home at **a quarter to five.**

EXAMPLE The first bell rang at **8:42 A.M.,** and the last one rang at **3:12 P.M.**

RULE 8 Use numerals to write dates, house numbers, street numbers above ninety-nine, apartment and room numbers, telephone numbers, page numbers, amounts of money of more than two words, and percentages. Write out the word *percent.*

EXAMPLE On June **10, 1999,** I met Jan at **41** East **329th** Street in Apartment **3**G. Her telephone number is **555-2121.**

EXAMPLE Our class meets in Room **12; 55 percent** of the students are girls.

EXAMPLE I found **two dollars** between page **250** and page **251** in this book. The book's original price was **$12.95.**

GRAMMAR / USAGE / MECHANICS

PRACTICE Writing Numbers

Write each sentence. Use the correct form for each number. If the sentence is already correct, write correct.

1. Members of the Bookworm Club read 60 books a year.
2. In 1900 Mexico's population was about thirteen million, but in 2000, it was about one hundred million—an increase of over seven hundred percent.
3. The trip from Houston to Dallas is 238 miles.
4. The first month of school, Ms. Huta took 8 students who completed all their homework to lunch; by November, the number had grown to 20.
5. Mickey borrowed $20 on Friday, August twenty-first; on the following Monday he repaid $15.60.
6. The Clothes Horse, at 192 East 12th Street, is having a twenty % off sale.
7. The cooking class will meet in Room 155 at six o'clock; the first class is November 12, 2002.
8. There were 3,140 seats in the auditorium, but twelve thousand sixty people wanted to attend the concert.
9. 91 percent is still an A, and I got 92 percent of the test answers right.
10. Messages were recorded at ten-twenty A.M. and 4:15 P.M.

PRACTICE Proofreading

Rewrite the following passage, correcting errors in spelling, capitalization, grammar, and usage. Add any missing punctuation. Write legibly to be sure one letter is not mistaken for another. There are ten mistakes.

Abraham Lincoln

[1]Abraham Lincoln was our 16th president. [2]He was born on February 12, 1809 in a log cabin. [3]When he was nine, his mother died however, his father remarried. [4]Lincoln loved his stepmother who was good and kind.

[5]Lincoln had little formal education but loved to read. [6]The self taught Lincoln impressed people with his honesty, hard work, and good character. [7]In his spare time, at home and work Lincoln studied and became a lawyer in 1836. [8]He served his state and nation several ways as an Illinois legislator, as a member of Congress, and as president.

[9]As president Lincoln saved the Union. [10]Lincoln was assassinated on April 14, 1865, as he watched a play, Our American Cousin. [11]He died the next morning at 722 A.M.

POSTTEST Commas, Semicolons, Colons, and End Punctuation

Write each sentence. Add commas, semicolons, colons, and end punctuation where needed.

1. Hey Who do you think you are cutting in line in front of me

2. The long line of shoppers looked tired hungry and irritated about waiting

3. Before the play rehearsal starts will you go over my lines with me

4. "This play takes place in 1931" said Mr. Haddad "during the Great Depression."

5. "This was a time of great hardship for many Americans"

he continued. "Millions lost their jobs their homes and their self-respect too."

6. Helen Traglia Ed.D. knows a great deal about American history moreover she is an expert on the Depression.
7. "Do you know what happened in November 1932 in our country" Helen asked.
8. It could have been one of the following the stock market crash the election of FDR or the start of World War II
9. "Ms. Traglia was it the presidential election?" asked Robert who enjoys reading history.
10. Indeed it was. Does anyone know what the initials FDR CCC and PWA stand for?
11. Franklin Delano Roosevelt was elected by a landslide in 1932 the people liked what they heard about his New Deal for the United States
12. Beginning with emergency measures the New Deal first set about providing relief
13. Acadia National Park Maine is one example of the fine work done by the Civilian Conservation Corps
14. Roosevelt's programs provided jobs improved our park system and gave the American people confidence again but it took World War II to end unemployment boost production and restore prosperity
15. FDR is remembered for his New Deal programs which became the basis for today's social policy.

POSTTEST Quotation Marks, Italics, and Apostrophes

Write each sentence. Add quotation marks, underlining (for italics), apostrophes, and other punctuation marks where they're needed. If the sentence is already correct, write correct.

16. For every action stated Mr. Smith there is an equal and opposite reaction.
17. What happens when a cat jumps he asked.
18. Its paws push against the ground, and the ground pushes against its paws with an equal and opposite force.

19. This diagram shows how it moves forward and how Earth moves in the opposite direction he added.
20. Did you say Earth moves
21. Youve got to be kidding said Tara.
22. The reason you dont notice Earths motion is that its mass is so large he explained.
23. Chapter 2, Balanced and Unbalanced Forces, in the book Understanding Physical Science will help you understand.
24. This statement by the way he added is known as Newtons third law of motion.
25. Someones lost cat got quite a reaction at the childrens reading room.

POSTTEST Hyphens, Dashes, Parentheses, and Numbers

Write each sentence. Add hyphens, dashes, and parentheses where they're needed. Use the correct form for each number.

26. In a city of 25,000 residents, 1/5 of them worked at the university and 1/4 of them at local businesses.
27. The house at 123 Downey Street had a well stocked pantry containing 8 shelves of food.
28. 5 self help books lay on her nightstand, and not one had been finished.
29. Mike was made managing editor of the *Star,* at Forty-six East One Hundred Tenth Street, on June 30, 1994, when he was only 32.
30. If a $100 coat is 33% off, does it cost $66.67?
31. My doctor's appointment is at 1:15 P.M.; however, I may not see the doctor until about 2 o'clock.
32. The day I bought the book I read to page 75; that night I read four hours and made it to page two hundred twelve.
33. The Explorers that's the name of our nature club has twenty dollars and seventy cents in its treasury.
34. Does a two liter bottle hold more than two quarts?
35. The world population exceeds 6,000,000,000 people.

Chapter 13

Sentence Combining

PRETEST Compound Elements

Combine the sentences in each numbered item by using a coordinating conjunction. Add commas where they're needed. (Hint: Combine the elements listed in brackets at the end of each pair of sentences.)

1. a. Maritza signed up for the drama club.
b. Robert signed up for the drama club. [subjects]

2. a. Louise Fitzhugh wrote *Harriet the Spy.*
b. She also wrote *The Long Secret.* [direct objects]

3. a. Joy-Lee went to the beach with Beverly.
b. Joy-Lee went to the beach with Lin. [objects of prepositions.]

4. a. Antonio ironed his shirt.
b. Antonio polished his shoes. [predicates]

5. a. Nolan fed the parakeet some seed.
b. Nolan fed the parrot some seed. [indirect objects]

6. a. Summer vacation had begun.
b. The school was deserted. [sentences]

7. a. Rita will blow up the balloons.
b. Ben will make a banner. [sentences]

8. a. Katie plays first base.
b. Tameeka is the starting pitcher. [sentences]

9. a. Gina really liked the red sandals.
b. They cost $20 too much. [sentences]

10. a. You could go to the mall with me.
b. You could go to the pool with Dad. [objects of prepositions]

GRAMMAR / USAGE / MECHANICS

PRETEST Prepositional Phrases and Appositive Phrases

Combine the sentences in each numbered item by adding the new information in the second sentence to the first sentence in the form of a prepositional phrase or an appositive phrase.

11. a. Bo lost his jacket.
b. It is in the park.

12. a. Gail Devers won two gold medals at the 1996 Olympics.
b. She is a runner.

13. a. Wilbur and Orville Wright made the first powered flight in 1903.
b. They were brothers from Dayton, Ohio.

14. a. Mattie gave us bag lunches.
b. They were for the field trip.

15. a. London is located in southeast England.
b. London is the most important city in Great Britain.

16. a. Let's study together tonight.
b. Let's study at my house.

17. a. The teacher introduced Mr. Betz.
b. Mr. Betz is a nuclear engineer.

18. a. Arya gave a great report.
    b. The report was on killer whales.
19. a. They bought six Frisbees.
    b. They bought them for the class picnic.
20. a. Sacajawea guided the Lewis and Clark expedition.
    b. She was a Shoshone Indian and the only woman on the trip.

PRETEST Adjective and Adverb Clauses

Combine the sentences in items 21–25 by changing the new information in the second sentence to an adjective clause and adding it to the first sentence. Begin your clause with the word in brackets. Add commas if they're needed.

Combine the sentences in items 26–30 by changing the information in one sentence to an adverb clause and adding it to the other sentence. Begin your clause with the word in brackets. Add a comma if it's needed.

21. a. Coach Wright will speak at the assembly.
    b. Jenna will introduce him. [whom]
22. a. George Washington Carver experimented with peanuts.
    b. He was considered a brilliant scientist. [who]
23. a. We took Smithfield Trail to the top of the mountain.
    b. The trail was steep and rocky. [which]
24. a. Grandma has a large collection of bottles.
    b. The bottles are colorful and old. [that]
25. a. J. R. R. Tolkien wrote fantasy novels.
    b. His works are loved by many adults. [whose]
26. a. Enrique started doing more chores. [When]
    b. He got a raise in his allowance.
27. a. You should always brush your teeth.
    b. You go to bed. [before]
28. a. I finish this chapter. [As soon as]
    b. I will take a shower.

29. a. You exercised every day. [Because]
    b. You became stronger.
30. a. The crowd stood in silence.
    b. The soloist sang the anthem. [as]

13.1 COMPOUND SENTENCES CCSS L.6.3a

When you have written a few simple sentences that are closely related in meaning, try combining them to form compound sentences. A compound sentence often states your meaning more clearly than a group of simple sentences. By using some compound sentences, you can also vary the length of your sentences.

EXAMPLE **a.** Sam had three sisters.

b. Matt had only one. **[but]**

Sam had three sisters**, but** Matt had only one.

In this example, simple sentence *a* is joined to simple sentence *b* with the coordinating conjunction *but.* Note that a comma is used before the conjunction.

A **compound sentence** is made up of two or more simple sentences. You can combine two or more simple sentences in a compound sentence by using the conjunction *and, but,* or *or.*

GRAMMAR / USAGE / MECHANICS

PRACTICE Combining Simple Sentences

Combine the sentences in each numbered item by using a comma and a coordinating conjunction. For the first three items, use the coordinating conjunction shown in brackets at the end of the first sentence.

1. a. Jamaal may play trombone in the school band. [or]
   b. He may take private lessons instead.
2. a. The hurricane season has begun. [and]
   b. Fewer people are visiting Caribbean islands.

3. a. Ellen loves Mexican food. [but]
   b. Her twin sister, Liz, prefers Italian food.

4. a. My best friend walks to school with me.
   b. I walk home with my little sister.

5. a. The audience cheered wildly.
   b. The cast bowed to them.

6. a. The lawn needs mowing.
   b. The bird feeders should be filled.

7. a. For extra space, our school might buy portable classroom units.
   b. An addition might be built.

8. a. Romana opened a tortilla stand.
   b. Soon it grew into a big business.

9. a. You shouldn't live in fear.
   b. You should be cautious around strangers.

10. a. I might make spaghetti for dinner.
   b. I might order pizza.

13.2 COMPOUND ELEMENTS CCSS L.6.3a

Sometimes several sentences share information—for example, the same subject or verb. By combining such sentences and using compound elements, you can avoid repeating words. Sentences with compound elements also add variety to your writing.

EXAMPLE **a.** Helen wore a purple dress.

b. She **carried a red handbag.** **[and]**

Helen wore a purple dress **and carried a red handbag.**

Sentences *a* and *b* share information about Helen. The combined version takes the new information from sentence *b*, *carried a red handbag*, and joins it to sentence *a*, using the coordinating conjunction *and.*

You can avoid repeating information by using **compound elements.** Join compound elements with the conjunctions *and, but,* or *or.*

PRACTICE Combining Sentences with Compound Elements

Combine the sentences in each numbered item by using a coordinating conjunction to form a compound element. Add the new information from the second sentence to the first sentence. For the first three items, the new information is in italics, and the conjunction you should use is shown in brackets at the end of the first sentence.

1. a. Our group picked up paper in the ditch. [and]
b. We also picked up *cans* in the ditch.

2. a. I found the right glove. [but]
b. I did *not* find *the left one*.

3. a. Conchita wanted to make jewelry. [or]
b. She wanted to make *greeting cards*.

4. a. Mom's new pin is made of carved wood.
b. It is also made of seashells.

5. a. This morning we may visit the Empire State Building.
b. We may visit the Statue of Liberty.

6. a. Mr. Takemoto has a passport.
b. He does not have a driver's license.

7. a. My room was now neat.
b. It was clean.

8. a. Janice could wear the red shoes with that dress.
b. She could wear the black shoes with that dress.

9. a. Joaquin graded papers for the teacher.
b. Jean also graded papers for the teacher.

10. a. Mr. Hammerlink gave Pedro a hall pass.
b. He also gave Winnie a hall pass.

GRAMMAR / USAGE / MECHANICS

13.3 PREPOSITIONAL PHRASES CCSS L.6.3a

Prepositional phrases are useful in sentence combining. Like adjectives and adverbs, they present more information about nouns and verbs. Because prepositional phrases show relationships, they can often express complicated ideas effectively.

GRAMMAR / USAGE / MECHANICS

EXAMPLE **a.** The family took a trip.

b. It was a **hot summer day. [on]**

c. They went **to the beach.**

On a hot summer day, the family took a trip **to the beach.**

The new information in sentence *b* is added to sentence *a* as a prepositional phrase, and the new information in sentence *c* is moved to sentence *a.* In the new sentence, the prepositional phrase *On a hot summer day* modifies the verb, *took.* The phrase *to the beach* modifies the noun *trip.* Notice that a prepositional phrase that modifies a noun follows the noun it modifies. Prepositional phrases that modify verbs can occupy different positions in a sentence. (For a list of common prepositions, see page 174.)

A **prepositional phrase** is a group of words that begins with a preposition and ends with a noun or a pronoun. Prepositional phrases most often modify nouns and verbs.

PRACTICE Combining Sentences with Prepositional Phrases

Combine the sentences in each numbered item by adding the prepositional phrase from the second sentence to the first sentence. For the first three items, the prepositional phrase in the second sentence is shown in italics. In the last item, you will need to combine three sentences.

1. a. The custard shop is very popular.
b. The custard shop is *in our town*.

2. a. We found it hard to swim.
b. We were swimming *against the current*.

3. a. Several wild horses were running.
b. They were *on the beach*.

4. a. Mrs. Katz teaches aerobics.
b. She teaches at the YMCA.

5. a. My brother got his acceptance letter today.
   b. The letter was from Yale.
6. a. My cat leapt.
   b. She leapt onto the refrigerator.
7. a. The cross-country race was held Saturday.
   b. The race was at Annie's Woods.
8. a. My best friend is moving.
   b. He is moving to Spokane, Washington.
9. a. There will be a surprise birthday party.
   b. The party is for Ahmed.
10. a. Here is an interesting article.
    b. It is about ice fishing.
    c. It is in the *Tribune.*

13.4 APPOSITIVES CCSS L.6.3a

Appositives and appositive phrases identify or rename nouns. Using appositives is another way to vary the length and structure of sentences and to make writing more interesting.

EXAMPLE **a.** Maya Lin designed the Vietnam Veterans Memorial.

b. She was **an architecture student.**

Maya Lin, **an architecture student,** designed the Vietnam Veterans Memorial.

The appositive phrase *an architecture student* identifies the noun *Maya Lin.* Note that the appositive phrase is set off with commas because it gives nonessential information about Maya Lin. If an appositive or an appositive phrase gives information that is essential for identifying a noun, it's not set off with commas. (For more information about appositives, see pages 89–90.)

An **appositive** is a noun placed next to another noun to identify it or give additional information about it. An **appositive phrase** includes an appositive and other words that modify it.

PRACTICE Combining Sentences with Appositives

Combine the sentences in each numbered item by changing the new information in the second sentence to an appositive or an appositive phrase and adding it to the first sentence. For the first three items, the appositive or appositive phrase in the second sentence is shown in italics. Add commas where they're needed.

1. a. John F. Kennedy was killed by an assassin's bullet in November 1963.
b. He was *the thirty-fifth U.S. president.*

2. a. Bella Washington is running for city council.
b. She is *my favorite aunt.*

3. a. Secretariat was one of the greatest racehorses ever.
b. He was *a powerful thoroughbred.*

4. a. Chlorophyll allows a plant to make food.
b. Chlorophyll is a green pigment in plant cells.

5. a. The Nile River runs through Egypt.
b. It is the longest river in the world.

6. a. The gerbil is a popular pet.
b. It is a burrowing desert rodent.

7. a. Our car is parked in row 3G.
b. Our car is a deluxe sedan.

8. a. I have to find my lucky charm.
b. It is a 1938 penny.

9. a. The Chicago Cubs play their home games at Wrigley Field.
b. Wrigley Field is an open-air baseball park.

10. a. Julia has twelve years of experience.
b. She is the news anchor for WBLR.

13.5 ADJECTIVE AND ADVERB CLAUSES

CCSS L.6.3a

When two sentences share information, one of the sentences can often be made into an adjective clause modifying a word in the other sentence.

EXAMPLE **a.** Carla and Darla entered the dance contest.

b. Carla and Darla **are identical twins.** **[, who . . . ,]**

Carla and Darla, **who are identical twins,** entered the dance contest.

The new information (in blue type) in sentence *b* becomes an adjective clause modifying *Carla and Darla*. *Who* now connects the clauses. Notice the commas in the new sentence. Adjective clauses that add nonessential information are set off with commas. Those that add essential information are not. (For more information about adjective clauses, see page 195.)

An **adjective clause** is a subordinate clause that modifies a noun or a pronoun in the main clause. A relative pronoun, such as *who, whom, whose, which,* or *that,* is used to tie the adjective clause to the main clause. The words *where* and *when* can also be used as connectors.

You can also use adverb clauses to combine sentences. Adverb clauses are especially effective in showing relationships between actions. For example, an adverb clause can show when one action takes place in relation to another.

EXAMPLE **a.** Lee read a great deal as a boy.

b. He was recovering from an accident. **[while]**

Lee read a great deal as a boy **while he was recovering from an accident.**

In the new sentence, the adverb clause *while he was recovering from an accident* modifies the verb *read.* The adverb clause tells when Lee read a great deal. Note that the subordinating conjunction *while* makes the relationship between the two actions clear. An adverb clause may occupy different positions within a sentence. If it begins the sentence, it's followed by a comma. (For more information about adverb clauses, see pages 198–199.)

An **adverb clause** is a subordinate clause that often modifies the verb in the main clause. Adverb clauses are introduced by subordinating conjunctions, such as *after, although, as, because, before, if, since, unless, until, when, whenever, where, wherever,* and *while.*

PRACTICE Combining Sentences with Adjective and Adverb Clauses

Combine the sentences in items 1–5 by changing the new information in the second sentence to an adjective clause and adding it to the first sentence. For items 1–3, the new information in the second sentence is shown in italics. Begin your clause with the word in brackets. Add commas if they're needed.

Combine the sentences in items 6–10 by changing the information in one sentence to an adverb clause and adding it to the other sentence. Begin your clause with the word in brackets. Add a comma if it's needed.

1. a. Leonardo da Vinci designed a flying device.
b. The device was *ingenious but impractical.* [that]

2. a. An electric motor does not pollute.
b. It *is clean and silent.* [which]

3. a. The Nelsons are close family friends.
b. Their *son is a professional actor.* [whose]

4. a. The children were invited to a pool party.
b. They helped clean up. [who]

5. a. The Birch twins were quite a handful.
b. My father taught them last year. [whom]

6. a. The grass will have to be mowed by Wednesday.
b. It rains again. [if]

7. a. The children waited quietly on the curb.
b. The parade began. [until]

8. a. The band played a Fourth of July concert. [After]
b. There was a display of fireworks.

9. a. The beetles were found. [Wherever]
   b. The trees had been attacked and destroyed.
10. a. Rory usually wins his races.
   b. He practices so hard. [because]

GRAMMAR / USAGE / MECHANICS

PRACTICE Proofreading

The following passage is about the talented writer Shel Silverstein. Rewrite each paragraph, combining sentences that are closely related in meaning.

Shel Silverstein

Shel Silverstein is best known for his children's books. They have been translated into twenty languages. Silverstein was a playwright, cartoonist, composer, and folk singer. He was a man of many talents.

Silverstein was born in 1930. He was born in Chicago, Illinois. He wrote from the time he was a young boy. He developed a unique writing style. He had not planned to write for children. An editor talked him into trying it.

In 1964 he published *The Giving Tree.* It was one of his earliest books. It was also one of his most successful books. *The Giving Tree* is an inspiring fable. It is about a character who gives. It is also a story about a character who takes. It is a story children love. Adults like the story too.

A Light in the Attic is a famous book of poetry. Silverstein wrote it. *Where the Sidewalk Ends* is another one. His poetry was often silly. Sometimes it was a bit bizarre. He also wrote the hit song "A Boy Named Sue." It was recorded by Johnny Cash. He also wrote several plays. Silverstein died in the spring of 1999.

POSTTEST Compound Elements

Combine the sentences in each numbered item by using a coordinating conjunction. Add commas where they're needed. (Hint: Combine the elements listed in brackets at the end of each pair of sentences.)

1. a. Leah is on the honor roll.
b. José is on the honor roll. [subjects]

2. a. The Riveras planted sunflowers along the fence.
b. The Riveras planted daisies along the fence. [direct objects]

3. a. Luke Skywalker is a hero in *Star Wars.*
b. He is also a hero in *Return of the Jedi.* [objects of preposition]

4. a. Grandpa gave the horses some water.
b. Grandpa gave the cows some water. [indirect objects]

5. a. Loretta Young produced a TV show.
b. Loretta Young starred in that TV show. [predicates]

6. a. Brittany doesn't like Mexican food.
b. That's what everyone else wanted to order. [sentences]

7. a. Mary wrote the music.
b. Troy wrote the lyrics. [sentences]

8. a. Janet might work at a fast-food restaurant.
b. She might volunteer at the hospital. [sentences]

9. a. The library will be open later on weeknights.
b. It will be closed on weekends. [sentences]

10. a. I enjoy riding horses.
b. I like using an English saddle. [sentences]

POSTTEST Prepositional Phrases and Appositive Phrases

Combine the sentences in each numbered item by adding the new information in the second sentence to the first sentence in the form of a prepositional phrase or an appositive phrase.

11. a. The sixth grade held an election.
b. The election was for class officers.

12. a. Alexander the Great lived from 356 to 323 B.C.
b. He was a king of Macedonia and a world conqueror.

13. a. Marcie put the glass away.
b. She put it in the cupboard.

14. a. Kevin learned algebra.
b. He learned it with ease.

15. a. The waterfall spilled a thousand feet down a cliff.
b. The waterfall was a symbol of untamed natural beauty and purity.

16. a. This poem tells of a highwayman and his love.
b. The poem is by Alfred Noyes.

17. a. Our class trip was fun and educational.
b. Our class trip was an outing to Russell's Woods.

18. a. Mimi's cat won the Best of Show award.
b. Mimi's cat is a blue Persian.

19. a. Aunt Cloma's cottage is a rustic place.
b. The cottage is on Green Lake.

20. a. The trainer worked all afternoon with the promising new filly.
b. A filly is a young female horse.

POSTTEST Adjective and Adverb Clauses

Combine the sentences in items 21–25 by changing the new information in the second sentence to an adjective clause and adding it to the first sentence. Begin your clause with the word in brackets. Add commas if they're needed.

Combine the sentences in items 26–30 by changing the information in one sentence to an adverb clause and adding it to the other sentence. Begin your clause with the word in brackets. Add a comma if it's needed.

GRAMMAR / USAGE / MECHANICS

21. a. The firefighter was brave.
b. He saved two children from a burning building. [who]

22. a. My braces are a little tight.
b. They were put on just last week. [which]

23. a. The school district will buy new buses.
b. They will have seat belts and video cameras. [that]

24. a. My sister is going to take singing lessons at the university.
b. Her voice is beautiful. [whose]

25. a. Robin Williams has made another comedy.
b. The viewing public always seems to love him. [whom]

26. a. A whale resembles a fish in some ways. [Although]
b. It is really an air-breathing mammal.

27. a. We reached our hotel.
a. The others had arrived. [before]

28. a. The baby fell asleep. [Until]
b. Mei could not read her book.

29. a. The birds watch hungrily.
b. The squirrels raid the feeder. [while]

30. a. Chris couldn't find her math homework.
b. Her locker was so messy. [because]

Chapter 14

Spelling and Vocabulary

14.1 SPELLING RULES CCSS L.6.2b

English spelling often seems to make no sense. Usually there are historical reasons for the spellings we use today, but you don't need to study the history of the English language to spell correctly. The rules in this section work most of the time, but there are exceptions to every rule. When you're not sure how to spell a word, the best thing to do is check a dictionary.

Spelling *ie* and *ei*

An easy way to learn when to use *ie* and when to use *ei* is to memorize a simple rhyming rule. Then learn the common exceptions to the rule.

RULE	EXAMPLES
WRITE *I* BEFORE *E*	achieve, believe, brief, chief, die, field, friend, grief, lie, niece, piece, pier, quiet, retrieve, tie, yield
EXCEPT AFTER *C*	ceiling, conceit, conceive, deceit, deceive, receipt, receive
OR WHEN SOUNDED LIKE *A*, AS IN *NEIGHBOR AND WEIGH.*	eight, eighty, freight, neigh, reign, sleigh, veil, vein, weigh, weight

Some exceptions: caffeine, either, foreign, forfeit, height, heir, leisure, neither, protein, seize, species, their, weird; words ending in *cient (ancient)* and *cience (conscience);* plurals of nouns ending in *cy (democracies);* the third-person singular form of verbs ending in *cy (fancies);* words in which *i* and *e* follow *c* but represent separate sounds *(science, society)*

Words Ending in *cede, ceed,* and *sede*

The only English word ending in *sede* is *supersede.* Three words end in *ceed: proceed, exceed,* and *succeed.* You can remember these three words by thinking of the following sentence.

EXAMPLE If you **proceed** to **exceed** the speed limit, you will **succeed** in getting a ticket.

All other words ending with the "seed" sound are spelled with *cede: precede, recede, secede.*

Adding Prefixes

Adding prefixes is easy. Keep the spelling of the root word and add the prefix. If the last letter of the prefix is the same as the first letter of the word, keep both letters.

un- + happy = unhappy	co- + operate = cooperate
dis- + appear = disappear	il- + legal = illegal
re- + enlist = reenlist	un- + natural = unnatural
mis- + spell = misspell	im- + migrate = immigrate

Adding Suffixes

When you add a suffix beginning with a vowel, double the final consonant if the word ends in a **single consonant following a single vowel *and***

- the word has one syllable

mud + -y = muddy	sad + -er = sadder
put + -ing = putting	stop + -ed = stopped

- the word is stressed on the last syllable and the stress remains on the same syllable after the suffix is added

occur + -ence = occurrence	repel + -ent = repellent
regret + -able = regrettable	commit + -ed = committed
begin + -ing = beginning	refer + -al = referral

Don't double the final letter if the word ends in *s, w, x,* or *y: buses, rowing, waxy, employer.*

Don't double the final consonant before the suffix *-ist* if the word has more than one syllable: *druggist* but *violinist, guitarist.*

Adding suffixes to words that end in *y* can cause spelling problems. Study these rules and note the exceptions.

When a word ends in a **vowel and *y*,** keep the *y*.

play + -s = plays
obey + -ed = obeyed
buy + -ing = buying
employ + -er = employer
joy + -ful = joyful
joy + -less = joyless
joy + -ous = joyous
annoy + -ance = annoyance
enjoy + -ment = enjoyment
enjoy + -able = enjoyable
boy + -ish = boyish
coy + -ly = coyly

SOME EXCEPTIONS: gay + -ly = gaily, day + -ly = daily, pay + -d = paid, lay + -d = laid, say + -d = said

When a word ends in a **consonant and *y*,** change the *y* to *i* before any suffix that doesn't begin with *i*. Keep the *y* before suffixes that begin with *i*.

carry + -es = carries
dry + -ed = dried
easy + -er = easier
merry + -ly = merrily
happy + -ness = happiness
beauty + -ful = beautiful
fury + -ous = furious
defy + -ant = defiant
vary + -ation = variation
deny + -al = denial
rely + -able = reliable
mercy + -less = merciless
likely + -hood = likelihood
accompany + -ment = accompaniment
carry + -ing = carrying
baby + -ish = babyish
lobby + -ist = lobbyist

SOME EXCEPTIONS: shy + -ly = shyly, dry + -ly = dryly, shy + -ness = shyness, dry + -ness = dryness, biology + -ist = biologist, economy + -ist = economist, baby + -hood = babyhood

GRAMMAR / USAGE / MECHANICS

Usually a **final silent *e*** is dropped before a suffix, but sometimes it's kept. The following chart shows the basic rules for adding suffixes to words that end in silent *e*.

ADDING SUFFIXES TO WORDS THAT END IN SILENT *E*	
RULE	**EXAMPLES**
Drop the *e* before suffixes that begin with a vowel.	care + -ed = cared dine + -ing = dining move + -er = mover type + -ist = typist blue + -ish = bluish arrive + -al = arrival desire + -able = desirable accuse + -ation = accusation noise + -y = noisy
Some exceptions	mile + -age = mileage dye + -ing = dyeing
Drop the *e* and change *i* to *y* before the suffix *-ing* if the word ends in *ie*.	die + -ing = dying lie + -ing = lying tie + -ing = tying
Keep the *e* before suffixes that begin with *a* and *o* if the word ends in *ce* or *ge*.	dance + -able = danceable change + -able = changeable courage + -ous = courageous
Keep the *e* before suffixes that begin with a vowel if the word ends in *ee* or *oe*.	see + -ing = seeing agree + -able = agreeable canoe + -ing = canoeing hoe + -ing = hoeing
Some exceptions	free + -er = freer free + -est = freest
Keep the *e* before suffixes that begin with a consonant.	grace + -ful = graceful state + -hood = statehood like + -ness = likeness encourage + -ment = encouragement care + -less = careless sincere + -ly = sincerely

GRAMMAR / USAGE / MECHANICS

RULE	EXAMPLES
Some exceptions	awe + -ful = awful judge + -ment = judgment argue + -ment = argument true + -ly = truly due + -ly = duly whole + -ly = wholly
Drop *le* before the suffix *-ly* when the word ends with a consonant and *le.*	possible + -ly = possibly sniffle + -ly = sniffly sparkle + -ly = sparkly gentle + -ly = gently

When a word ends in *ll,* drop one *l* when you add the suffix *-ly.*

dull + -ly = dully

chill + -ly = chilly

full + -ly = fully

hill + -ly = hilly

Compound Words

Keep the original spelling of both parts of a compound word.

Remember that some compounds are one word, some are two words, and some are hyphenated. Check a dictionary when in doubt.

foot + lights = footlights

busy + body = busybody

book + case = bookcase

light + house = lighthouse

fish + hook = fishhook

with + hold = withhold

book + keeper = bookkeeper

heart + throb = heartthrob

Spelling Plurals

A singular noun names one person, place, thing, or idea. A plural noun names more than one. To form the plural of most nouns, you simply add *-s.* The following chart shows other basic rules.

GENERAL RULES FOR FORMING PLURALS

NOUNS ENDING IN	TO FORM PLURAL	EXAMPLES
ch, s, sh, x, z	Add *-es.*	lunch → lunches bus → buses dish → dishes box → boxes buzz → buzzes
a vowel and *y*	Add *-s.*	boy → boys turkey → turkeys
a consonant and *y*	Change *y* to *i* and add *-es.*	baby → babies penny → pennies
a vowel and *o*	Add *-s.*	radio → radios rodeo → rodeos
a consonant and *o*	Usually add *-es.*	potato → potatoes tomato → tomatoes hero → heroes echo → echoes
	Sometimes add *-s.*	zero → zeros photo → photos piano → pianos
f or *fe*	Usually change *f* to *v* and add *-s* or *-es.*	wife → wives knife → knives life → lives leaf → leaves half → halves shelf → shelves wolf → wolves thief → thieves
	Sometimes add *-s.*	roof → roofs chief → chiefs cliff → cliffs giraffe → giraffes

The plurals of **proper names** are formed by adding *-es* to names that end in *ch, s, sh, x,* or *z.*

EXAMPLE The **Woodriches** live on Elm Street.

EXAMPLE There are two **Jonases** in our class.

EXAMPLE Have you met your new neighbors, the **Gomezes**?

Just add *-s* to form the plural of all other proper names, including those that end in *y.*

EXAMPLE The **Kennedys** are a famous American family.

EXAMPLE I know three **Marys.**

EXAMPLE The last two **Januarys** have been especially cold.

To form the plural of a **compound noun written as one word,** follow the general rules for plurals. To form the plural of **hyphenated compound nouns** or **compound nouns of more than one word,** usually make the most important word plural.

EXAMPLE A dozen **mailboxes** stood in a row at the entrance to the housing development.

EXAMPLE The two women's **fathers-in-law** have never met.

EXAMPLE The three **post offices** are made of brick.

Some nouns have **irregular plural forms** that don't follow any rules.

man → men

woman → women

child → children

foot → feet

tooth → teeth

mouse → mice

goose → geese

ox → oxen

Some nouns have the same singular and plural forms. Most of these are the names of animals, and some of the plural forms may be spelled in more than one way.

deer → deer

sheep → sheep

head (cattle) → head

Sioux → Sioux

series → series

species → species

fish → fish *or* fishes

antelope → antelope *or* antelopes

buffalo → buffalo *or* buffaloes *or* buffalos

PRACTICE Spelling Rules

Find the misspelled word in each group and write it correctly.

1. piece, ceiling, wierd
2. fatest, sitter, recurring
3. boxes, oxes, foxes
4. concede, recede, procede
5. obeyed, fryed, enjoyed
6. Februarys, Aldrichs, Sallys
7. shoveing, crying, poised
8. bedroom, handhold, lifline
9. brunchs, crannies, leaves
10. dissappoint, impossible, unnecessary

14.2 IMPROVING YOUR SPELLING CCSS L.6.2b

You can improve your spelling by improving your study method. You can also improve your spelling by thoroughly learning certain common but frequently misspelled words.

HOW TO STUDY A WORD

By following a few simple steps, you can learn to spell new words. Pay attention to unfamiliar or hard-to-spell words in your reading. As you write, note words that you have trouble spelling. Then use the steps below to learn to spell those difficult words.

1. Say It

Look at the word and say it aloud. Say it again, pronouncing each syllable clearly.

2. See It

Close your eyes. Picture the word in your mind. Visualize the word letter by letter.

3. Write It

Look at the word again and write it two or three times. Then write the word without looking at the printed spelling.

4. Check It

Check your spelling. Did you spell the word correctly? If not, repeat each step until you can spell the word easily.

Get into the habit of using a dictionary to find the correct spelling of a word. How do you find a word if you can't spell it? Write down letters and letter combinations that could stand for the sound you hear at the beginning of the word. Try these possible spellings as you look for the word in a dictionary.

SPELLING PROBLEM WORDS

The following words are often misspelled. Look for your problem words in the list. What words would you add to the list?

Often Misspelled Words

absence	cemetery	February
accidentally	changeable	foreign
accommodate	choir	forty
achievement	college	fulfill
adviser	colonel	funeral
alcohol	commercial	genius
all right	convenient	government
analyze	courageous	grammar
answer	curiosity	guarantee
athlete	definite	height
attendant	descend	humorous
ballet	develop	hygiene
beautiful	discipline	imaginary
beginning	disease	immediate
believe	dissatisfied	incidentally
beneficial	eligible	incredibly
blaze	embarrass	jewelry
business	envelope	judgment
cafeteria	environment	laboratory
canceled	essential	leisure
canoe	familiar	library

license
maintenance
medicine
mischievous
misspell
modern
molasses
muscle
necessary
neighborhood
niece
ninety
noticeable
nuisance
occasion
original
pageant
parallel
permanent
physical
physician
picnic
pneumonia
privilege
probably
pronunciation
receipt
receive
recognize
recommend
restaurant
rhythm
ridiculous
schedule
sense
separate
similar
sincerely
souvenir
succeed
technology
theory
tomorrow
traffic
truly
unanimous
usually
vacuum
variety
various
Wednesday

PRACTICE Spelling Problem Words

Find each misspelled word and write it correctly.

1. Only fourty people attended the ballay.
2. Bad hygene can spread desease.
3. His advizer memorizes humerous poems.
4. The genyus was admitted to collige at the age of six.
5. I remain disatisfied with the schejule.
6. Her mischevous antics are truly rediculus.
7. If I had more lesure, I would probably join a quire.
8. We usually pack a veriety of picnick items.
9. The traffic was incredably heavy last Wensday.
10. I did not recieve a receipt from the attendent.

14.3 USING CONTEXT CLUES

The surest way to learn the meaning of a new word is to use a dictionary. However, you won't always have a dictionary handy. You can often figure out the meaning of an unfamiliar word by looking for clues in the words and sentences around it. These surrounding words and sentences are called the context.

USING SPECIFIC CONTEXT CLUES

Writers often give clues to the meaning of unfamiliar words. Sometimes they even tell you exactly what a word means. The following chart shows five types of specific context clues. It also gives examples of words that help you identify the type of context clue.

INTERPRETING CLUE WORDS IN CONTEXT

TYPE OF CONTEXT CLUE	CLUE WORDS	EXAMPLES
Definition The meaning of the unfamiliar word is given in the sentence.	in other words or that is which is which means	Jamake *inscribed* his name; **that is,** he wrote his name on the card. Jaleesa put the wet clay pot in the *kiln,* **or** oven, to harden.
Example The meaning of the unfamiliar word is explained through familiar examples.	for example for instance including like such as	Some people are afraid of *arachnids,* **such as** spiders and ticks. The new program has been *beneficial* for the school; **for example,** test scores are up, and absences are down.

chart continued on next page

TYPE OF CONTEXT CLUE	CLUE WORDS	EXAMPLES
Comparison The unfamiliar word is compared to a familiar word or phrase.	also identical like likewise resembling same similarly too	Maria thought the dress was *gaudy.* Lisa, **too,** thought it was flashy. A *rampant* growth of weeds and vines surrounded the old house. The barn was **likewise** covered with uncontrolled and wild growth.
Contrast The unfamiliar word is contrasted to a familiar word or phrase.	but however on the contrary on the other hand unlike	Robins are *migratory* birds, **unlike** sparrows, which live in the same region all year round. Martin didn't *bungle* the arrangements for the party; **on the contrary,** he handled everything smoothly and efficiently.
Cause and effect The unfamiliar word is explained as part of a cause-and-effect relationship.	as a result because consequently therefore thus	**Because** this rubber raft is so *buoyant,* it will float easily. Kevin is very *credulous;* **consequently,** he'll believe almost anything.

USING GENERAL CONTEXT

Sometimes there are no special clue words to help you understand an unfamiliar word. However, you can still use the general context. That is, you can use the details in the words or sentences around the unfamiliar word. Read the following sentences:

> Joel was chosen student **liaison** to the faculty. Everyone hoped his appointment would improve communication between the students and the teachers.

The first sentence tells you that Joel is serving as a kind of connection between the students and the faculty. The word *communication* helps you figure out that being a liaison means acting as a line of communication between two groups.

PRACTICE Using Context Clues

Use context clues to figure out the meaning of the italicized word. Write the meaning. Then write definition, example, comparison, contrast, cause and effect, *or* general *to tell what type of context clue you used to define the word.*

1. Meredith was *ecstatic* about her performance; Milly, on the other hand, was bitterly disappointed.
2. Because clouds had *obscured* the sky all day, we feared we would not get to view the eclipse.
3. The police arrived to quiet down the *clamor* at the party across the street.
4. Like an over-inflated balloon, the *obese* pig waddled out of its pen.
5. The castaway had not shaved for two years; consequently, his beard was extremely *scraggly*.
6. The captain stood at the *helm*, which is the big wheel used for steering, as the tall ship left the harbor.
7. People had said that Miss Brill never cracked a smile, but we found her quite *jovial*.
8. Our club contributes money to *benevolent* causes, such as food programs, homeless shelters, hospitals, and international aid organizations.
9. He is so *loquacious* that you will be lucky to get a word in edgewise.
10. The driver of the car was angry and aggressive; the motorcyclist was similarly *bellicose*.

14.4 ROOTS, PREFIXES, AND SUFFIXES

You can often figure out the meaning of an unfamiliar word by dividing it into parts. The main part of the word is called the root, and it carries the word's basic meaning. A root is often a word by itself. For example, *read* is a word. When a prefix or a suffix is added to it, *read* becomes a root, as in *unreadable.*

Prefixes and suffixes can be added to a root to change its meaning. A prefix is added to the beginning of a root. A suffix is added to the end of a root. A word can have both a prefix and a suffix: *un* + *read* + *able* = *unreadable.*

ROOTS

The root of a word carries the main meaning. Some roots, like *read,* can stand alone. Other roots may have parts added to make a complete word. For example, the root *port* ("carry") by itself is a place to which ships carry goods. Combined with a prefix, it can become *report, deport,* or *transport.* Add a suffix and you can get *reporter, deportment,* or *transportation.*

Learning the meanings of common roots can help you figure out the meanings of many unfamiliar words. The following chart shows some common roots.

ROOTS

ROOTS	WORDS	MEANINGS
bio means "life"	biography	a written story of a person's life
	biosphere	the part of the atmosphere where living things exist
dec or *deca* means "ten"	decade	ten years
	decathlon	an athletic contest consisting of ten events
dent means "tooth"	dentist	a doctor who treats the teeth
	trident	a spear with three prongs, or teeth
dict means "to say"	dictionary	a book of words
	dictator	one who rules absolutely
	predict	to say before (something happens)
duc or *duct* means "to lead"	conductor	one who leads or directs
	produce	to bring into existence
flect or *flex* means "to bend"	flexible	able to bend
	reflect	to bend back (light)
graph means "to write" or "writing"	autograph	one's own signature
	biography	a written story of a person's life
lect means "speech"	lecture	a speech
	dialect	the speech of a certain region
miss or *mit* means "to send"	omit	to fail to send or include
	missile	something sent through the air or by mail
phon means "sound" or "voice"	phonograph	an instrument for playing sounds
	telephone	a device for transmitting voices over a distance
port means "to carry"	transport	to carry across a distance
	porter	one who carries baggage

GRAMMAR / USAGE / MECHANICS

ROOTS	WORDS	MEANINGS
script means "writing"	prescription	a written order for medicine
	postscript	a message added at the end of a letter
spec or *spect* means "to look" or "to watch"	spectator	one who watches
	inspect	to look closely
	prospect	to look for (mineral deposits)
tele means "distant"	telephone	a device for transmitting voices over a distance
	television	a device for transmitting pictures over a distance
tri means "three"	triathlon	an athletic contest consisting of three events
	tricycle	a three-wheeled vehicle
vid or *vis* means "to see"	vision	the ability to see
	videotape	a recording of visual images
voc or *vok* means "to call"	vocation	an inclination, or call, to a certain pursuit
	revoke	to recall or take back

PREFIXES

The following chart shows some prefixes and their meanings. Notice that some prefixes, such as *dis-*, *in-*, *non-*, and *un-*, have the same or nearly the same meaning. A single prefix may have more than one meaning. The prefix *in-*, for example, can mean "into," as in *inject,* as well as "not," as in *indirect.* The prefix *re-* can mean "again" or "back."

Note that *il-*, *im-*, *in-*, and *ir-* are variations of the same prefix. *Il-* is used before roots that begin with *l (illegal);* *im-* is used before roots that begin with *m (immature);* and *ir-* is used before roots that begin with *r (irregular). In-* is used before all other letters.

PREFIXES

CATEGORIES	PREFIXES	WORDS	MEANINGS
Prefixes that reverse meanings	*de-* means "remove from" or "reduce"	defrost devalue	to remove frost to reduce the value of
	dis- means "not" or "do the opposite of"	disagreeable disappear	not agreeable to do the opposite of appear
	in-, il-, im-, and *ir-* mean "not"	incomplete illegal immature irregular	not complete not legal not mature not regular
	mis- means "bad," "badly," "wrong," or "wrongly"	misfortune misbehave misdeed misjudge	bad fortune to behave badly a wrong deed to judge wrongly
	non- means "not" or "without"	nonathletic nonfat	not athletic without fat
	un- means "not" or "do the opposite of"	unhappy untie	not happy to do the opposite of tie
Prefixes that show relationship	*co-* means "with," "together," or "partner"	coworker coexist coauthor	one who works with another to exist together an author who writes as a partner with another
	inter- means "between"	interscholastic	between schools
	post- means "after"	postseason	after the regular season
	pre- means "before"	preseason	before the regular season

GRAMMAR / USAGE / MECHANICS

CATEGORIES	PREFIXES	WORDS	MEANINGS
	re- means "back" or "again"	repay recheck	to pay back to check again
	sub- means "under" or "below"	submarine substandard	under the sea below standard
	super- means "more than"	superabundant	more than abundant
	trans- means "across"	transport	to carry across a distance
Prefixes that show judgment	*anti-* means "against"	antiwar	against war
	pro- means "in favor of"	progovernment	in favor of the government
Prefixes that show number	*bi-* means "two"	bicycle	a two-wheeled vehicle
	semi- means "half" or "partly"	semicircle semisweet	half a circle partly sweet
	uni- means "one"	unicycle	a one-wheeled vehicle

SUFFIXES

A suffix added to a word can change the word's part of speech as well as its meaning. For example, adding the suffix *-er* to *read* (a verb) makes *reader* (a noun). Adding *-less* to *faith* (a noun) makes *faithless* (an adjective).

The following chart shows some common suffixes and their meanings. Notice that some suffixes, such as *-er, -or,* and *-ist,* have the same or nearly the same meaning. A single suffix may have more than one meaning. The suffix *-er,* for example, can also mean "more," as in *bigger.*

SUFFIXES

CATEGORIES	SUFFIXES	WORDS	MEANINGS
Suffixes that mean "one who" or "that which"	*-ee, -eer*	employee charioteer	one who is employed one who drives a chariot
	-er, -or	worker sailor	one who works one who sails
	-ian	physician musician	one who practices medicine (once called physic) one who plays or studies music
	-ist	pianist chemist	one who plays the piano one who works in chemistry
Suffixes that mean "full of" or "having"	*-ful*	joyful suspenseful beautiful	full of joy full of suspense having beauty
	-ous	furious famous courageous	full of fury having fame having courage
Suffixes that show a state, a condition, or a quality	*-hood*	falsehood	quality of being false
	-ness	happiness	state of being happy
	-ship	friendship	condition of being friends
Suffixes that show an action or process or its result	*-ance, -ence*	performance conference	action of performing process of conferring
	-ation, -ion	flirtation invention	action of flirting result of inventing
	-ment	argument arrangement enjoyment	result of arguing result of arranging process of enjoying

GRAMMAR / USAGE / MECHANICS

CATEGORIES	SUFFIXES	WORDS	MEANINGS
Suffixes that mean "relating to," "characterized by," or "like"	*-al*	musical comical	relating to music relating to comedy
	-ish	childish foolish	like a child like a fool
	-y	witty hairy	characterized by wit characterized by hair
Other common suffixes	*-able* and *-ible* mean "capable of," "fit for," or "likely to"	breakable collectible agreeable	capable of being broken fit for collecting likely to agree
	-ize means "to cause to be" or "to become"	visualize familiarize	to cause to be made visual to become familiar
	-less means "without"	hopeless careless	without hope done without care
	-ly means "in a (certain) manner"	easily sadly	in an easy manner in a sad manner

Notice that sometimes the spelling of a word changes when a suffix is added. For example, when *-ous* is added to *fury*, the *y* in *fury* changes to *i*. See pages 289–292 to learn more about spelling words with suffixes.

More than one suffix can be added to a single word. The following examples show how suffixes can change a single root word.

peace **[noun]**

peace + ful = peaceful **[adjective]**

peace + ful + ly = peacefully **[adverb]**

peace + ful + ness = peacefulness **[noun]**

PRACTICE Roots, Prefixes, and Suffixes

Divide the following words. Write their parts in three columns headed prefix, root, *and* suffix. *In a fourth column, write another word that has the same prefix or the same suffix or both. Then write a definition for each word.*

1. reporter
2. predictable
3. interdental
4. ungrateful
5. biannual
6. submergible
7. coworker
8. misdirection
9. antidepressant
10. semidarkness

Part Three

Composition

The time to begin writing an article is when you have finished it to your satisfaction. By that time you begin to clearly and logically perceive what it is you really want to say.

—Mark Twain

Chapter 15

Persuasive Essay

Look around you. Magazines, newspapers, books, posters, letters, e-mails, blogs, radio and television programs—almost anything you read, see, or hear can include persuasion. **Persuasion** is writing that tries to convince readers, listeners, or viewers to think, feel, or act in a certain way. An **argument** is a type of persuasive writing that uses logic and reasoning to do this.

Good persuasive writing fits the form of the genre, addresses your purpose, and catches and holds the attention of your audience.

- The **genre** is the writing mode, such as essay, story, poem, or play.
- Your **purpose** is your reason for writing. In a persuasive essay, your purpose is to convince your audience to think or act in a particular way.
- The **audience** includes the people who will read your essay. CCSS W.6.4

Often persuasive writing begins by stating the writer's goal or purpose. Then the writer includes evidence—information to support that goal. Strong supporting evidence makes the reader think or feel a certain way. Finally, the writer usually includes a reminder of what the audience should do or think.

The instruction on the pages that follow will guide you through the process of writing a persuasive essay and meeting the Common Core State Standards for persuasive, or argumentative, writing. For a list of the writing and grammar Common Core State Standards, see pages 431–438. CCSS W.6.10

15.1 PLAN

Graphic Organizers

During the Plan stage, you will gather and organize writing ideas. To help you do this, you may wish to use a graphic organizer, such as the Persuasive Essay Map on page 373.

Identify Your Position

Write the topic or issue that you want readers of your persuasive essay to think about or act on. A **topic** is a general subject you wish to write about. An **issue** is a subject under discussion or consideration.

Next, think about your position on the topic or issue. Your **position**, or claim, is the opinion that you will try to persuade your audience to accept or the action you will try to persuade your audience to take.

The statement you make about your position will be the **controlling idea**, or thesis, of your essay. A controlling idea is usually stated in one or two sentences. Your controlling idea is related to your purpose and audience. Remember that your purpose is your reason for writing. Your audience includes the people who will read your essay.

To identify your position, ask yourself:

- What do I want my audience to think about the topic?
- What actions do I want my audience to take after reading my essay?

Write one or two sentences explaining your position on the topic. These sentences will be the controlling idea, or thesis, of your essay. CCSS W.6.1a

Gather Reasons and Evidence

One way to build an argument is to identify clear reasons and relevant evidence that you will use to support your controlling idea. **Clear reasons** explain why someone should accept your position, or claim. **Relevant evidence** addresses your claim through facts, expert opinions, and examples that are directly related to your argument.

TYPE OF RELEVANT EVIDENCE	DEFINITION
Fact	a statement that can be proved to be true
Opinion	what someone believes, based on his or her personal viewpoint; opinions cannot be proven true or false
Example	an instance that serves as an illustration or sample

Begin by listing evidence you know from your own experience or background. Then gather more information from

- community newsletters
- newspaper and magazine articles
- credible Web sites
- interviews with experts

Make sure each source you use is credible. A **credible** source presents current, or up to date, information on the topic and is written by an authority or expert who knows a lot about the topic. A credible source presents information objectively and names other sources to back up information.

List your evidence clearly. Take notes about how your evidence supports your position and controlling idea. Then identify whether each piece of evidence is a fact, an opinion, or an example. CCSS W.6.1a, b

Consider Alternative Positions

In order to create strong arguments, writers of persuasive essays must anticipate, or make guesses about, opinions other than their own. Think about your topic, position, and audience. Then anticipate the **views**, **concerns**, and **counter-arguments** that others might have about your topic.

TERM	DEFINITION
View	a belief
Concern	a worry
Counter-argument, or opposing claim	a statement that counters or opposes another argument

Take notes about how you would respond to your readers' views, concerns, and counter-arguments. CCSS W.6.1a

15.2 DRAFT

Write the Introduction

Write your introductory, or opening, paragraph. Your introduction should

- grab your readers' attention
- introduce your focus or topic
- state your controlling idea, or thesis
- briefly explain why your audience should care about the issue CCSS W.6.1a

Write the Body: Organize Your Ideas

Use your planning notes to write the body, or main paragraphs, of your essay. In the body, guide and inform your readers' understanding of your main ideas. To show your understanding of the topic, relate each paragraph to your controlling idea. Be sure that each paragraph clearly expresses one main idea and only includes details that support the idea.

You will want to organize your ideas and evidence clearly and logically so readers can identify your claim, counterarguments, and supporting reasons and evidence. You might use one of the following organizational strategies:

STRATEGY	DEFINITION
Order of importance	to put the most important information first or last
Cause and effect	to describe an event or action and what results from it
Comparison and contrast	to describe similarities and differences between things or ideas

The organizational strategy you use should create a focused and coherent essay. An essay is **focused** and **coherent** when each paragraph clearly expresses a main idea and supporting details that relate to the controlling idea, or thesis. CCSS W.6.1a, b

Writing Tip

As you write, be sure to use and maintain a formal style. In formal writing, you usually write from the third-person point of view and avoid using slang, contractions, and conversational language. CCSS W.6.1d

Write the Body: Link the Ideas

Use transitions to link the main idea and supporting details in a paragraph. Also use transitions to help the reader understand how each new paragraph relates to the argument. **Transitions** are words, phrases, and clauses that show how ideas, such as your claim and counter-arguments, and evidence, such as facts, opinions, and examples, are related. The chart that follows shows some transitions you can use to clearly link your ideas. CCSS W.6.1c

RELATIONSHIP	TRANSITIONS
Addition	*also, and, besides, both . . . and, furthermore, in addition*
Contrast	*but, however, instead, nevertheless, on the contrary, on the other hand, still, yet*
Choice	*either . . . or, neither . . . nor, nor, or, otherwise*
Importance	*first, last, mainly, most important, most of all*
Cause and effect	*as a result, consequently, for, so, so that, then, therefore, thus*
Sequence	*after, as, before, next, since, then, until, when, while*

Write the Conclusion

Write an effective conclusion to your essay. An effective conclusion follows from and supports the argument you are making. The conclusion should

- restate your controlling idea, or thesis
- summarize your main ideas
- encourage readers to agree with your position
- encourage readers to take action CCSS W.6.1e

15.3 REVISE

Introduction to Revision

The word *revise* means "to see again." To revise your essay, you will look at it again to make sure that it is clear and well organized and that it accomplishes your goal. You will focus on the development, organization, and style of your writing by applying these four revision strategies:

- **Add** details to make your main point clearer.
- **Delete** unnecessary words or ideas.
- **Replace** boring or overused words with precise language that is more exact and strong.
- **Rearrange** or **combine** phrases and sentences so your ideas and supporting details are presented logically.

Use these revision strategies with the questions and checklists that follow. The questions will help you think about how well your essay addresses the genre as well as your purpose and audience. CCSS W.6.4, W.6.5

Focus and Coherence

Ask yourself:

✓ Does my essay have a clear focus?

✓ Does each paragraph relate to the controlling idea, or thesis?

✓ Do all parts work together so that my argument is clear and persuasive for readers?

Organization

Ask yourself:

✓ Does the introduction present my controlling idea, or thesis?

✓ Does the body follow a logical order?

✓ Does the conclusion follow from and support my argument? CCSS W.6.1a, b, e

COMPOSITION

Development of Ideas

Ask yourself:

✓ Does the essay show my understanding of the topic?

✓ Do my body paragraphs develop my claims and counter-arguments fairly?

✓ Does each paragraph give clear reasons and relevant evidence to support the paragraph's claim or counter-argument?

✓ Are my reasons and evidence compiled from credible sources? CCSS W.6.1b

Voice–Word Choice

Ask yourself:

✓ Does my essay include precise language?

✓ Does my essay include transitions that clarify the relationships between ideas in sentences and paragraphs?

✓ Does my essay include formal language from beginning to end? CCSS W.6.1c, d

Voice–Sentence Fluency

Ask yourself:

✓ Does my essay include a mix of short sentences and long sentences that make the paragraphs interesting to read?

✓ Have I made my sentences more interesting by combining some of them, using prepositional phrases, appositive phrases, and adjective and adverb clauses?

✓ Does my writing include a consistent style and tone that make it flow smoothly? CCSS L.6.3a, b

COMPOSITION

Revising Tip

As you revise, use a thesaurus to find exactly the right words to communicate your ideas. Vary your words and sentences to avoid wordiness and **redundancy**, or words and sentences that say the same thing twice. CCSS L.6.3b

15.4 EDIT

Correct Errors in Grammar

Editing involves correcting errors in grammar, usage, mechanics, and spelling. Begin editing by taking a careful look at your sentences. Make sure that each sentence states a complete thought and is grammatically correct. Use the checklist below to edit your sentences. CCSS W.6.5, L.6.1

Sentence-Editing Checklist

Ask yourself:

- ✓ Have I avoided sentence fragments?
- ✓ Have I avoided run-on sentences?
- ✓ Do verbs agree with their subjects?
- ✓ Have I used verb tenses and forms correctly?
- ✓ Have I used pronouns in the proper case (subjective, objective, possessive)?
- ✓ Have I correctly used intensive pronouns (*yourself, yourselves*) for emphasis?
- ✓ Have I used adjectives and adverbs correctly?
- ✓ Are my sentences parallel so that elements that have the same function in a sentence are written in the same form or verb tense? CCSS L.6.1a, b

Correct Errors in Mechanics and Spelling

Next, check for and correct any errors in mechanics (punctuation and capitalization) and spelling. Use the proofreading checklist below to edit your essay. You should also use a dictionary to check and confirm spellings.
CCSS L.6.2, b

Proofreading Checklist

Ask yourself:

- ✓ Have I used correct punctuation?
- ✓ Have I written possessives correctly?
- ✓ Have I spelled all words correctly?
- ✓ Have I used capital letters as needed?

Peer and Teacher Review

After you have revised and edited your essay yourself, you will revise it through peer review and teacher review. During **peer review**, you will share your writing with a partner or classmates. Then you will discuss how to improve your writing. During **teacher review**, you will give your essay to your teacher. Your teacher will read it and suggest how you can make your essay better. The ideas and opinions of your peers and teacher will tell you whether you're achieving your goals.

You can use the **Peer Review Guide** on page 382 to respond to a classmate's writing. CCSS W.6.5, L.6.1e

15.5 PUBLISH

Now that you have written and polished your essay, you will publish and present it. This is the stage when you share your final essay with others. You may wish to consider the following publishing and presenting options. Some of these options require you to collaborate with your classmates and use technology:

- Submit your essay to your school newspaper.
- Send your essay as a letter to an appropriate Web site or online newspaper.
- Present your essay orally in a small group.
- Create a blog and use your essay to start an online class debate. CCSS W.6.6

Reflecting on, or thinking about, your own writing can help you improve your writing skills. Use the **Reflection Guide** on page 383 to reflect on the writing you did in this workshop.

Chapter 16

Response Essay

The goal of expository writing is to explain or inform. There are many types of expository writing, such as essays, research reports, and magazine articles. A response essay is also a type of expository writing. In a response essay, you write a personal response that explains and defends your interpretation, or understanding, of something you have read.

Good expository writing fits the form of the genre, addresses your purpose, and catches and holds the attention of your audience.

- The **genre** is the writing mode, such as essay, story, poem, or play.
- The **purpose** is your reason for writing. In a response essay, your purpose is to explain and defend your interpretation of a literary or expository text.
- The **audience** includes the people who will read your essay. CCSS W.6.4

Writing a response essay involves careful thought, planning, and organization. The instruction on the pages that follow will guide you through the process of writing a response essay and meeting the Common Core State Standards for informative/explanatory writing. For a list of the writing and grammar Common Core State Standards, see pages 431–438. CCSS W.6.10

16.1 PLAN

Graphic Organizers

During the Plan stage, you will gather and organize writing ideas. To do this, you may wish to use a graphic organizer, such as the Evidence Chart on page 374.

Identify Your Controlling Idea

Choose a literary or expository selection that you would like to respond to in an essay. Think about the text, your reaction to it, and the topic you wish to discuss. The **topic** is the general subject you wish to write about. The main point you want to make about the topic will be the **controlling idea**, or thesis, of your essay. Sum up the controlling idea in one or two sentences. When you draft your essay, you will give details and examples from the text to support your controlling idea. CCSS W.6.2a

Writing Tip

In the Plan stage, your controlling idea is a starting point. As you gather evidence and draft your essay, you can narrow or broaden your controlling idea. CCSS W.6.2a

Gather Evidence

Look in the selection for evidence that supports your controlling idea. **Evidence** includes facts, definitions, details, quotations, examples, and other information that provide proof in support of your main point. For example, if you are analyzing the author's style, you might look for sentences that help create a specific tone. **Style** is a writer's personal way of using language. The **tone** expresses the writer's feelings and attitude toward a topic or theme.

With your controlling idea in mind, write evidence from the text that you will include in your response. Explain how the evidence supports your controlling idea. CCSS W.6.2b, W.6.9a, b

Synthesize Ideas

When you **synthesize** ideas, you combine ideas to create a new idea or reach a new understanding. You may synthesize ideas from several sources in order to support your controlling idea and key points. **Sources** may include

- personal experience
- books, stories, essays, and articles
- Web sites

Continue recording evidence. Take notes about the related ideas from your sources. Then synthesize these ideas with details from the text. After you synthesize, you may need to revise your controlling idea. CCSS W.6.2b, W.6.9a, b

16.2 DRAFT

Write the Introduction

When you write your draft, your goal is to organize the evidence you have gathered into unified paragraphs. The **introduction** is the opening paragraph of your essay. An effective introduction grabs the readers' attention and tells what your essay is about. It also states your controlling idea and sets the tone.

The art of communicating your thoughts and feelings effectively through words is called **rhetoric.** You might begin your response essay with a rhetorical element to grab your readers' attention from the start. The chart on the next page describes various rhetorical elements you might use.

ELEMENT	DEFINITION
Quotation	well-chosen words from the selection
Description	words that describe a setting, character, person, or event by appealing to the senses
Rhetorical question	a question to which no answer is expected
Anecdote	a brief story based on an interesting or amusing event from a person's life
Analogy	a comparison between two things that may not be similar
Parallelism	the use of a series of words, phrases, or sentences that have similar grammatical structure
Repetition	the repeated use of a word, phrase, sound, or other part of a text

Write your introduction. You might freewrite several introductions using different rhetorical elements before deciding on the best introduction. Freewriting means just what it says: writing freely without worrying about grammar, punctuation, spelling, logic, or anything. You just write what comes to your mind. Choose a rhetorical element and set a time limit for freewriting your introduction. Then just start writing ideas as they come to you. CCSS W.6.2a

Write the Body Paragraphs

In the body, or main paragraphs, of your essay, you guide and inform your readers' understanding of your key ideas. Each paragraph includes a **topic sentence** that states the key idea of the paragraph. The rest of the paragraph includes facts, definitions, concrete details, quotations, examples, and other information that support the topic sentence. Similarly, each topic sentence should support the controlling idea of the paper.

Writing Tip

An essay is **focused** and **coherent** when each paragraph clearly relates to the controlling idea, or thesis. Make sure the key idea and supporting facts and details you include in each paragraph relate to your controlling idea. CCSS W.6.2b, W.6.9a, b

After you write the body paragraphs, organize them using a logical structure. You may use one of the strategies in the following chart. CCSS W.6.2a, b

STRATEGY	DEFINITION
Order of importance	to explain the most important ideas first or last
Comparison and contrast	to describe similarities and differences between things or ideas
Cause and effect	to describe an event and what results from it
Sequence of events	to discuss events in the order that they happened

Maintain a Formal Style

Throughout your essay, use vocabulary and precise words that are specific to your topic. Be sure to use and maintain a formal style. In formal writing, you usually write from the third-person point of view and avoid using slang, contractions, and conversational language. CCSS W.6.2d, e

Use Transitions

To make your writing flow smoothly, use transitions to link the ideas in sentences and paragraphs. **Transitions** are words, phrases, and clauses that show the relationship between ideas or events. Use some of the following transitions to clearly link the ideas or events described in your sentences and paragraphs. CCSS W.6.2c

RELATIONSHIP	EXAMPLES OF TRANSITIONS
Addition	*also, and, besides, both . . . and, furthermore, in addition*
Contrast	*but, however, instead, nevertheless, on the contrary, on the other hand, still, yet*
Importance	*first, last, mainly, most important, most of all*
Cause and effect	*as a result, consequently, for, so, so that, then, therefore, thus*
Sequence	*after, as, before, next, since, then, until, when, while*

Write the Conclusion

Write an effective conclusion that follows from the information or explanation you presented in your response. Your conclusion should

- restate your controlling idea
- summarize your key points
- give your readers something further to think about CCSS W.6.2f

16.3 REVISE

Introduction to Revision

The word *revise* means "to see again." To revise your response essay, you will look at it again to make sure that it is clear and well organized and that it accomplishes your goal. You will focus on the development, organization, and style of your writing by applying all or some of these four revision strategies:

- **Add** details and information to make your main point clearer.
- **Delete** unnecessary words or ideas.
- **Replace** boring or overused words with precise language that is more exact and strong.
- **Rearrange** or **combine** phrases and sentences so your ideas and supporting details are presented logically.

Use these revision strategies with the questions and checklists that follow. The questions will help you think about how well your essay addresses the genre as well as your purpose and audience. CCSS W.6.4, W.6.5

Focus and Coherence

Ask yourself:

✓ Does my essay have a clear focus?

✓ Does each paragraph relate to the controlling idea, or thesis?

✓ Do all parts work together so that my main point is explained and well supported? CCSS W.6.2a, b

Organization

Ask yourself:

✓ Does the introduction present my controlling idea, or thesis?

✓ Do the body paragraphs follow a logical order?

COMPOSITION

✓ Does the conclusion follow from and support the information or explanation that I presented? CCSS W.6.2a, b, f

Development of Ideas

Ask yourself:

✓ Does each paragraph express a key idea about the controlling idea, or thesis?

✓ Is each key idea supported by appropriate evidence? CCSS W.6.2b, W.6.9a, b

Voice–Word Choice

Ask yourself:

✓ Does my essay include precise words and vocabulary that are specific to my topic?

✓ Does my essay include transitions that link the ideas in sentences and paragraphs?

✓ Does my essay include formal language from beginning to end? CCSS W.6.2c–e

Voice–Sentence Fluency

Ask yourself:

✓ Does my essay include a mix of short sentences and long sentences that make the paragraphs interesting to read?

✓ Have I made my sentences more interesting by combining some of them, using prepositional phrases, appositive phrases, and adjective and adverb clauses?

✓ Does my writing include a consistent style and tone that make it flow smoothly? CCSS L.6.3a, b

16.4 EDIT

Correct Errors in Grammar

Editing involves correcting errors in grammar, usage, mechanics, and spelling. Begin editing by taking a careful look at your sentences. Make sure that each sentence expresses a complete thought and is grammatically correct. Use the checklist below to edit your sentences.
CCSS W.6.5, L.6.1

Sentence-Editing Checklist

Ask yourself:

✓ Have I avoided sentence fragments?

✓ Have I avoided run-on sentences?

✓ Do verbs agree with their subjects?

✓ Have I used verb tenses and forms correctly?

✓ Have I used pronouns in the proper case (subjective, objective, possessive)?

✓ Have I correctly used intensive pronouns (*myself*, *ourselves*) for emphasis?

✓ Have I used adjectives and adverbs correctly?

✓ Are my sentences parallel so that elements that have the same function in a sentence are written in the same form or verb tense? CCSS L.6.1a, b

Correct Errors in Mechanics and Spelling

Next, check for and correct any errors in mechanics (punctuation and capitalization) and spelling. Use the checklist below to edit your essay. You should also use a dictionary to check spellings. CCSS L.6.2, b

Proofreading Checklist

Ask yourself:

✓ Have I used correct punctuation?
✓ Have I written possessives correctly?
✓ Have I spelled all words correctly?
✓ Have I used capital letters as needed?

Peer and Teacher Review

After you have revised and edited your essay yourself, you will revise it through peer review and teacher review. During **peer review**, you will share your writing with a partner or classmates. Then you will discuss how you can each improve your writing. During **teacher review**, you will give your essay to your teacher. Your teacher will read it and suggest how to improve your response essay. The ideas and opinions of your peers and teacher will tell you whether you're achieving your goals.

You can use the **Peer Review Guide** on page 382 to respond to a classmate's writing. CCSS W.6.5; L.6.1e

16.5 PUBLISH

After you have written and revised your essay, you will publish and present it. This is the stage when you share your final essay with others. You may wish to consider the following publishing and presenting options. Some of these options require you to collaborate with your classmates and use technology:

- Create a class collection of response essays.
- Enter your essay into a writing contest.
- Share your essay in a small group.
- Post your essay on your school or class Web site.
- Publish your essay as a blog entry and invite other students to comment on it. CCSS W.6.6

Reflecting on, or thinking about, your own writing can help you improve your writing skills. Use the **Reflection Guide** on page 383 to reflect on the writing you did in this workshop.

Chapter 17

Multi-Paragraph Essay

The goal of expository writing is to explain or inform. There are many types of expository writing, including essays, research reports, and magazine articles. Since all good essays include introductory, body, and concluding paragraphs, all good essays are multi-paragraph, or made of more than one paragraph. Good expository writing fits the form of the genre, addresses your purpose, and catches and holds the attention of your audience.

- The **genre** is the writing mode, such as essay, story, poem, or play.
- The **purpose** is your reason for writing. In a multi-paragraph essay, your purpose is to explain and inform.
- The **audience** includes the people who will read your essay. CCSS W.6.4

The instruction on the pages that follow will guide you through the process of writing an expository multi-paragraph essay while meeting the Common Core State Standards for informative/explanatory writing. For a list of the writing and grammar Common Core State Standards, see pages 431–438. CCSS W.6.10

17.1 PLAN

Graphic Organizers

During the Plan stage, you will gather and organize writing ideas. To do this, you may wish to draw and use a graphic organizer, such as the Evidence Chart on page 375.

Identify Your Controlling Idea

Write down the topic of your essay. The **topic** is the general subject you wish to write about. The main point you want to make about the topic will be the **controlling idea**, or thesis, of your multi-paragraph essay. You usually sum up the controlling idea in one or two sentences. In this Plan stage, your controlling idea is a starting point. As you gather evidence and draft your paper, you may narrow or broaden your controlling idea. CCSS W.6.2a

Gather Evidence

Now that you have identified your controlling idea, you need to get information, or evidence, to support it. **Evidence** includes facts, definitions, details, quotations, examples, and other information. You can begin the process of gathering evidence with one or more of the following activities: asking questions, doing research, observing, and interviewing. You may find that you'll want to use all four of these methods to gather evidence.

Write down evidence related to your controlling idea that you know from your own experience or background. Explain how the evidence supports your controlling idea. Then do research to find more evidence. You may look for information in

- reference books, such as encyclopedias
- magazine or newspaper articles
- Web sites that are trustworthy, objective, and up to date

Analyze the research and take notes about how the evidence supports your controlling idea. CCSS W.6.2b

Writing Tip

Do not **plagiarize** information, or take ideas from someone else and present them as your own. Plagiarizing is against the law. Always credit the source of the information with an in-text citation. See pages 384–387 for information about citing sources. CCSS W.6.8

Synthesize Ideas

When you **synthesize** ideas, you combine ideas to create a new idea or reach a new understanding. You may synthesize ideas from several sources in order to support your controlling idea and key points. **Sources** may include

- personal experience
- background knowledge
- books, essays, and articles
- Web sites

Continue recording evidence. Take notes about the related ideas from your sources. Then synthesize the ideas from your experience and background and from your research. After you synthesize, you may need to revise your controlling idea. CCSS W.6.2b, W.6.9b

17.2 DRAFT

Write the Introduction

When you write your draft, your goal is to organize the evidence you have gathered into unified paragraphs. The **introduction** is the opening paragraph of a multi-paragraph essay. An effective introduction grabs the readers' attention and introduces the topic. It also states your controlling idea.

The art of communicating your thoughts and feelings effectively through words is called **rhetoric.** The chart below describes different rhetorical elements.

ELEMENT	DEFINITION
Quotation	well-chosen words from the selection
Interesting fact	a statement that can be proven as true
Rhetorical question	a question to which no answer is expected
Anecdote	a brief story based on an interesting or amusing event from a person's life
Analogy	a comparison between two things that may not be similar
Parallelism	the use of a series of words, phrases, or sentences that have similar grammatical structure
Repetition	the repeated use of a word, phrase, sound, or other part of a text

In your introduction, you might include a rhetorical element to grab your readers' attention from the start.
CCSS W.6.2a

Writing Tip

If you are stuck, just start writing. Your first attempt will not be perfect. You might freewrite more than one introduction before deciding on the best one. CCSS W.6.2a

COMPOSITION

Write the Body Paragraphs

In the body, or main paragraphs, of your essay, you guide and inform your readers' understanding of your key ideas. Each paragraph includes a **topic sentence** that states the key idea of the paragraph. The rest of the paragraph includes facts, definitions, concrete details, quotations, examples, and other information that support the topic sentence. Similarly, each topic sentence should support the controlling idea of the paper.

Write the body of your essay so it is focused and coherent. An essay is **focused** and **coherent** when each paragraph clearly relates to the controlling idea, or thesis. Make sure the key idea and supporting evidence in each paragraph relate to your controlling idea.

Now organize the body paragraphs using a logical structure. You may organize the paragraphs using one of the strategies in the following chart. CCSS W.6.2a, b, W.6.9a, b

STRATEGY	DEFINITION
Definition	to explain technical or specialized vocabulary and terms related to specific areas of study or work
Classification	to group information by type
Comparison and contrast	to describe similarities and differences between things
Process	to explain the order of an action or an event
Cause and effect	to describe an event and what results from it
Sequence of events	to discuss events in the order that they happened

COMPOSITION

Maintain a Formal Style

Throughout your essay, use precise language and vocabulary that is specific to your topic. Be sure to use and maintain a formal style. In formal writing, you usually write from the third-person point of view and avoid using slang, contractions, and conversational language. CCSS W.6.2d, e

Use Transitions

To make your writing flow smoothly, use transitions to link the ideas in sentences and paragraphs. **Transitions** are words, phrases, and clauses that show the relationship between ideas or events. Use some of the following transitions to clearly link the ideas or events described in your sentences and paragraphs. CCSS W.6.2c

RELATIONSHIP	EXAMPLES OF TRANSITIONS
Addition	*also, and, besides, both . . . and, furthermore, in addition*
Contrast	*but, however, instead, nevertheless, on the contrary, on the other hand, still, yet*
Importance	*first, last, mainly, most important, most of all*
Cause and effect	*as a result, consequently, for, so, so that, then, therefore, thus*
Sequence	*after, as, before, next, since, then, until, when, while*

Include Visual Elements

To help readers better understand the ideas in your essay, you may wish to include

- graphics, such as images, maps, and charts
- formatting, such as heads and subheads
- multimedia elements, such as links to video clips CCSS W.6.2a

Write the Conclusion

Write an effective conclusion that follows from the information or explanation you presented in the introduction and body. Your conclusion will be effective if it clearly and concisely does the following:

- restates your controlling idea
- summarizes your key points
- gives your readers something further to think about CCSS W.6.2f

17.3 REVISE

Introduction to Revision

The word *revise* means "to see again." To revise your multi-paragraph essay, you will look at it again to make sure that it is clear and well organized and that it accomplishes your goal. You will focus on the development, organization, and style of your writing by applying all or some of these four revision strategies:

- **Add** details and information to clarify your main point.
- **Delete** unnecessary words or ideas.
- **Replace** boring or overused words with precise language that is more exact and strong.
- **Rearrange** or **combine** phrases and sentences so your ideas and supporting details are presented logically.

Use these revision strategies with the questions and checklists on the following pages. The questions will help you think about how well your essay addresses the genre as well as your purpose and audience. CCSS W.6.4, W.6.5

COMPOSITION

Focus and Coherence

Ask yourself:

✓ Does my essay have a clear focus?

✓ Does each paragraph relate to the controlling idea, or thesis?

✓ Do all parts work together so that my main point is explained and well supported? CCSS W.6.2a, b

Organization

Ask yourself:

- ✓ Does the introduction present my controlling idea, or thesis?
- ✓ Do the body paragraphs follow a logical order?
- ✓ Does the conclusion follow from and support the information or explanation that I presented? CCSS W.6.2a, b, f

Development of Ideas

Ask yourself:

- ✓ Does each paragraph express a key idea about the controlling idea, or thesis?
- ✓ Is each key idea supported by appropriate evidence? CCSS W.6.2b, W.6.9a, b

Voice–Word Choice

Ask yourself:

- ✓ Does my essay include precise words and vocabulary that are specific to my topic?
- ✓ Does my essay include transitions that link the ideas in sentences and paragraphs?
- ✓ Does my essay include formal language from beginning to end? CCSS W.6.2c–e

Voice–Sentence Fluency

Ask yourself:

- ✓ Does my essay include a mix of short sentences and long sentences that make the paragraphs interesting to read?
- ✓ Have I made my sentences more interesting by combining some of them, using prepositional phrases, appositive phrases, and adjective and adverb clauses?
- ✓ Does my writing include a consistent style and tone that make it flow smoothly? CCSS L.6.3a, b

Revising Tip

As you revise, use a thesaurus to find exactly the right words to communicate your ideas. Vary your words and sentences to avoid wordiness and **redundancy**, or words and sentences that say the same thing twice. CCSS L.6.3b

17.4 EDIT

Correct Errors in Grammar

Editing involves correcting errors in grammar, usage, mechanics, and spelling. Begin the editing stage by taking a careful look at your sentences. Make sure that each sentence expresses a complete thought and is grammatically correct. Use the checklist that follows to edit your sentences. CCSS W.6.5, L.6.1

Sentence-Editing Checklist

Ask yourself:

✓ Have I avoided sentence fragments?

✓ Have I avoided run-on sentences?

✓ Do verbs agree with their subjects?

✓ Have I used verb tenses and forms correctly?

✓ Have I used pronouns in the proper case (subjective, objective, possessive)?

✓ Have I correctly used intensive pronouns (*himself, themselves*) for emphasis?

✓ Have I used adjectives and adverbs correctly?

✓ Are my sentences parallel so that elements that have the same function in a sentence are written in the same form or verb tense? CCSS L.6.1a, b

COMPOSITION

Correct Errors in Mechanics and Spelling

Next check for and correct any errors in mechanics (punctuation and capitalization) and spelling. Use the checklist below to edit your essay. You should also use a dictionary to check spellings. **CCSS L.6.2, b**

Proofreading Checklist

Ask yourself:

✓ Have I used correct punctuation?
✓ Have I written possessives correctly?
✓ Have I spelled all words correctly?
✓ Have I used capital letters as needed?

Peer and Teacher Review

After you have revised and edited your essay yourself, you will revise it through peer review and teacher review. During **peer review**, you will share your writing with a partner or classmates. Then you will discuss how to improve your writing. During **teacher review**, you will give your essay to your teacher. Your teacher will read it and suggest how you can make your essay better. The ideas and opinions of your peers and teacher will tell you whether you're achieving your goals.

You can use the **Peer Review Guide** on page 382 to respond to a classmate's writing. **CCSS W.6.5, L.6.1e**

COMPOSITION

17.5 PUBLISH

After you have written and polished your essay, you will publish and present it. This is the stage when you share your final essay with others. You may wish to consider the following publishing and presenting options. Some of these options require you to collaborate with your classmates and use technology:

- Create a class collection of essays.
- Enter your essay into a writing contest.
- Share your essay in a small group.
- Post your essay on your school or class Web site.
- Publish your essay on the Internet. CCSS W.6.6

Reflecting on, or thinking about, your own writing can help you improve your writing skills. You can use the **Reflection Guide** on page 383 to reflect on the writing you did in this workshop.

Chapter 18

Research Report

When you write a research report, you investigate a topic and present information about the topic to your readers. You've probably seen reports in newspapers and magazines. Journalists write these reports to investigate such topics as politics, environmental issues, and business concerns. They use a variety of sources to find information, and then they present this information to their readers.

To write a report, you should

- choose a topic that interests you
- decide on a purpose for your report
- gather information from sources
- take notes, organize your notes, and write an outline
- explain your purpose and main idea in a written thesis statement
- present the information about your topic to your readers in your own words
- prepare a list of your sources

The instruction on the pages that follow will guide you through the process of writing a research report and meeting the Common Core State Standards for research as well as for informative/explanatory writing. For a list of the writing and grammar Common Core State Standards, see pages 431–438. CCSS W.6.10

18.1 PLAN

Graphic Organizers

During the Plan stage, you will gather and organize writing ideas. To do this, you may wish to draw and use graphic organizers, such as the Main Idea Map, Source Card, and Note Card on pages 376–378.

Do Preliminary Research

Write down the topic of your research report. The **topic** is the general subject you wish to write about. Then do some preliminary, or beginning, research. Look up your topic in a reference work, such as an encyclopedia, to find general information. Then find more information by using a search engine. CCSS W.6.7

Write Research Questions

Write questions about your topic that you may want to answer in your report. Good questions begin with the words *who, what, when, where, why,* and *how.*

From your list of questions, choose one question to be your **major research question.** You may also combine related questions to form the major research question. Write down the major research question that you will answer through further research. CCSS W.6.7

Write a Research Plan

Now that you have your major research question, write a research plan. Your plan should list

- other information that you need
- the types of sources you will use, including both print and digital sources
- any questions you want to answer through further research and investigation **CCSS W.6.7**

Gather Sources

Follow your research plan to gather sources through the Internet and from your school and local libraries or media centers. Remember to search for a wide variety of print and digital sources. When possible, search for a mix of primary and secondary sources. **CCSS W.6.8**

TYPE OF SOURCE	DEFINITION AND EXAMPLES
Primary source	• written by people who actually experienced the events they write about • original documents (diaries, autobiographies, speeches, letters, interviews, news film footage), creative works (poems, dramas, novels, music, art), and artifacts (buildings, clothing, furniture, pottery)
Secondary source	• based on information gathered from primary sources and others • publications (magazine and newspaper articles, biographies, textbooks, encyclopedias, books, critical reviews)

COMPOSITION

Evaluate Sources

You should use only valid and reliable print and digital sources. **Valid sources** are related to your topic and contain information that can be verified in another source. **Reliable sources** are credible, or trustworthy, such as encyclopedias or quotations from experts in the field. Reliable sources also are objective and current, or up to date.

To evaluate the quality of your sources, ask yourself the questions in the following chart:

EVALUATION TERM	QUESTIONS
Relevant	Is the information related to my topic? Does it help answer my questions about the topic?
Accurate	Can I verify the information in another source?
Credible	Is the information written by an author or organization with a good reputation? Is the author considered an expert?
Objective	Is the information a fact or an opinion? Is the source biased, or show favoritism toward or against something?
Current	Is the information current or out of date?

As you evaluate your sources, get rid of any sources that you don't think are valid or reliable. When you decide not to use a source, think about why you are dropping it. Then search for a source that will be more useful.

Create Source Cards

Once you have evaluated your sources, create a source card for each source you will use. Make sure you write down information about each source using a standard format. On each source card, include the following information:

- author
- title
- publication information (For books, include the city in which the source was published, name of publisher, and year of publication. For magazines, also include the issue number and volume number.)
- date on which you accessed the Web site
- location of the source (for example, the name of the library or Web site where you found the source)
- library call number or Web site URL

Number each source card in the upper right-hand corner. Your first source will be number 1, your second source will be number 2, and so on. You will use these cards when you write your Works Cited list. CCSS W.6.8

Create Note Cards

After you have created source cards, skim and scan the sources for relevant information. **Relevant information** includes facts, definitions, concrete details, quotations, examples, and other information related to your major research question.

Take notes on a note card for each piece of relevant information you find. On the note card, write a key word or phrase that describes the information. Then, write a summary or a paraphrase of the information, or record a quotation from the source. See the chart on the next page for an explanation of each type of note.

TYPE OF NOTE	HOW TO DO IT
Write a summary	Restate only the main ideas of a passage. A summary should be shorter than the passage from the source.
Paraphrase	Restate the passage in your own words. It should be about the same length as the original passage.
Record a quotation	Copy a passage word for word. For example, if you think information in a source is expressed in an interesting way, you may want to copy the author's own words. If you quote a source directly, use quotation marks around the words.

Next, note whether the information is fact or opinion. Write down the page number or the URL of the Web site page so you can find the information again, if you need to. Finally, refer to your source cards for the source numbers and record the appropriate source number in the upper right-hand corner of each note card. CCSS W.6.7, W.6.8

Write Your Thesis Statement

Take another look at your major research question. Ask yourself:

- Will I have enough to write about? If not, your major research question is too narrow. You should revise your research question to be broader.
- Will I have too much to write about? If so, your major research question is too broad. You should revise your research question to be more specific.

When your major research question is not too narrow or too broad, write your answer to the research question in one or two sentences. Make sure that your answer includes a clear statement of your viewpoint on the research topic. Your answer will be the **thesis statement**, or main point of the research report.

Organize Information

Now that you have your thesis statement, you need to make an organizational plan for the main ideas and details that you want to present in your report. To identify the main ideas of your report, look again at the note cards you wrote. Use the key word or phrase on each card to sort the cards into categories, or groups. Sorting the cards into categories will help you see the main ideas in the information you gathered. Write down one main idea about the details in each category of cards. Be sure that the main ideas support your thesis statement.

Next, organize the main ideas in a logical order. This will be the order in which you write the body paragraphs of your report.

Now go back to your groups of note cards and organize the groups according to the order you listed for your main ideas. The note cards in each group contain the details that you will use to support the main idea of the group. You may organize the details using one of the strategies defined on the next page.

STRATEGY	DEFINITION
Definition	to explain technical or specialized vocabulary and terms related to specific areas of study or work
Classification	to group information by type
Comparison and contrast	to describe similarities and differences among things or ideas
Process	to explain the order of an action or an event
Cause and effect	to describe an event and what results from it
Sequence of events	to discuss events in the order that they happened

Finally, use your organized groups of cards to create an outline using the structure shown below.

I.

A.

B.

C.

II.

A.

B.

C.

COMPOSITION

List your main ideas in order using Roman numerals I, II, III, IV, and so on. Beneath each main idea, list the appropriate supporting details in order using capital letters A, B, C, and so on. You will follow the order of main ideas and details in your outline when you write the body paragraphs of your research report.
CCSS W.6.2a

18.2 DRAFT

Write the Introduction

When you write a draft, your goal is to organize the information you have gathered into unified paragraphs. The **introduction** is the opening paragraph of your research report. An effective introduction introduces your topic and presents your thesis statement. The introduction should also grab your readers' attention, possibly by including

- an interesting anecdote, or brief story
- a surprising fact, or
- a thought-provoking question CCSS W.6.2a

Write Topic Sentences

Follow your outline to write the body paragraphs of your research report. Each paragraph should contain a **topic sentence** that states the main idea of the paragraph. Be sure that each main idea supports your thesis statement.

Present Findings

Next, develop the body paragraphs by presenting a summary, a paraphrase, or a quotation of the information from your sources. The facts, definitions, details, quotations, and examples you include in each paragraph should focus on and either explain or expand upon the topic sentence. Organize the topic sentence and supporting details of each paragraph in a way that best develops your thesis.

Do not copy information word for word and present it as your own. This is called **plagiarism.** Plagiarizing is against the law. Always credit the source of the information with an in-text citation, as described below.

- Write the author's last name and the page number(s) on which you found the information in parentheses. Place this information at the end of the last sentence or idea taken from the author's work.
- If the source is a Web site that does not include page numbers, do not write a page number in your citation.
- If the source does not list the author's name, use a shortened form of the work's title instead. If you mention the title and author in the paragraph, include only the page number in parentheses.

After you present information from your sources, draw a conclusion about the information in your paragraph. A **conclusion** is a general statement based on specific ideas. CCSS W.6.2b, W.6.8

Writing Tip

Don't worry about punctuation, spelling, or grammar as you write your draft. You can fix those later. The important thing when you draft is to state your ideas in a clear, organized way.

COMPOSITION

Maintain a Formal Style

Throughout your report, use precise language and vocabulary that is specific to your topic. Be sure to use and maintain a formal style. In formal writing, you usually write from the third-person point of view and avoid using slang, contractions, and conversational language. CCSS W.6.2d, e

Use Transitions

To make your writing flow smoothly, use transitions to link the ideas in sentences and paragraphs. **Transitions** are words, phrases, and clauses that show the relationship between ideas or events. Some of the following transitions may help you to clearly link the ideas presented in the sentences and paragraphs of your report. CCSS W.6.2c

RELATIONSHIP	EXAMPLES OF TRANSITIONS
Addition	*also, and, besides, both . . . and, furthermore, in addition*
Contrast	*but, however, instead, nevertheless, on the contrary, on the other hand, still, yet*
Importance	*first, last, mainly, most important, most of all*
Cause and effect	*as a result, consequently, for, so, so that, then, therefore, thus*
Sequence	*after, as, before, next, since, then, until, when, while*

Include Visual Elements

To help readers better understand the ideas in your report, you may wish to include

- graphics, such as images, maps, and charts
- formatting, such as heads and subheads
- multimedia elements, such links to video clips CCSS W.6.2a

Write the Conclusion

Finally, write the conclusion to your research report. The conclusion should state your thesis statement in a different way. It should also follow from and support the information in your report by summarizing the main points you made. End your conclusion with a strong closing statement that leaves a lasting impression. CCSS W.6.2f

Create a Works Cited List

At the end of your report, list all the sources of information cited in your report. Alphabetize the sources by the author's last name. If there is no author, then alphabetize the source by the first word in the title. CCSS W.6.8

For help with citing sources and creating a Works Cited list, see pages 384–389.

18.3 REVISE

Introduction to Revision

The word *revise* means "to see again." To revise your report, you will look at it again to make sure that it is clear and well organized and that it accomplishes your goal. You will focus on the development, organization, and style of your writing by applying these four revision strategies:

- **Add** details and information to make your main point clearer.
- **Delete** unnecessary words or ideas.
- **Replace** boring or overused words with precise language that is more exact and strong.
- **Rearrange** or **combine** phrases and sentences so your ideas and supporting details are presented logically.

Use these revision strategies with the questions and checklists that follow. The questions will help you think about how well your research report addresses the genre as well as your purpose and audience.

- The **genre** is the writing mode, such as research report, story, poem, or play.
- Your **purpose** is your reason for writing. In a research report, your purpose is to explain and inform.
- The **audience** includes the people who will read your report. CCSS W.6.4

Focus and Coherence

Ask yourself:

✓ Does my research report have a clear focus?

✓ Does each paragraph relate to the thesis, or controlling idea?

✓ Do all parts work together so that my main point is explained and well supported? CCSS W.6.2a, b

Organization

Ask yourself:

✓ Does the introduction present my thesis, or controlling idea?

✓ Does each body paragraph present the main idea and details in a way that best develops the thesis?

✓ Are the body paragraphs ordered logically?

✓ Does the conclusion follow from and support the information or explanation that I presented? CCSS W.6.2a, b, f

Development of Ideas

Ask yourself:

✓ Does each paragraph express a main idea about the thesis, or controlling idea?

✓ Is each main idea supported by appropriate evidence? CCSS W.6.2b, W.6.9a, b

Voice–Word Choice

Ask yourself:

✓ Does my report include vocabulary and precise words that are specific to my topic?

✓ Does my report include transitions that link the ideas in sentences and paragraphs?

✓ Does my report include formal language from beginning to end? CCSS W.6.2c–e

Voice–Sentence Fluency

Ask yourself:

✓ Does my report include a mix of short sentences and long sentences that make the paragraphs interesting to read?

✓ Have I made my sentences more interesting by combining some of them, using prepositional phrases, appositive phrases, and adjective and adverb clauses?

✓ Does my writing include a consistent style and tone that make it flow smoothly? CCSS L.6.3a, b

Revising Tip

As you revise, use a thesaurus to find exactly the right words to communicate your ideas. Vary your words and sentences to avoid wordiness and **redundancy**, or words and sentences that say the same thing. CCSS L.6.3b

18.4 EDIT

Correct Errors in Grammar

Editing involves correcting errors in grammar, usage, mechanics, and spelling. Begin editing by taking a careful look at your sentences. Make sure that each sentence expresses a complete thought and is grammatically correct. Use the checklist on the next page to edit your sentences. CCSS W.6.5, L.6.1

Sentence-Editing Checklist

Ask yourself:

- ✓ Have I avoided sentence fragments?
- ✓ Have I avoided run-on sentences?
- ✓ Do verbs agree with their subjects?
- ✓ Have I used verb tenses and forms correctly?
- ✓ Have I used pronouns in the proper case (subjective, objective, possessive)?
- ✓ Have I correctly used intensive pronouns (*herself, themselves*) for emphasis?
- ✓ Have I used adjectives and adverbs correctly?
- ✓ Are my sentences parallel so that elements that have the same function in a sentence are written in the same form or verb tense? **CCSS L.6.1a, b**

Correct Errors in Mechanics and Spelling

Next check for and correct any errors in mechanics (punctuation and capitalization) and spelling. Use the checklist below to edit your report. You should also use a dictionary to check spellings. **CCSS L.6.2, b**

Proofreading Checklist

Ask yourself:

- ✓ Have I used correct punctuation?
- ✓ Have I written possessives correctly?
- ✓ Have I spelled all words correctly?
- ✓ Have I used capital letters as needed?

Peer and Teacher Review

After you have revised and edited your report yourself, you will revise it through peer review and teacher review. During **peer review**, you will share your writing with a partner or classmates. Then you will discuss how to improve your writing. During **teacher review**, you will give your report to your teacher. Your teacher will read it and suggest how you can make your report better. The ideas and opinions of your peers and teacher will tell you whether you're achieving your goals.

You can use the **Peer Review Guide** on page 382 to respond to a classmate's writing. CCSS W.6.5, L.6.1e

18.5 PUBLISH

After you have written and polished your research report, you will publish and present it. This is the stage when you share your final research report with others. You may wish to consider the following publishing and presenting options. Some of these options require you to collaborate with your classmates and use technology:

- Create a class collection of research reports.
- Enter your report into a writing contest.
- Give an oral presentation of your report to classmates.
- E-mail your report to an organization associated with your topic.
- Publish a multimedia version of your report online with images and video clips. CCSS W.6.6

Reflecting on, or thinking about, your own writing can help you improve your writing skills. You can use the **Reflection Guide** on page 383 to reflect on the writing you did in this workshop.

Chapter 19

Narrative

A **narrative** is a story or an account of an event. There are historical narratives, fictional narratives, and real-life narratives. When you write a story, or narrative, you answer the question *What happened?* Your story will need a beginning, a middle, and an end. It will also need a setting, a conflict and resolution, characters, and dialogue.

The basic elements of a narrative are defined below.

ELEMENT	DEFINITION
Setting	the time and place in which the events of a narrative occur
Mood	the general feeling of a narrative
Characters	the people or animals in a literary work
Plot	the sequence of events
Conflict	a problem that the character(s) must face
Resolution	the outcome of the conflict
Theme	the overall message about life presented in the narrative

The instruction on the pages that follow will guide you through the process of writing a narrative while meeting the Common Core State Standards for narrative writing. For a list of the writing and grammar Common Core State Standards, see pages 431–438. CCSS W.6.10

19.1 PLAN

Graphic Organizers

During the Plan stage, you will gather and organize writing ideas. To do this, you may wish to use graphic organizers, such as the Story Map, Character Chart, and Setting and Mood Diagram on pages 379–381.

Identify Key Elements

Write the topic of your story. The **topic** of most good stories is a problem faced by a character. Examples of story topics are "an unusual babysitting experience" and "the drama of a science fair project."

Now write a possible theme for your story. The **theme** is the central message about life that a writer expresses. For example, if your story is about an unusual babysitting experience, your theme might be "It takes a calm manner and clear thinking to deal with a babysitting crisis." You can revise your theme as you draft, if you want to.

Writing down some details about the important story elements can ease you into writing. Think about the characters and events and how the setting affects them. Write down the names of your characters and identify the setting of your story. The **setting** is the time and place in which the events of the narrative occur. The setting often helps create the **mood**, or atmosphere.

In narrative writing, the point of view is important. **Point of view** is the perspective, or standpoint, from which a story is told. The chart on the next page describes the two main points of view for a narrative. Read the chart and then identify your story's point of view. CCSS W.6.3a

POINT OF VIEW	NARRATOR	USE
First-person	The narrator is a character in the story and uses the word *I*.	Use first-person point of view if you want to reveal the action through the main character's eyes.
Third-person	The narrator is not a character in the story but tells the story from outside the action. The narrator refers to characters as *he* and *she*.	Use third-person point of view if you want readers to see the action from outside the story.

Develop Interesting Characters

Look at your list of characters. Decide which of the characters is a main character and which are minor characters. A **main character** is central to the story and is usually fully developed. A **minor character** has few personality traits and is used to help move the plot along. For each character, give examples of

- the way the character looks
- what the character thinks, feels, and says
- how the character acts and interacts with others
- what the narrator or other characters think and say about the character

Write precise words or phrases about each character. Then think of descriptive details that help develop each word or phrase. Good descriptive details include specific nouns, vivid verbs, and exact adjectives. Make sure the details are related to the story. CCSS W.6.3a, b, d

COMPOSITION

Create the Main Events

To develop your **plot**, or sequence of events, of your story, identify the main conflict and resolution. The **conflict** is the central struggle or problem that the main character faces. The **resolution** is the outcome of the conflict.

Next, write down the events of your narrative. Chronological order is an effective way to organize a story so the events unfold naturally and logically. **Chronological order** is the time order in which events happen. When you use chronological order, you tell what happens first, second, and so on. Include well-paced action to keep your readers engaged in the story.

Transitions will help your readers follow your story. **Transitions** are words, phrases, and clauses that help show the relationship between events or ideas. Some examples of transitions are *before, after, next, first, later, afterward, nearby, in the distance, finally,* and *while.* Write down three transitions that you can use to clarify the sequence of events in your narrative. Then write down three transitions that you can use to signal shifts from one time frame or setting to another. CCSS W.6.3a, c

COMPOSITION

Describe the Setting

Writers use descriptive details and sensory language to create specific, believable settings. **Sensory language** describes how people and things look, sound, feel, smell, or taste. The setting helps create the **mood**, or atmosphere, of a story. For example, a writer might create a frightening mood by describing a dark, stormy night booming with loud claps of thunder.

Write notes about the setting and mood of your story. Then write precise words and phrases, descriptive details, and sensory language that describe the setting. Make sure that your sensory details help create the mood. CCSS W.6.3b, d

Use Literary Strategies and Narrative Techniques

Writers use literary strategies and narrative techniques to develop experiences, events, characters, style, and tone. These strategies and techniques include foreshadowing, dialogue, pacing, and description, which are defined below.

STRATEGY OR TECHNIQUE	DEFINITION
Foreshadowing	the writer's use of clues to prepare the audience for events that will happen later in the story
Dialogue	the conversation between characters in a literary work
Pacing	the speed in which the plot events and action unfold
Description	vivid writing that helps readers **visualize,** or see in their minds, the characters, settings, events, and experiences

Identify literary strategies and narrative techniques that you can use in your story. Describe how you will use them. Then explain how they will help develop the experiences, events, characters, style, and tone. CCSS W.6.3b, d

19.2 DRAFT

Write the Opening

Begin your draft by writing the opening, or beginning, to your story. Your opening should grab your readers' attention so they want to keep reading. In the opening, you should

- introduce the main character
- introduce the conflict that drives the plot, or story line

- include descriptive details and sensory language that help create the setting

Include interesting details about your main character from your planning notes. Choose sensory details from your planning notes that will help create the setting.
CCSS W.6.3a, b, d

Writing Tip

If you can't decide how to begin your story, just get your ideas on paper. After you have written the first draft of your opening, you can revise it as many times as needed until you are satisfied with it.

Write Dialogue

Choose a place in your story where you can use dialogue. **Dialogue** is a conversation between characters in a literary work. Dialogue can serve many purposes. For example, it can be used to introduce the conflict and move along the plot. It can also be used to develop characters and events. What characters say—and how they say it—will often reveal what they're like.

Identify the purpose of the dialogue. Then think of the language you will use to show the ages, personalities, thoughts, and feelings of the characters that are speaking. Your dialogue will sound natural if your characters talk the way real people talk. You can use slang, sentence fragments, and contractions in dialogue. Begin a new paragraph each time the speaker changes. CCSS W.6.3b

Writing Tip

Use quotation marks and tag lines so that it is clear which character is speaking. **Tag lines** are the words that identify the speaker, such as "said Charlie." However, do not use the word *said* too often in tag lines. Instead use more descriptive words, such as *questioned, cried*, or *whispered.*

Write the Body

Next, use your planning notes to write the body, or middle, of your story. Include action and details that will keep readers engaged. Remember to

- follow the plot you created
- include a well-paced sequence of events related to the conflict, with events unfolding naturally and logically
- use transition words, phrases, and clauses to show sequence and to signal shifts from one time frame or setting to another
- use descriptive details to create interesting characters
- use sensory language to create a specific, believable setting and mood
- include literary strategies and narrative techniques to develop experiences, events, characters, style, and tone CCSS W.6.3a–d

Write the Ending

Finally, write the ending, or conclusion, of your story. Make sure that your ending follows from the narrated experiences or events by presenting the resolution to the conflict and relating to the theme of your story. The conclusion should give your audience the feeling that the story is complete. CCSS W.6.3e

19.3 REVISE

Introduction to Revision

The word *revise* means "to see again." To revise your narrative, you will look at it again to make sure that it is clear and well organized and that it accomplishes your goal. You will focus on the development, organization, and style of your writing.

Apply one or more of the four revision strategies that follow to revise your narrative:

- **Add** details and information to make the theme, or message about life, clearer.
- **Delete** unnecessary words or ideas.
- **Replace** boring or overused words with precise language that is more exact and strong.
- **Rearrange** or **combine** phrases and sentences to be sure readers can understand the theme.

Use these revision strategies with the questions and checklists that follow. The questions will help you think about how well your narrative addresses the genre as well as your purpose and audience.

- The **genre** is the writing mode, such as story, poem, play, or essay.
- Your **purpose** is your reason for writing. Your purpose might be to describe, explain, narrate, amuse, or persuade. In this workshop, your purpose is to narrate a story.
- The **audience** includes the people who will read your story. CCSS W.6.4, W.6.5

Focus and Coherence

Ask yourself:

✓ Does the story have a clear purpose and focus?

✓ Does the story use the same point of view from beginning to end?

✓ Does the story engage my readers? CCSS W.6.3a

Organization

Ask yourself:

✓ Does the opening introduce the main character and conflict?

- ✓ Does the body, or middle, present events in chronological order, with events unfolding naturally and logically?
- ✓ Does the ending offer a clear resolution to the conflict? CCSS W.6.3a, c, e

Development of Ideas

Ask yourself:

- ✓ Can the readers easily identify the narrator and point of view?
- ✓ Is the main character fully developed, interesting, and believable?
- ✓ Does my story include literary strategies and narrative techniques to develop experiences, events, and ideas? CCSS W.6.3a, b

Voice–Word Choice

Ask yourself:

- ✓ Does my writing include precise words and phrases, descriptive details, and sensory language so that readers can visualize characters, setting, and events?
- ✓ Does my writing include transitions that link the events and signal shifts in time or setting? CCSS W.6.3c, d

Voice–Sentence Fluency

Ask yourself:

- ✓ Does my story include a mix of short sentences and long sentences that make the events and characters seem real?
- ✓ Have I made my sentences more interesting by combining some of them, using prepositional phrases, appositive phrases, and adjective and adverb clauses? CCSS L.6.3a, b

19.4 EDIT

Correct Errors in Grammar

Editing involves correcting errors in grammar, usage, mechanics, and spelling. Begin the editing stage by taking a careful look at your sentences. Make sure that each sentence expresses a complete thought and is grammatically correct. Use the checklist below to edit your sentences. **CCSS W.6.5, L.6.1**

Sentence-Editing Checklist

- ✓ Have I avoided sentence fragments?
- ✓ Have I avoided run-on sentences?
- ✓ Do verbs agree with their subjects?
- ✓ Have I used verb tenses and forms correctly?
- ✓ Have I used pronouns in the proper case (subjective, objective, possessive)?
- ✓ Have I correctly used intensive pronouns (*myself*, *ourselves*) for emphasis?
- ✓ Have I used adjectives and adverbs correctly?
- ✓ Are my sentences parallel so that elements that have the same function in a sentence are written in the same form or verb tense? **CCSS L.6.1a, b**

Correct Errors in Mechanics and Spelling

Next, check for and correct any errors in mechanics (punctuation and capitalization) and spelling. Use the checklist on the next page to edit your narrative. You should also use a dictionary to check and confirm spellings. **CCSS L.6.2, b**

Proofreading Checklist

✓ Have I used correct punctuation?
✓ Have I written possessives correctly?
✓ Have I spelled all words correctly?
✓ Have I used capital letters as needed?

Peer and Teacher Review

In addition to revising and editing your own story, you will revise your work through peer review and teacher review. During **peer review**, you will share your writing with a partner or classmates in a writing group. Then you will discuss how to improve your writing. During **teacher review**, you will give your story to your teacher. Your teacher will also suggest ways to make your story better.

You can use the **Peer Review Guide** on page 382 to respond to a classmate's writing. CCSS W.6.5, L.6.1e

19.5 PUBLISH

After you have written and polished your story, you will publish and present it. This is the stage when you share your final narrative with others. You may wish to consider the following options, some of which require you to collaborate with your classmates and use technology:

- Enter your story into a writing contest.
- Create a class collection of stories.
- Perform your story as Readers Theater.
- Publish a multimedia version of your story online with images and video clips. CCSS W.6.6

Reflecting on your own writing can help you improve your writing skills. You can use the **Reflection Guide** on page 383 to reflect on the writing you did in this workshop.

Chapter 20

Graphic Organizers

The graphic organizers on the following pages will help you plan your writing as you complete the workshops on pages 312–371. The chart below shows which graphic organizers go with which workshops.

WRITING WORKSHOP	GRAPHIC ORGANIZERS
Persuasive Essay	• Persuasive Essay Map
Response	• Evidence Chart–Response Essay
Multi-Paragraph Essay	• Evidence Chart–Multi-Paragraph Essay
Research Report	• Main Idea Map • Source Card • Note Card
Narrative	• Story Map • Character Chart • Setting and Mood Diagram
All workshops	• Peer Review Guide • Reflection Guide

Copy this graphic organizer onto a separate sheet of paper. Then fill it out.

PERSUASIVE ESSAY MAP

Topic or Issue:

↓

Position or Controlling Idea:

↓

Reason 1/Evidence:	Reason 2/Evidence:	Reason 3/Evidence:

↓	↓	↓
☐ Fact	☐ Fact	☐ Fact
☐ Opinion	☐ Opinion	☐ Opinion
☐ Example	☐ Example	☐ Example
↓	↓	↓

Other Views, Concerns, Counter-Arguments	Other Views, Concerns, Counter-Arguments	Other Views, Concerns, Counter-Arguments

COMPOSITION

Copy this graphic organizer onto a separate sheet of paper. Then fill it out.

EVIDENCE CHART–RESPONSE ESSAY

Focus:
Controlling Idea:

Evidence from the Text	
Evidence (details, quotations, facts, examples, statistics)	**How It Supports Controlling Idea**

Evidence from Other Sources (personal experience, books, essays, articles, Web sites)		
Evidence	**How It Supports Controlling Idea**	**Primary or Secondary Source**

Related Ideas from Sources:	**Synthesized Idea:**

COMPOSITION

Copy this graphic organizer onto a separate sheet of paper. Then fill it out.

EVIDENCE CHART—MULTI-PARAGRAPH ESSAY

Topic:		
Controlling Idea:		
Evidence (details, quotations, facts, examples, statistics)	**How It Supports Controlling Idea**	**Source**
Related Ideas from Sources:	**Synthesized Idea:**	

COMPOSITION

Copy this graphic organizer onto a separate sheet of paper. Then fill it out.

MAIN IDEA MAP

Thesis Statement:	
Main Idea	**Category**

COMPOSITION

Copy this graphic organizer onto a separate sheet of paper for each source. Then fill it out.

SOURCE CARD

Author: **Source Number:**

Title:

City of Publication and Publisher:

Date of Publication:

Access Date:

Location of Source (e.g., name of library or Web site):

Library Call Number or Web Site URL:

COMPOSITION

Copy this graphic organizer onto a separate sheet of paper for each piece of relevant information. Then fill it out.

NOTE CARD

Key Word or Phrase About Information:	**Source Number:**
Specific Information/Details from Source:	
Page Number on Which Information Was Found:	

COMPOSITION

Copy this graphic organizer onto a separate sheet of paper. Then fill it out.

STORY MAP

Topic:	**Theme:**
Main Characters:	**Minor Characters:**
Setting (time and place):	**Point of View:**

Conflict:		
Event 1:	**Event 2:**	**Event 3:**
Resolution:		

Strategy/Device to Enhance Style, Tone, or Plot:

COMPOSITION

Copy this graphic organizer onto a separate sheet of paper. Then fill it out.

CHARACTER CHART

Character's Name:	
Looks:	
Thinks:	
Feels:	
Says:	
Acts:	
Interacts:	
Narrator or Other Characters Say:	

Copy this graphic organizer onto a separate sheet of paper. Then fill it out.

SETTING AND MOOD DIAGRAM

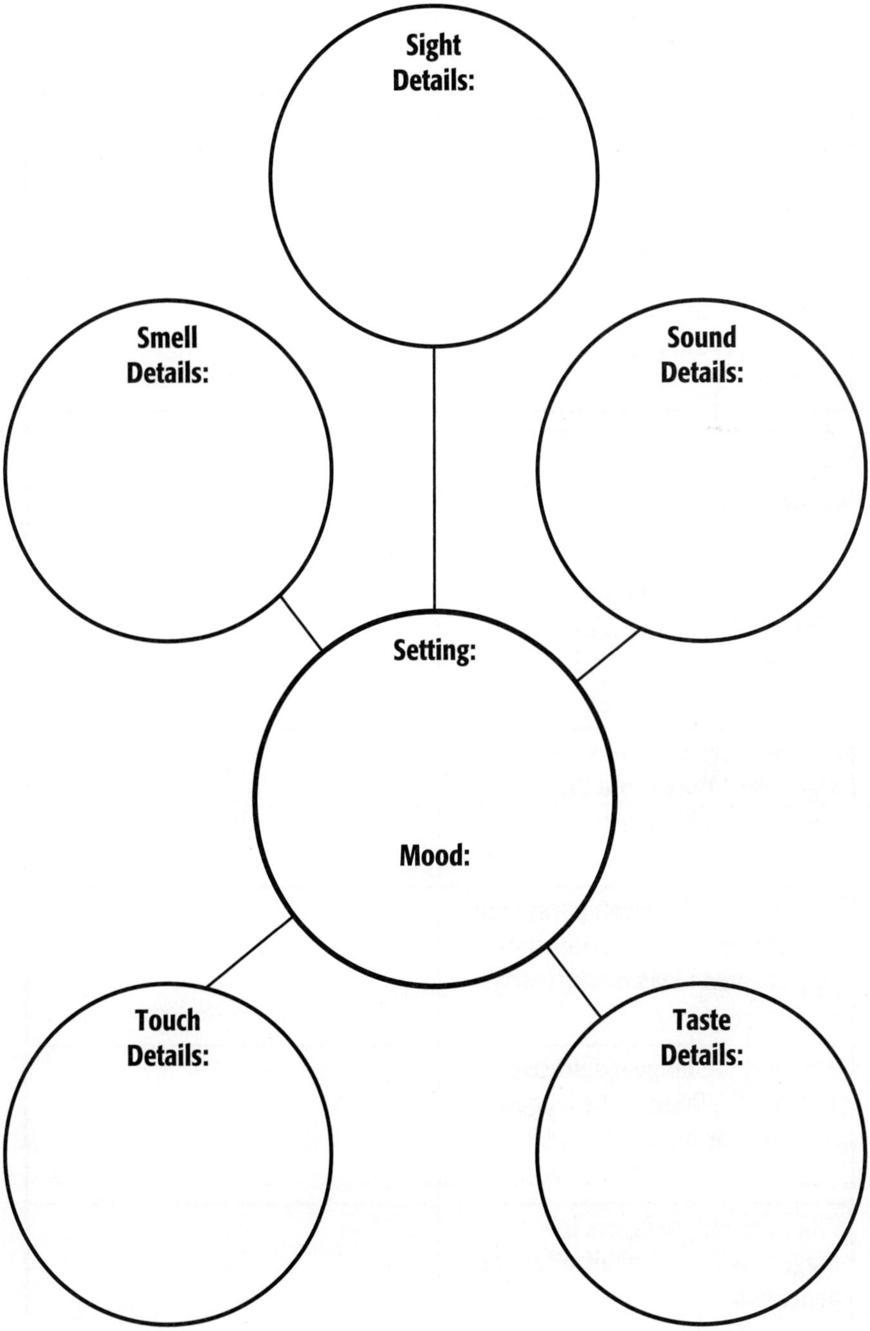

Copy this graphic organizer onto a separate sheet of paper. Then fill it out.

PEER REVIEW GUIDE

During peer review, you will express your opinions about a classmate's writing. You will also share your ideas about how to improve the writing. These questions can help guide you through the process of peer review.

What is best about this piece of writing?	
Is the opening interesting and attention getting? What, if anything, could make it better?	
What is the focus, or main point, of this piece? Do all of the key ideas relate to that point?	
Has the writer explained or supported each key idea? Where are more details needed?	
Are the ideas or events clearly organized? How could the organization be improved?	
Are the ideas between paragraphs related? Where could transitions help connect ideas more clearly?	
Where is the language precise and vivid? Where is the language confusing or unclear?	
Where are there errors in usage, spelling, capitalization, or punctuation?	

Copy this graphic organizer onto a separate sheet of paper. Then fill it out.

REFLECTION GUIDE

Reflecting on your own writing can help you improve your writing skills. You can reflect on your own writing by completing these sentence starters:

What I like best about this piece of writing is . . .	
When I look back at the project, the part I most enjoyed working on was . . .	
The most difficult part of the project was . . .	
One thing I learned from this project was . . .	
I would assess my work on this project as (outstanding, good, fair, weak) . . .	
One thing I need to improve in my next writing project is . . .	
One goal I would like to focus on in the future is . . .	

Chapter 21

MLA Style Guide

CITING SOURCES

When you write an informative, explanatory, or persuasive text, you should cite, or name, the sources of the information you present. You need to cite sources for all ideas, statements, quotations, and facts that are not common knowledge. One reason for citing your sources is to allow your readers to check a source and judge how believable or important a piece of information is.

Another reason to cite your sources is to avoid plagiarism. **Plagiarism** is the act of taking an author's words or ideas and presenting them as your own. Plagiarism is against the law. You must cite a source not only for words you quote directly but also for facts or ideas you take from it.

IN-TEXT CITATIONS

In-text citations are sources that you cite within the body of your paper. You should include in-text citations for sources from which you use information in your paper. Insert the author's last name or the title of the work (if the author's last name is not available) and a page reference in parentheses after the information. For online sources without page numbers, use the title of the Web site. Always put the period outside the parentheses. See the example of an in-text citation on the next page.

Every in-text citation must connect to one of the entries in your Works Cited list. This connection should be by the author's last name or the title of the work—whichever is listed first in the entry in parentheses. For example, the in-text citation shown below in parentheses refers to the author's last name and the page number where the information was found; the Works Cited entry for that source begins with the author's last name. This connection helps readers easily locate sources in a Works Cited list.

In-Text Citation:

Sundiata would later be known by such titles as "Lord Lion," "Lion of Mali," and "Father of the Bright Country" (Koslow 12).

Works Cited:

Kozlow, Philip. *Mali: Crossroads of Africa.* New York: Chelsea House, 1995. Print.

The chart on the next two pages explains how to cite different sources within the body of your paper, as recommended by the Modern Language Association of America (MLA). These guidelines relate to both print and digital sources.

DOCUMENTING SOURCES WITHIN A PAPER	
Kind of Source	**Example**
Author named in text Insert the page number in parentheses. If there is no page number (as with many Web sources), simply leave off the citation in parentheses.	According to Philip Koslow, Sundiata would be known by such titles as "Lord Lion," "Lion of Mali," and "Father of the Bright Country" (12).
Work with two (or three) authors Insert each author's last name in parentheses before the page number.	Sundiata faced one of his biggest challenges when he was a young child. He had been born with a disability. He crawled around like a baby until he was seven years old (McKissack and McKissack 49).
Work with more than three authors Give the last name of the first author listed, followed by *et al.* ("and others") and the page number.	The Gold of Africa Museum contains probably the most important collection of gold artworks, including precious masks, crocodiles, birds, a gold crown, and human figures, from Mali and other African nations (Pinchuck et al. 131).
Work with no author or editor Use the title or a shortened version of the title, and give the page number. If there is no page number (as with some Web pages), include only the title of the work.	According to legend, when Sundiata learned that Dankaran Touman was to be king because Sundiata was disabled, he took an iron rod and used the rod to stand upright ("Sundiata").

More than one work by the same author Use the author's last name, the title or a shortened version of the title, and the page number.	After Sundiata's death, Mali lacked strong leadership for several decades. (McKissack, *The Royal Kingdoms* 56).
More than one source at a time Include both sources and their page numbers, separated by a semicolon.	Much of what we know about Sundiata comes from griots, the African storytellers (Koslow 12; Eisner 3).

WORKS CITED LIST

Use your source cards and note cards to document, or record, the publishing information about your sources in a Works Cited list. This list will appear at the end of your paper. The list should be alphabetized by the authors' last names. If a work has no author, alphabetize it by the title.

Technology Tip

There are online programs that can help you build your Works Cited list. Enter "Works Cited generator" in your search engine to find such a program.

The chart on the following pages shows the proper style to use for different types of sources in a Works Cited list or bibliography, as recommended by the MLA.

DOCUMENTING SOURCES IN A WORKS CITED LIST

Kind of Source	Example
Book with one author	Koslow, Philip. *Mali: Crossroads of Africa*. New York: Chelsea House, 1995, Print.
Book with two or three authors (If a book has more than three authors, name only the first author, followed by *et al.*)	McKissack, Pat, and Fredrick McKissack. *The Royal Kingdoms of Ghana, Mali, and Songhay: Life in Medieval Africa.* New York: H. Holt, 1994. Print.
Book with editor(s)	Lehman, David, and Heather McHugh, eds. *The Best American Poetry 2007*. New York: Scribner's, 2007. Print.
Book with an organization or a group as author or editor	Adobe Creative Team. *Adobe Photoshop CS3 Classroom in a Book*. Berkeley: Adobe, 2007. Print.
Work from an anthology	Desai, Anita. "Games at Twilight." 1978. *The Penguin Book of International Women's Stories.* Ed. Kate Figes. London: Penguin, 1996. 204-11. Print.
Introduction in a published book	Jackson, Peter. Introduction. *The Making of* Star Wars: *The Definitive Story Behind the Original Film*. By J. W. Rinzler. New York: Del Rey, 2007. iii. Print.
Encyclopedia article	"Jazz." *The New Encyclopaedia Britannica: Micropaedia*. 15th ed. 1998. Print.
Weekly magazine article	Sacks, Oliver. "A Bolt from the Blue." *New Yorker* 23 July 2007: 38–42. Print.

Monthly magazine article	Plotnikoff, David. "Hungry Man." *Saveur* July 2007: 35–36. Print.
Newspaper article If no author is named, begin the entry with the title of the article.	Long, Ray, and Jeffrey Meitrodt. "Some Budget Progress Made." *Chicago Tribune* 26 July 2007, B3 sec. Print.
Online newspaper article Include a URL only when the reader cannot locate the source without it or when your teacher requires it.	Onion, Amanda. "Americans Embracing 'Green' Cleaning." *ABC News*. ABC News Internet Ventures, 30 Jan. 2006. Web. Aug. 2007. <http://abcnews.go.com/Technology/Business/story?id=1544322>.
Online magazine article Include a URL only when the reader cannot locate the source without it or when your teacher requires it.	Parks, Bob. "Robot Buses Pull In to San Diego's Fastest Lane." *Wired Magazine*. July 2007. Web. 25 Oct. 2007. <http://www.wired.com/cars/futuretransport/magazine/15-08/st_robot>.
Web page Include a URL only when the reader cannot locate the source without it or when your teacher requires it.	Everett, Glenn. "Utilitarianism." *The Victorian Web*. Ed. George P. Landow. U Scholars Programme, Natl. U of Singapore, 11 Oct. 2002. Web. 18 May 2007.
Radio or TV program	"Jungles." *Planet Earth*. Dir. Alastair Fothergill. Discovery Channel. 19 Nov. 2006. Television.
Videotape or DVD For a videotape (VHS) version, replace "DVD" with "Videocassette."	*An Inconvenient Truth*. Dir. Davis Guggenheim. Paramount, 2006. DVD.

Part Four

Resources

Knowledge is of two kinds: we know a subject ourselves, or we know where we can find information on it.

–Samuel Johnson

PHOTO: Comstock Images/Jupiterimages/Getty Images

Chapter 22

The Library or Media Center

Although you've probably been in a library, you might not realize how many print, digital, and media resources that the library has to offer or how to find them. This chapter will guide you through the library and help you understand how and where to find what you need.

CARD SERVICES, HELP DESKS, AND CHECKOUT

The staff of librarians and library workers can direct you to resources on any subject you're interested in. Workers at a desk in card services can help you obtain or renew a library card, which you'll need in order to check out books and other materials. Librarians at the help desks can answer your questions about library resources or the research you are doing. The library also has a checkout desk or a self-checkout station where you can use your library card to check out library books and other materials and to pay fines.

CATALOGS

Catalogs tell you which books and materials are available and where to find them. A computer or card catalog will tell you about books and materials that are available in your particular library. An online catalog will tell you about books and materials that are available through a network of libraries in your city or state. You'll learn more about using catalogs in Chapter 23.

AREAS FOR ADULTS, TEENS, AND KIDS

Many libraries are divided into separate areas for adults, teens (sometimes called the "young adults area"), and children. Although it's called the "adult area," you don't have to be an adult to use these books and materials. All three areas usually contain similar sections and materials, such as fiction and nonfiction books, DVDs and CDs, reference materials, and computers. The areas for teens and children may also include chapter books, textbooks, leveled readers for beginning readers, and picture books for very young readers.

STACKS

The stacks are rows of bookshelves in the library. The stacks are often divided into these sections:

- fiction (novels, short stories, mysteries, and science fiction)
- nonfiction (biographies and subjects such as sports, history, and science)

REFERENCE SECTION

The reference section often includes both print and digital encyclopedias, dictionaries, almanacs, atlases, and other materials. The areas for teens and children might also include textbooks for subject areas such as literature, math, science, and social studies. Books and digital materials in the reference section can be used only in the library. By not allowing people to check out these materials, the library helps to ensure that they are always available when someone needs to consult them.

NEWSPAPERS AND MAGAZINES

In the section of newspapers and magazines (sometimes called the "periodicals" section), you can read local newspapers as well as papers from major cities in the United States and perhaps from other countries. You can also look through magazines and journals. You may not be able to check out the current issues, but you can usually take older issues home to read. You'll learn more about finding articles in newspapers and magazines in Chapter 23.

DVDs AND CDs

The DVDs and CDs section of the library may also be called the audio-visual section. This section may contain audiobooks, eBooks, computer games, movies, videos, and music that you can check out and enjoy at home.

COMPUTERS

The areas for adults, teens, and children may have computer sections of laptops and desktop computers with high-speed Internet access. You may be able to use these computers for research or to check e-mail. The computers may also contain software programs that you can use to write reports, résumés, and letters or to create spreadsheets and presentations. For a small fee per page, you can usually print the articles you've found online or in the library's databases or the papers you've written.

STUDY AREAS

Most libraries have quiet areas containing desks that are set aside for people who want to read or study individually. Some libraries also have group study rooms in which students and other people can gather for group study or discussions. You might need to reserve the group study rooms ahead of time.

SPECIAL COLLECTIONS AND STACKS

Some libraries set aside a special room or section for collections of rare books, manuscripts, and items of local interest, including works by local students and artists. Libraries may also have a "popular topics" section of stacks. These stacks are organized so readers can find books by popular topics such as cooking, finance, gardening, green living, sports, and jobs and careers.

Chapter 23

Using Print and Digital Resources

In the course of doing research for a report, you will look at print and digital books as well as magazines, also known as periodicals. Books are tremendous sources because they give you access to information and opinions from the past. Magazines and journals are good sources of current information and opinions because they are published more often than books. In this chapter, you'll learn about some of the different kinds of print and digital resources available to you.

23.1 UNDERSTANDING CATALOGING SYSTEMS

Maybe you're looking for information on a particular subject. Maybe you want to see books by a certain author, or you want to check out a specific book. The library's catalog will help you find what you're looking for. The catalog will be either an online computer catalog or a paper card catalog. If it's an online catalog, you might be able to access it from your home computer as well as in the library.

COMPUTER CATALOGS

Each computer catalog is different. Before you use one for the first time, read the instructions. They might be printed on the screen or posted beside the computer. If you need help, ask a library worker.

Using Search Techniques

Most catalog programs allow you to search by subject using a keyword or by title or author. Computer catalogs may also allow you to do advanced keyword searches. Read the computer screen carefully to be sure the catalog is set for the type of search you want to do. For example, the screen below shows that the catalog will search for a subject by keyword. If you wanted to search this catalog by title or author or if you wanted to do an advanced keyword search, you would click on the Title, Author, or Advanced tab to change the setting.

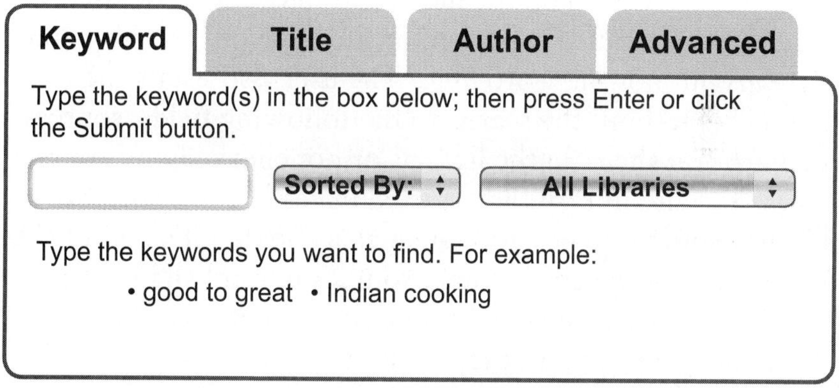

Subject Search For a subject search, you will type the keyword(s) for the subject. A **keyword** is a word or phrase that names or describes your topic. Whenever you search a computer database, including the Internet, the keyword you use will greatly affect the results you get.

Search Tip

Be specific. A general keyword, such as *experiments,* will get you a long list of sources, sometimes called **hits** or **matches.** Although these sources will relate in some way to your keyword, few of them are likely to focus on your specific subject. To save time, choose a keyword that better names or describes your topic, such as *cloning.* You will get a much shorter list of sources, but more of the sources will be useful to you.

Advanced Keyword Search If the simple keyword search lists too many sources for your subject, you can narrow the list by doing an advanced keyword search. An advanced search allows you to set field limits so the computer searches for only the keywords and fields you have specified. For example, the screen on the next page shows that the user wants the computer to search for the keywords *cloning* and *animals* but not the word *dogs.* The user also wants the computer to limit the search to the following fields: sources that are "on shelf" in the library, or not checked out; sources located in any library that is listed instead of one specific library; sources in any format, such as book, CD, and DVD, instead of one specific format; sources in English instead of another language; and sources published between the years 2000 and 2011. The user chose not to limit the search to a specific publisher.

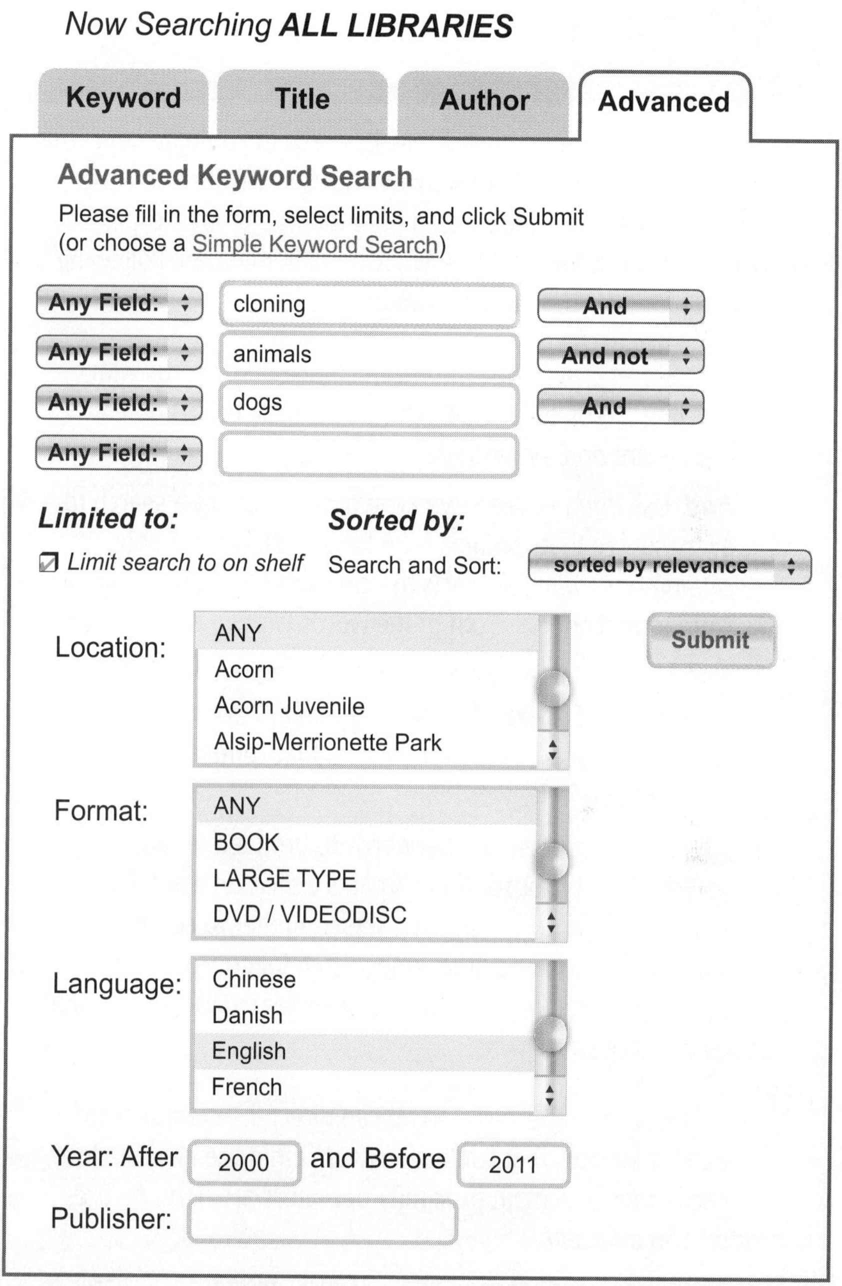
Now Searching ALL LIBRARIES
Keyword
Title
Author
Advanced
Advanced Keyword Search
Please fill in the form, select limits, and click Submit
(or choose a Simple Keyword Search)
Any Field:
cloning
And
Any Field:
animals
And not
Any Field:
dogs
And
Any Field:
Limited to:
Limit search to on shelf
Sorted by:
Search and Sort:
sorted by relevance
Submit
Location:
ANY
Acorn
Acorn Juvenile
Alsip-Merrionette Park
Format:
ANY
BOOK
LARGE TYPE
DVD / VIDEODISC
Language:
Chinese
Danish
English
French
Year: After
2000
and Before
2011
Publisher:

Search Tip

Many online and computer catalogs allow you to combine keywords in various ways to broaden or narrow your search. Such searches, called Boolean searches, are based on a method of logic expressed by George Boole, a 19th-century English mathematician. Following are descriptions of some Boolean search techniques you can use.

Use Boolean Operators. You can combine keywords with connecting words called **operators.** The three basic Boolean operators are *and, or,* and *not.*

- ***And:*** Use *and* between two keywords to narrow a search to every source that contains *both* keywords. For example, *cloning and animals* directs the computer to search only for sources that contain both of the words *cloning* and *animals.*
- ***Not:*** Use *not* to narrow a search by excluding terms that you do not want. For example, *cloning and not dogs* directs the computer to search only for sources that contain the word *cloning* but not the word *dogs.*
- ***Or:*** Use *or* between two keywords to broaden, or widen, a search to every source that contains *either* keyword. For example, *cloning or twins* tells the computer to conduct two searches at the same time–one search for sources that contain the word *cloning* and another search for sources that contain the word *twins.*

Use Proximity Operators. You can direct the computer to search for sources that contain keywords that are near or close to each other. The main proximity operators are *near, before, after,* and *adjacent.*

- ***Near:*** Use *near* between two keywords to narrow a search to every source that contains *both* keywords when they are close to each other, in any order. For example, *cloning near animals* directs the computer to search only for sources that contain the words *cloning* and *animals,* in either order, when the words are near each other.

- ***Before*** or ***After:*** Use *before* or *after* between two keywords to narrow a search to every source that contains one keyword before (or after) another keyword. For example, *cloning before sheep* directs the computer to search only for sources that contain the word *cloning* when it appears before the word *sheep. Cloning after sheep* directs the computer to search only for sources that contain the word *cloning* when it appears after the word *sheep.*
- ***Adj:*** Use *adj* between two keywords to narrow a search to every source that contains both keywords when they are adjacent, or next to each other, in the exact order they were entered in the search box. For example, *cloning adj sheep* tells the computer to search only for sources that contain the word *cloning* when it appears before and next to the word *sheep.* **Note:** Some computer databases use adjacency as the default setting, so *cloning sheep* will produce the same search results as *cloning adj sheep.*

Use Wildcards. You can expand a search, but in a focused way, using one or more asterisks (*) to truncate, or shorten, your keyword. Then the computer will search for all words that begin with the letters before the asterisk.

- **One asterisk (*):** Type an asterisk after the first key letters of a word to direct the computer to search for sources that contain the first key letters followed by 1–5 other characters. For example, *clon** tells the computer to search for sources that contain *clon* followed by 1 to 5 other letters, such as in *clone, clones, cloned,* and *cloning.*

  You can also use this technique when you aren't sure how to spell a word. For example, you could use *Doll** if you weren't sure whether the first cloned sheep was named *Dollie* or *Dolly.*

- **Two asterisks (**):** Type two asterisks after the first key letters of a word to direct the computer to conduct an open-ended search. For example, *clon*** tells the computer to search for sources that contain *clon* followed by any number of letters and characters. The sources will include the words *clone, clones, cloned,* and *cloning,* as well as such terms as *clone wars, cloning: the science of, cloning pets, clone codes,* and *clone saga epic.*
- **Question mark (?):** Use a question mark (?) anywhere in a keyword to replace one letter or character. Using a question mark is helpful when you want to search for various spellings of a word. For example, a search for *wom?n* will produce sources that contain both *woman* and *women.*

Title Search For a title search, you will enter the title, starting with the first two or three important words in the title. Ignore *A, An,* and *The* at the beginning of a title. For example, for the book *The Digital Age: 1947–Present Day,* you would type the following:

Digital Age

Author Search For an author search, you will enter the author's last name first, followed by a comma and the first name. For example, for author Charlie Samuels, you would type the following:

Samuels, Charlie

When you enter titles and names, be sure the words you type are spelled correctly. A computer catalog can't recognize misspelled words. It will search for exactly what you type.

If you need help with the computer catalog of your library, you can always ask a librarian for help. Many libraries also offer classes on how to use the library's computer catalog and other databases.

Understanding Search Results

After you enter the keyword(s) of a subject, the title, or the author's name, the screen will show you a list of related sources that are available at the library or libraries you selected. Let's say you're doing research on cloning and you've started a subject search by typing in the keyword *cloning.* The screen will show you a list similar to the one that follows.

Keywords (1-12 of 21)		
Afterschool charisma / Kumiko Suekane; [translation, Camellia Nieh]. Suekane, Kumiko. San Francisco, Calif. : Viz Media, c2009- v. : chiefly ill. (some col.) ; 21 cm	Find It Request It Add to List	c2009-
Star Wars, the Clone Wars, Clone commandos [videorecording] / Lucasfilm, Ltd. [United States] : Warner Home Video, 2009. 1 videodisc (88 min.) : sd., col. ; 4 3/4 in. DVD, widescreen.	Find It Request It Add to List	2009 DVD
Genetics in medicine / Andrew Solway. Solway, Andrew Milwaukee, WI : World Almanac Library, 2007 64 p. : col. ill. ; 27 cm. Website	Find It Request It Add to List	2007
Point blank / Anthony Horowitz Horowitz, Anthony, 1955- New York Speak, 2006. 274, 17 p. ; 20 cm.	Find It Request It Add to List	2006
Artemis Fowl. 4, The Opal deception [sound recording] / Eoin Colfer. Colfer, Eoin New York : Random House/Listening Library, p2005 6 sound discs (ca. 72 min. each) : digital; 4 3/4 in.	Find It Request It Add to List	p2005

RESOURCES

The first row in the screen on page 403 shows that the computer found 21 sources about the keyword *cloning*. The screen shows entries for five of those sources. The title in each entry appears in blue and is underlined to show that it is a link. You can click on the link to see more information. If the source is in a format other than a book, the title line identifies the format in brackets. For example, the entry for the *Star Wars* entry shows *[videorecording]* after the title and a DVD icon in the last column to indicate the format.

Beneath the title line in each entry is the author and/or publishing information. The entry may also include the number of pages in a book; the size of a book; whether it has illustrations, an index, a glossary, or a bibliography; the number of discs in a video or sound recording; and the run time of each disc, indicated by the number of minutes.

To find facts about cloning, you will want to look for nonfiction sources. Because only the title, author, format, and publishing information appear on this screen, you should click on the title link to see a more detailed description of the source. The screen on the next page shows the detailed description that appears when the link *Genetics in medicine / Andrew Solway* is clicked.

RESOURCES

Author	Solway, Andrew.
Title	**Genetics in medicine**
Pub. Info.	Milwaukee, WI: World Almanac Library, 2007.
Edition	North American ed.

LIBRARY / LOCATION	CALL NUMBER	AVAILABILITY
Calumet Park Juv	616.042 SOL/Y	ON SHELF
Elmhurst Juv	J 616.042 SOL	ON SHELF
Grande Prairie Juv	J 616.042 SOL	ON SHELF
Harvey Juv	J 616.042 SOL	ON SHELF
Homewood Juv	J 576.5 SOL	ON SHELF
Justice Juv	J 616.042 SOL	ON SHELF
Lyons Juv	JUV 616.042 SOL	ON SHELF
Northlake Juv	J 616.042 SOL	ON SHELF
Orland Park Juv	J 616.042 SOL	ON SHELF
Palos Hghts Juv	J 616.042 SOL	ON SHELF

View additional copies or search for a specific volume/copy

Edition	North American ed.
Phys.Desc.	64 p. : col. ill. ; 27 cm.
Series	Cutting edge medicine. Cutting edge medicine.
Note	Includes bibliographical references (p. 62) and index.
Contents	What is genetics? -- From genes to characteristics -- Genetic engineering -- Genetic disorders -- Cloning -- Combating aging -- The future of genetic engineering.
Subject	Medical genetics -- Juvenile literature.
Standard #	9780836878653 (lib. bdg.) 0836878655 (lib. bdg.)

The detailed description may include a list of libraries that contain the source, as well as the call numbers for that source and a description of its availability. (**Call numbers** are numbers and letters used to classify books. They're explained on pages 407–411.) If the source isn't marked "fiction," then you know that it is nonfiction. Library catalogs often use the word *juvenile* to indicate books that are suitable for teens and children. If the word *juvenile* or the letters *JUV* or *J* don't appear, then you know that the source is meant for adults. For example, the screen on page 405 shows that the nonfiction book *Genetics in Medicine* is available on the shelf in juvenile literature at the ten libraries listed.

The detailed description may also include links to other sources related to your subject or author. For example, the screen on page 405 shows that the author's name, *Solway, Andrew,* is a link. You would click on that link to see other books and materials written by Andrew Solway. The screen also shows that *Cutting edge medicine* and *Medical genetics —Juvenile literature* are links to other sources on these subjects.

Either print out or write down the call numbers for the sources you want. Then go to the location in the library, such as the teens (or young adults) nonfiction section, and find the shelf with call numbers for the source you want. For example, for a book with call number *J 616.042 SOL,* you would find the shelf with call numbers between 610 and 620. Then look down the rows for the book marked *616.042 SOL.* The books are in numerical and alphabetical order, so it's easy to find the one you're looking for. Glance through the table of contents or index to be sure this book will help you learn more about cloning.

RESOURCES

CARD CATALOGS

Some libraries have card catalogs instead of online computer catalogs. The cards list the same information as found in the computer catalog. However, they don't tell you whether someone has checked out the book.

Card catalogs are stored in long, narrow drawers. The drawers hold two or more small cards for every book in the library. The cards are arranged in alphabetical order. Fiction books have two cards each. One lists the book by its author, and one lists the book by its title. Nonfiction books have at least three cards each. These cards list the book by its author, its title, and its subject or subjects.

A library may separate its card catalog into two categories: subject cards in one category and author and title cards in another. Often cards are cross-referenced, listing other available sources on the same subject or a related topic. A card catalog might also have separate cross-reference cards, filed alphabetically and listing related topics.

23.2 LOCATING BOOKS

The purpose of call numbers is to help you locate books. Most school and community libraries use call numbers based on the Dewey decimal system. Many college and university libraries use call numbers based on the Library of Congress system.

DEWEY DECIMAL SYSTEM

The Dewey decimal system was created in 1876 by a librarian named Melvil Dewey. This system divides nonfiction books into ten categories. The Dewey categories are described in the chart on the next page.

DEWEY CATEGORIES		
NUMBERS	**CATEGORY**	**EXAMPLES OF SUBCATEGORIES**
000–099	General Works	encyclopedias, bibliographies, periodicals, journalism
100–199	Philosophy	philosophy, psychology, personality
200–299	Religion	mythology, bibles
300–399	Social Sciences	sociology, education, government, law, economics, vocations, customs
400–499	Language	dictionaries, languages, grammar
500–599	Pure Sciences	chemistry, astronomy, biology, mathematics
600–699	Technology and Applied Sciences	medicine, engineering, agriculture, home economics, business, radio, television, aviation
700–799	Arts	architecture, painting, music, photography, recreation
800–899	Literature	poetry, plays, essays, criticism
900–999	Geography and History	geography, history, travel

Let's say you want to know more about author James Thurber. You'd begin by entering his last name as a keyword in a computer catalog or by looking under *T* in a card catalog.

The library might have many books by Thurber and about Thurber. One book might be *My Life and Hard Times*, a book by James Thurber. This book is placed in the 800 category, literature. Literature is broken into subcategories; for example, 810 is American literature, and 820 is English literature. James Thurber was an American author, so *My Life and Hard Times* has a call number in the 810s: *817 THU*.

Some subcategories of the Dewey system contain hundreds of books. To make sure each book has its own call number, a decimal point and more numbers (and sometimes letters) are added to the number of the subcategory. For example, the book about genetics by Andrew Solway has a call number of *616.042 SOL.* Many libraries add the first three letters of the author's last name to the call number, such as *SOL* for Solway or *THU* for Thurber.

Library Tip

Two librarians may assign the same book to different Dewey categories. That's why books in your library may have different call numbers than those noted here.

Our imaginary library has another book, a biography called *Remember Laughter: A Life of James Thurber,* by Neil A. Grauer. Its call number is *B Thurber James.* The *B* (or *BIOG* or *BIOGRAPHY*) at the beginning of a Dewey decimal call number identifies the book as biography. Some libraries group their biographies together in a separate section of the library. Often there is a biography section in the adult stacks as well as in the teens and children sections. Biographies are shelved alphabetically according to the subject of the book. James Thurber is the subject of the book *Remember Laughter: A Life of James Thurber.* So the book is located in the *T* section of the biographies.

The library also has a book called *Thurber: A Biography,* by Burton Bernstein. It, too, has a call number of *B Thurber James.* Two biographies with the same call number but different authors are shelved alphabetically by the last name of the author. That puts Bernstein's book before Grauer's book in the *T* section of the biographies.

One book of short stories by James Thurber, *92 Stories,* is located in the fiction section. Most libraries using the Dewey system identify fiction in the call number with the letters *F, Fic,* or *Fiction.* The call number also includes the first three letters of the author's last name or the author's entire last name. For example, the call number of *92 Stories* is *Fic Thurber.*

Fiction is shelved alphabetically by the authors' last names. Books by the same author are shelved by the first important word in each title, ignoring *A, An,* and *The.* (The book *92 Stories* is shelved as if the number were spelled out: *Ninety-two.*)

Reference books, such as encyclopedias, have an *R* or *Ref* in their call numbers. When you see *R* or *Ref*, remember that you cannot check out these sources. You must use them in the library.

LIBRARY OF CONGRESS SYSTEM

The Library of Congress system divides books into twenty-one categories. Each category is represented by a letter as shown in the chart on the next page. Like the Dewey decimal system, the Library of Congress system has subcategories identified by a second letter. For example, *N* is the category for fine arts. You would look under *NA* for books about architecture, *NB* for sculpture, *ND* for painting, and so on. Numbers added to the letter combinations identify more specific categories.

RESOURCES

LIBRARY OF CONGRESS CATEGORIES

LETTER	CATEGORY	LETTER	CATEGORY
A	General Works	N	Fine Arts
B	Philosophy and Religion	P	Language and Literature
C–F	History	Q	Science
G	Geography and Anthropology	R	Medicine
H	Social Sciences	S	Agriculture
J	Political Science	T	Technology
K	Law	U	Military Science
L	Education	V	Naval Science
M	Music	Z	Bibliography and Library Science

In one library using the Library of Congress system, Neil A. Grauer's book, *Remember Laughter: A Life of James Thurber,* has a call number of *PS 3539.H94.* The *P* stands for the general category of Literature, while *S* indicates a work by an American author. The next letter and numbers, *.H94,* are a code that stands for the author and the specific book.

Note that in the Library of Congress system, biographies are not filed separately but with the other books. Therefore, the call numbers of the biographies for Thurber begin with *PS,* indicating an American author.

FINDING INFORMATION IN NONFICTION BOOKS

Nonfiction books contain various sections that you can use to decide whether a source will be useful to you. Not every book contains all the sections described below.

Information About a Book

To find information about a book, check the following parts:

The **title page** contains the book title, the author's name, and usually the publisher.

The **copyright page** gives the publication or copyright date. This page is usually printed on the back of the title page. Check the copyright date to see how current, or up to date, the information in the book is.

The **table of contents** lists the main topics covered in the book. This section may help you decide whether the book has the information you're looking for.

The **foreword, introduction,** or **preface** is written by the author or an expert on the topic or subject. This section may explain the purpose of the book or the author's outlook on the subject.

Information in a Book

To find information in a book, check the sections below:

The **index** lists the people, places, events, and other important topics mentioned in the book in alphabetical order. The pages in the book where you can find references to these topics are listed after each topic.

The **glossary** lists terms in the book in alphabetical order and defines them.

The **bibliography** suggests additional research sources that you might use. It may also include the sources for information found in the book itself.

The **appendix** contains additional information related to the book, such as maps, charts, illustrations, and graphs.

The **afterword** or **epilogue** is used by some authors to make a final statement about the book or offer additional findings.

23.3 LOCATING ARTICLES IN NEWSPAPERS AND MAGAZINES

You can find the latest information on a topic in newspapers, magazines, and journals. The two tools described below will make your search easier.

COMPUTER DATABASES

Many libraries have computers in a reference section that you can use for online references. These computers contain databases holding collections of magazine, journal, and newspaper articles. Most of these databases allow you to search by topic, by type of publication, or by specific publication. Some programs allow you to select the years you want to search, so you can see only the magazines or newspapers within that period of time. You usually can narrow your search to a specific magazine or newspaper, such as the *New York Times.* Some databases may allow you to review the table of contents of one issue of a magazine and read any of the articles that interest you.

To search for information in a database, begin by entering a keyword. The database will then list articles about that topic. The listing usually includes the title, the author, the publication, the date, and a sentence or two about the article. You can select any articles that seem useful. Then the database will allow you to read either a brief summary or the whole article on the computer screen. Usually for a small fee, you can print a copy of the article.

READERS' GUIDE TO PERIODICAL LITERATURE

In addition to computer databases, some libraries may have the print edition of the *Readers' Guide to Periodical Literature.* This guide includes titles of articles from about two hundred magazines and journals. Both subjects and authors are listed alphabetically and cross-referenced.

An update of the print edition of *Readers' Guide* is published every two weeks. Information about all the articles published that year is reprinted in a hardbound book at the end of the year. The guide is also available online so you can search using a computer.

Libraries often keep issues for the current year in their newspapers and magazines area. Issues from the previous one to five years may be stored in a different area. Older issues may be on **microfilm** (a roll or reel of film) or **microfiche** (a sheet of film). Both types of film must be inserted into special projectors that enlarge the pages so that you can read them easily. Many libraries have converted their microfilm and microfiche collections to digital microform versions that can be viewed on computers. Usually for a small fee, you can print copies of articles from microfilm, microfiche, and microform to take home.

Evaluating Tip

Not every book in the library or article in library databases offers current, reliable information. The tips below will help you avoid sources that have outdated information or biased opinions.

1. **Evaluate the author of each source of information.** Look for information about the author's background. Consider whether this person is an expert or just someone with many opinions.
2. **Make sure the information is directly related to your topic.** If you try to include facts that are slightly off your topic, your report will seem unorganized.
3. **Check the publication date.** You may use older sources for information that's not likely to change, such as facts about the battles of World War II. However, your sources must be as recent as possible for topics that are in today's headlines.

4. **Evaluate the author's thinking.** Are the "facts" in a source really facts, or are they just opinions? Can they be proved or disproved? Does the author offer evidence to support his or her ideas?
5. **Gather information on the same topic from several sources.** By doing this, you'll discover different opinions on the issue or topic, but the facts should remain the same.

23.4 USING OTHER REFERENCE SOURCES

GENERAL REFERENCE SOURCES

General reference sources are easy to use and provide information on thousands of topics. Many general reference sources are available in both print and digital formats. The chart that follows describes some excellent general references.

TYPE OF REFERENCE	EXAMPLES
General Encyclopedias General encyclopedias fill many volumes. Subjects are arranged alphabetically. An index at the end helps you find topics.	*World Book Encyclopedia* *Encyclopaedia Britannica* *Collier's Encyclopedia* *Grolier Encyclopedia*
Specialized Encyclopedias Specialized encyclopedias focus on specific topics. You might be surprised at the number of specialized encyclopedias available.	*Van Nostrand's Scientific Encyclopedia* *Encyclopedia of Opera* *Encyclopedia of Vitamins, Minerals, and Supplements* *Encyclopedia of the Geological Sciences*

TYPE OF REFERENCE	EXAMPLES
Almanacs and Yearbooks Almanacs and yearbooks are usually published annually. They provide current facts and statistics. Check the most recent issues for the latest information.	*Information Please Almanac* *World Almanac and Book of Facts* *Guinness Book of Records* *Statistical Abstract of the United States*
Atlases Atlases may contain current or historical information. They include maps and statistics about countries, climates, and other topics.	*Hammond World Atlas* *Cambridge Atlas of Astronomy* *Historical Atlas of the United States* *Goode's World Atlas* *National Geographic Atlas of the World* *Atlas of World Cultures*
Biographical References Biographical reference works include brief histories of notable people, living or dead.	*Contemporary Authors* *American Authors 1600–1900* *Cyclopedia of Literary Characters* *Webster's New Biographical Dictionary* *Biographical Dictionary of World War I* *Biographical Dictionary of World War II*
Government Publications Some large libraries have government publications on agriculture, population, economics, and other topics.	*Catalog of United States Government Publications* (Also available online.)
Books of Quotations In a book of quotations, you can find quotations by famous people or about certain subjects. The quotation from Samuel Johnson at the beginning of Part Four can be found in *The Harper Book of Quotations.*	*Bartlett's Familiar Quotations* *The Harper Book of Quotations* *The Oxford Dictionary of Quotations* *The International Thesaurus of Quotations*

PLANNING LIBRARY RESEARCH

You might use the guidelines below to plan your research.

1. Start early. If you wait, other students may have checked out the sources you want to use.
2. Begin with the general reference sources rather than those that deal with specific fields or topics. A general source will offer an overview of your topic. It may provide all the information you need, or it may guide you to additional sources.
3. List the sources you want to check and mark each one off your list after you've examined it so you won't check the same source twice.
4. Take careful notes and include the title, author, publisher, publication date, and page number of each source. (See pages 349–350 for more information about compiling source cards and note cards.)
5. Talk with the librarian about your project, its purpose, its length, and the kinds of sources you have been asked to use. Describe what you've done so far and be ready with specific questions you'd like answered. Librarians can often suggest valuable references you haven't considered and perhaps help you locate them.

23.5 MAKING THE MOST OF WORD RESOURCES

A dictionary and a thesaurus can help you put more words on the tip of your tongue and at the tip of your pencil. Both references are essential tools for writers, and both are available in print and digital formats.

KINDS OF DICTIONARIES

You may not know that there are many kinds of dictionaries. Most of the dictionaries you've seen in school, in public libraries, and online are general dictionaries that include words from general English for a general reader. There also are specialized dictionaries that define only words used in a particular field, profession, art, or craft.

General Dictionaries

General dictionaries fall into the following categories:

School dictionaries contain fewer than 90,000 entries. They focus on common words and offer easy-to-understand definitions.

College dictionaries have about 150,000 entries. These references are used in homes, schools, and businesses. They answer most questions about spelling, and they offer a variety of definitions.

Unabridged dictionaries contain more than 250,000 entries and often fill several volumes. They are generally located in libraries and include extensive definitions and word histories.

Digital dictionaries often contain millions of definitions and meanings that you can use your computer to access online at no cost. In addition to definitions, these online dictionaries often provide audio pronunciations, example sentences, and word origins.

Specialized Dictionaries

Specialized dictionaries list words used in a particular field. Following are some examples of the many kinds of specialized dictionaries.

Dictionary of Art Terms
Dictionary of Dog Terms
Dictionary of Inventions and Discoveries
Dictionary of Sports Idioms
Dictionary of Symbolism
Facts on File Dictionary of Allusions

WORD ENTRIES IN GENERAL DICTIONARIES

General print dictionaries contain entries in alphabetical order. Digital dictionaries usually present only the entry for the word you searched. An **entry** is a single word or term along with its pronunciation, definition, and other information. When you look up a word in a dictionary, you are looking for its word entry.

Finding Words in a Print Dictionary

The guide words at the top of each dictionary page can help you find words quickly. Guide words are the first and last words on the page. If the word you're looking for falls between these words alphabetically, it will be on that page.

For example, let's say the guide words on a page are *lintel* and *lisp.* You'll find the words *lioness, lip-synch,* and *liquid* on this page. However, *linguistic* comes before *lintel,* so it will be on an earlier page. *Lithium* comes after *lisp,* so it will be on a later page.

If you're looking for a phrase beginning with *St.,* the abbreviation will be spelled out: *Saint.* Look for *Saint Bernard,* not *St. Bernard.*

Search Tip

When you can't find the word you're looking for, consider these possibilities:

1. The word might have silent consonants, such as the *k* in *knight,* the *b* in *doubt,* or the *gh* in *blight.*
2. A consonant in the word might have an unusual spelling. For example, the *k* sound can be spelled with *k (kindness), c (contract, lecture), ck (mackerel),* or *ch (chrysanthemum, chrome).*
3. A vowel in the word might have an unusual spelling, such as the first vowel sound in *beautiful.*
4. Your dictionary might not contain enough entries. An unusual word might not be listed in a school dictionary, for example.

Understanding Dictionary Entries

Let's analyze a dictionary entry to see what kinds of information it offers.

in•fer (in fur´) *v.* **in•ferred, in•fer•ring 1.** to conclude by reasoning from facts known or assumed: *I infer from your frown that you're angry.* **2.** to guess: *We inferred that the stranger was our new teacher.* —**in•fer•able** (in fur´ ə bəl) *adj.* —**in•fer•rer** (in fur´ər) *n.* [from Middle French *inferer,* from Latin *inferre,* literally, "to carry or bring into," from *in-* + *ferre* "to carry"]

Synonyms: *Infer, deduce,* and *conclude* all mean "to arrive at a conclusion." *Infer* implies arriving at a conclusion based on specific facts. *Deduce* includes the special meaning of drawing a conclusion from a general idea. *Conclude* suggests arriving at an inference based on a chain of reasoning.

1. *The Entry Word:* The entry word itself shows the correct spelling of the word. A raised dot or a blank space within the entry word shows where the word may be divided at the end of a line of writing. The entry word will also show you when a compound word should be written as one solid word (as in **landfill**), when it should be hyphenated (as in **land-poor**), and when it should be written as two words (as in **land mine**).
2. *The Respelling:* The respelling, or pronunciation, is shown immediately after the entry word. An accent mark follows the second syllable in *infer* to show that the second syllable should be stressed when pronouncing the word. So that you can check the pronunciation of the letters and symbols in the respelling, a pronunciation key is shown on every page or every other page in most dictionaries.
3. *Part of Speech Label:* An abbreviation in italic type gives the part of speech of the entry word. The

abbreviation *v.* stands for *verb; adj.* stands for *adjective;* and *n.* stands for *noun.*

4. *Inflected Forms:* Inflected forms include plurals of nouns, principal parts of verbs (past, past participle, and present participle), and comparative and superlative forms of adjectives and adverbs. These forms are included in a dictionary entry only when they have irregular spellings. When the past and the past participle of a verb are the same, only one form is shown for both. The sample entry shows that *inferred* is the past form and the past participle of *infer,* and *inferring* is the present participle. These forms are considered irregular because the final consonant is doubled when the ending is added.

   This part of a dictionary entry can help you spell irregular plural forms, such as *quizzes* for *quiz* and *rodeos* for *rodeo.* This section will also show you when to double a final consonant *(stop, stopping; sad, sadder),* when to drop a final *e (dine, dining),* and when to change a final *y* to *i (easy, easiest)* before adding an ending.

5. *Definitions:* Definitions are the heart—and the longest part—of a dictionary entry. If an entry word has more than one meaning, each definition is numbered. Example sentences are often included to make meanings clearer.

6. *Run-on Entries:* Definitions in a dictionary entry may be followed by one or more run-on entries. A run-on entry is a form of the entry word to which a suffix has been added. In the sample dictionary entry, **in•fer•able** and **in•fer•er** are run-on entries. Each run-on entry is preceded by a dash and followed by its pronunciation and its part of speech. The meanings of these words can be inferred by combining the meaning of the entry word and the meaning of the suffix. (See the list of suffixes and their meanings on pages 307–308.)

7. *Etymology:* Many dictionary entries include the etymology, or origin or history of the word. The entry

for *infer* explains that this word is based on a Middle French word. The Middle French word was based on a Latin word with a literal meaning of "to carry or bring into." When you infer, you carry or bring your knowledge into a new situation. You use what you know to reach a conclusion. You can see that the Middle French and Latin versions of the word are both similar to the English spelling.

8. *Synonyms:* Some dictionary entries list synonyms, or words with the same or nearly the same meanings. Understanding small differences in meaning will help you use the right word in the right place. Some dictionaries also include antonyms, words with opposite meanings.

Some words have more than one meaning or word history; some may be used as more than one part of speech. In such cases, a dictionary may have multiple entries for a word. Let's look at three entries for the word *rest:*

> [1]**rest** (rest´) *n.* **1.** REPOSE, SLEEP **2.** freedom from activity or disturbance **3.** something that acts as a stand or a support **4.** a place for resting or lodging **5.** *Music.* a silence between musical notes **6.** a brief pause in reading [Middle English, from Old English; akin to Old High German *rasta* "rest"]
>
> [2]**rest** *v.* **1.** to get rest by lying down or stopping activity **2.** to lie dead **3.** *Farming.* to remain idle or without a crop **4.** *Law.* to finish presenting evidence in a legal case: *The defense rests, Your Honor.*
>
> [3]**rest** *n.* something that remains over; REMAINDER: *Jada ate the rest of the fruit salad.* [Middle English, from Middle French *reste,* from *rester* "to remain," from Latin *restare,* from *re-* + *stare* "to stand"]

Numbered Entries Notice the small raised numeral to the left of each entry word in the preceding dictionary sample. This number indicates there is more than one entry for the word. Some dictionaries show separate entries for each part of speech. Some show separate entries for each meaning that has a different word history, or etymology.

In the first and second entries, the meanings have to do with pausing, sleeping, or remaining idle, but the entry words are different parts of speech. The third entry word is the same part of speech as the first, but the word's meaning and its etymology are different.

Cross-References Synonyms within an entry are sometimes printed in small capital letters. In the entries for *rest,* the words *repose, sleep,* and *remainder* are synonyms for specific meanings of *rest.* You can learn more about these meanings of *rest* by looking up the words in small capital letters.

Subject Labels Some dictionary entries include subject labels. A subject label preceding a definition indicates that the definition applies to the subject named. In the sample entries for *rest,* there are three subject labels. In ^{1}*rest* definition 5 applies to music. In ^{2}*rest* definition 3 applies to farming, and definition 4 applies to law.

The chart on the next page gives examples of other kinds of information you may find in a dictionary entry.

TYPE OF INFORMATION	DESCRIPTION	EXAMPLE FROM AN ENTRY
Capitalization	Indicates that certain uses of a word should be capitalized	**earth** ... *Often capitalized.* the planet that is third in order from the sun
Out-of-date label	Identifies meanings that are no longer used or used only in special contexts	**anon** ... *Archaic.* at once; immediately
Style label	Indicates a meaning that is appropriate only in a very informal context	**cool** ... *Slang.* very good; EXCELLENT
Regional label	Indicates a meaning used in a certain geographical area	**bon•net** ... *British.* an automobile hood
Usage note	Offers guidelines for using–or not using–a word	**ain't** ... Although inappropriate in formal speech or writing, *ain't* is sometimes used to attract attention or add humorous emphasis.

OTHER KINDS OF INFORMATION IN GENERAL DICTIONARIES

You can find other kinds of information in the back of some dictionaries. Following is a list of some of the kinds of information you may find in a dictionary.

Biographical Names

Do you remember James Thurber? Who was he? When was he born? When did he die? A section of biographical names gives the spelling and pronunciation of thousands of people's names, from Berenice Abbott (an American photographer who lived from 1898 to 1991) to Stefan Zweig (an Austrian writer who was born in 1881 and died in 1942).

Geographical Names

How do you pronounce *Kilimanjaro*? What is it, and where is it? In a section of geographical names, you can find the correct spelling, pronunciation, and location of countries, cities, mountains, lakes, rivers, and other geographical features. Entries range from Lake Abitibi, in Ontario, Canada, to Zimbabwe, a country in southern Africa.

Abbreviations, Signs, and Symbols

Is the postal abbreviation for Maine MA, MN, or ME? A dictionary may include lists of abbreviations, signs, and symbols. Check this section if you can't remember, for example, what *NOAA* stands for (National Oceanic and Atmospheric Administration) or what the symbol *&* means *(and).*

Style Handbook

Some dictionaries include a style guide. This section may include rules for spelling, punctuation, and capitalization. It may also include other matters of writing style. Investigate your dictionary to find out what it has to offer.

THESAURUSES

A thesaurus lists **synonyms,** or words with the same or nearly the same meanings. Thesauruses are available in both print and digital formats. A print thesaurus may be organized in dictionary style or traditional style. A digital thesaurus may present entries in alphabetical order.

Print Format

A thesaurus in print, or book, format will be organized in either dictionary style or traditional style.

Traditional Style Let's say you've used the word *continue* several times in a report, and you want to find a synonym. To use a traditional thesaurus, begin by looking in the index. There you might find these choices:

continue endure 110.6
protract 110.9
go on 143.3
extend 201.9
persevere 623.2

Let's say that *extend* seems like a good word to replace *continue* in your report. You could use *extend,* or you could look in the front of the book under 201.9 for more choices. Guide numbers at the top of each page help you find the number you want quickly. They're similar to a dictionary's guide words.

On the page with the guide numbers 201.3–203.7, you find paragraph 201.9, a group of synonyms for *extend.* The most commonly used words are printed in bold type.

VERBS **9. lengthen, prolong,** prolongate, **elongate, extend,** produce [geom.], **protract,** continue, lengthen out, let out, **draw out,** drag out, string out [coll., U.S.], spin out; **stretch,** draw; tense, strain.

A page in the back of the thesaurus explains that *geom.* stands for *geometry* and *coll.* stands for *colloquial,* or *informal.*

Dictionary Style A dictionary-style thesaurus is organized much like a dictionary. Using the guide words at the top of the page, locate the word *continue.* Checking the front of the book, you learn that an asterisk (*) indicates that a term is colloquial or slang.

CONTINUE

Verb. **1.** [To persist] persevere, carry forward, maintain, carry *or* roll *or* keep *or* go *or* run *or* live on, never stop, sustain, remain, press onward, make headway, move ahead, *leave no stone unturned; see also ADVANCE.

Antonyms: cease, end, give up

2. [To resume] begin again, renew, begin *or* carry over, return to, take up again, begin where one left off, be reinstated *or* restored; see also RESUME.

Antonyms: discontinue, halt, postpone

RESOURCES

Digital Format

A digital thesaurus requires you to type into a search box the word for which you want a synonym. Although each thesaurus program presents synonym entries a little differently, most will display entries by definition with synonyms for that meaning listed alphabetically. Each entry identifies the part of speech, one or more definitions, and a list of synonyms with similar meanings. Some or all of the synonyms may link to other words. Linked words may be underlined or a different color. You can click on linked words to see additional entries for the word you clicked.

Let's say you've typed *continue* into the thesaurus search box. You might see the following entries:

Entry:	**continue**
Part of speech:	*verb*
Definition:	to extend
Synonyms:	drag out, draw out, elongate, extend, lengthen, lengthen out, let out, produce, prolong, prolongate, protract, spin out, stretch, string out

Entry:	**continue**
Part of speech:	*verb*
Definition:	to resume
Synonyms:	begin, begin again, begin over, begin where one left off, carry on, carry over, reinstate, renew, restart, resume, return to, take up again

Chapter 24

Accessing Digital Resources

When you're looking for up-to-date information, digital resources can provide an excellent starting point. The Internet is an increasingly important source of information for people of all ages around the world. CDs, DVDs, and other digital resources that are not connected to the Internet also offer vast amounts of information.

The Internet is a computer-based, worldwide information network. The World Wide Web, or WWW, is software that determines what is displayed on the Internet. Working together, the Internet and the World Wide Web allow you to gather information without leaving your home, school, or library.

UNDERSTANDING ADDRESSES

The information on the Internet is organized by locations, or sites. Each site has its own address. An address is also called a Uniform Resource Locator, or URL.

Most addresses begin with *http://,* which stands for "hypertext transfer protocol." The *http* identifies a way in which information is exchanged among computers that are connected by the Internet. The last part of an address, or its suffix, indicates the type of site it is. The chart on the next page identifies some of the suffixes in use.

SUFFIX	TYPE OF SITE
.com	commercial
.edu	educational
.gov	government
.mil	military
.net	network organization or Internet service provider
.org	organization

ACCESSING WEB SITES

Let's say you're connected to the Internet, and you want to view the information at a certain site or address. You can enter the address on the computer screen and be connected to the site.

You can also access specific reference sources, such as the *New York Times* or *Encyclopaedia Britannica,* in this way. Some of these sources are free. For others you must subscribe and perhaps pay a fee. A screen will explain any extra charges that are required. Then you can choose whether to continue.

The Evaluating Tip on the next page will help you decide whether the digital sources you find on the Internet are credible, or trustworthy.

Evaluating Tip

No one oversees Web sites to make sure they offer accurate information. You must evaluate each site yourself. First, review the "Evaluating Tip" on pages 414–415. The tips listed there also apply to Internet sources. The following tips will also help you evaluate Internet sources.

1. Determine whether a Web site actually relates to your topic. A search engine will use every possible meaning of your keyword to produce its list of sites.
2. Check the source of the information on a Web site. (You may have to press the "move back" key several times to identify a source.) Many Web sites are personal pages. Just because you find information on the Web doesn't mean the information is true or accurate.
3. Evaluate the accuracy and fairness of the information on a Web site. Is it based on more than one source? Are differing opinions included? After doing some of your own research elsewhere, are you aware of important information that was omitted from the site? Does the site include a bibliography and links to other sites? The answers to these questions can help you decide whether to use that source.

COMMON CORE STATE STANDARDS CORRELATION

Writing	
Text Types and Purposes	
1. Write arguments to support claims with clear reasons and relevant evidence.	Persuasive Essay, pp. 312–322
a. Introduce claim(s) and organize the reasons and evidence clearly.	Persuasive Essay, pp. 312–322
b. Support claim(s) with clear reasons and relevant evidence, using credible sources and demonstrating an understanding of the topic or text.	Persuasive Essay, pp. 312–322
c. Use words, phrases, and clauses to clarify the relationships among claim(s) and reasons.	Persuasive Essay, pp. 312–322
d. Establish and maintain a formal style.	Persuasive Essay, pp. 312–322
e. Provide a concluding statement or section that follows from the argument presented.	Persuasive Essay, pp. 312–322
2. Write informative/explanatory texts to examine a topic and convey ideas, concepts, and information through the selection, organization, and analysis of relevant content.	Response Essay, pp. 323–333 Multi-Paragraph Essay, pp. 334–344 Research Report, pp. 345–360

a. Introduce a topic; organize ideas, concepts, and information, using strategies such as definition, classification, comparison/contrast, and cause/effect; include formatting (e.g., headings), graphics (e.g., charts, tables), and multimedia when useful to aiding comprehension.	Response Essay, pp. 323–333 Multi-Paragraph Essay, pp. 334–344 Research Report, pp. 345–360
b. Develop the topic with relevant facts, definitions, concrete details, quotations, or other information and examples.	Response Essay, pp. 323–333 Multi-Paragraph Essay, pp. 334–344 Research Report, pp. 345–360
c. Use appropriate transitions to clarify the relationships among ideas and concepts.	Response Essay, pp. 323–333 Multi-Paragraph Essay, pp. 334–344 Research Report, pp. 345–360
d. Use precise language and domain-specific vocabulary to inform about or explain the topic.	Response Essay, pp. 323–333 Multi-Paragraph Essay, pp. 334–344 Research Report, pp. 345–360
e. Establish and maintain a formal style.	Response Essay, pp. 323–333 Multi-Paragraph Essay, pp. 334–344 Research Report, pp. 345–360
f. Provide a concluding statement or section that follows from the information or explanation presented.	Response Essay, pp. 323–333 Multi-Paragraph Essay, pp. 334–344 Research Report, pp. 345–360
3. Write narratives to develop real or imagined experiences or events using effective technique, relevant descriptive details, and well-structured event sequences.	Narrative, pp. 361–371
a. Engage and orient the reader by establishing a context and introducing a narrator and/or characters; organize an event sequence that unfolds naturally and logically.	Narrative, pp. 361–371

b. Use narrative techniques, such as dialogue, pacing, and description, to develop experiences, events, and/or characters.	Narrative, pp. 361–371
c. Use a variety of transition words, phrases, and clauses to convey sequence and signal shifts from one time frame or setting to another.	Narrative, pp. 361–371
d. Use precise words and phrases, relevant descriptive details, and sensory language to convey experiences and events.	Narrative, pp. 361–371
e. Provide a conclusion that follows from the narrated experiences or events.	Narrative, pp. 361–371
Production and Distribution of Writing	
4. Produce clear and coherent writing in which the development, organization, and style are appropriate to task, purpose, and audience. (Grade-specific expectations for writing types are defined in standards 1–3 above.)	Persuasive Essay, pp. 312–322 Response Essay, pp. 323–333 Multi-Paragraph Essay, pp. 334–344 Research Report, pp. 345–360 Narrative, pp. 361–371
5. With some guidance and support from peers and adults, develop and strengthen writing as needed by planning, revising, editing, rewriting, or trying a new approach. (Editing for conventions should demonstrate command of Language standards 1–3 up to and including grade 6.)	Persuasive Essay, pp. 312–322 Response Essay, pp. 323–333 Multi-Paragraph Essay, pp. 334–344 Research Report, pp. 345–360 Narrative, pp. 361–371
6. Use technology, including the Internet, to produce and publish writing as well as to interact and collaborate with others; demonstrate sufficient command of keyboarding skills to type a minimum of three pages in a single sitting.	Persuasive Essay, pp. 312–322 Response Essay, pp. 323–333 Multi-Paragraph Essay, pp. 334–344 Research Report, pp. 345–360 Narrative, pp. 361–371

Research to Build and Present Knowledge	
7. Conduct short research projects to answer a question, drawing on several sources and refocusing the inquiry when appropriate.	Research Report, pp. 345–360
8. Gather relevant information from multiple print and digital sources; assess the credibility of each source; and quote or paraphrase the data and conclusions of others while avoiding plagiarism and providing basic bibliographic information for sources.	Research Report, pp. 345–360
9. Draw evidence from literary or informational texts to support analysis, reflection, and research.	Response Essay, pp. 323–333 Multi-Paragraph Essay, pp. 334–344 Research Report, pp. 345–360
a. Apply *grade 6 Reading standards* to literature (e.g., "Compare and contrast texts in different forms or genres [e.g., stories and poems; historical novels and fantasy stories] in terms of their approaches to similar themes and topics").	Response Essay, pp. 323–333 Multi-Paragraph Essay, pp. 334–344 Research Report, pp. 345–360
b. Apply *grade 6 Reading standards* to literary nonfiction (e.g., "Trace and evaluate the argument and specific claims in a text, distinguishing claims that are supported by reasons and evidence from claims that are not").	Response Essay, pp. 323–333 Multi-Paragraph Essay, pp. 334–344 Research Report, pp. 345–360
Range of Writing	
10. Write routinely over extended time frames (time for research, reflection, and revision) and shorter time frames (a single sitting or a day or two) for a range of discipline-specific tasks, purposes, and audiences.	Persuasive Essay, pp. 312–322 Response Essay, pp. 323–333 Multi-Paragraph Essay, pp. 334–344 Research Report, pp. 345–360 Narrative, pp. 361–371

Language	
Conventions of Standard English	
1. Demonstrate command of the conventions of standard English grammar and usage when writing or speaking.	This standard is met throughout the book.
a. Ensure that pronouns are in the proper case (subjective, objective, possessive).	Personal Pronouns, pp. 125–126 Using Pronouns, pp. 126–128 Possessive Pronouns, pp. 131–132 Pronouns as Objects of Prepositions, pp. 176–177 Interrogative and Demonstrative Pronouns, pp. 135–137 Pronouns As Objects of Prepositions, pp. 176–177 Persuasive Essay, pp. 312–322 Response Essay, pp. 323–333 Multi-Paragraph Essay, pp. 334–344 Research Report, pp. 345–360 Narrative, pp. 361–371
b. Use intensive pronouns (e.g., *myself, ourselves*).	Reflexive and Intensive Pronouns, pp. 134–135 Persuasive Essay, pp. 312–322 Response Essay, pp. 323–333 Multi-Paragraph Essay, pp. 334–344 Research Report, pp. 345–360 Narrative, pp. 361–371

c. Recognize and correct inappropriate shifts in pronoun number and person.	Personal Pronouns, pp. 125–126 Pronouns and Antecedents, p. 130 Possessive Pronouns, pp. 131–132 Indefinite Pronouns, pp. 132–133 Reflexive and Intensive Pronouns, pp. 134–135 Interrogative and Demonstrative Pronouns, pp. 135–137 Making Subjects and Verbs Agree, pp. 206–208 Indefinite Pronouns as Subjects, pp. 212–213
d. Recognize and correct vague pronouns (i.e., ones with unclear or ambiguous antecedents).	Using Pronouns, pp. 127–128 Pronouns and Antecedents, pp. 128–130 Indefinite Pronouns, pp. 132–133
e. Recognize variations from standard English in their own and others' writing and speaking, and identify and use strategies to improve expression in conventional language.	Persuasive Essay, pp. 312–322 Response Essay, pp. 323–333 Multi-Paragraph Essay, pp. 334–344 Research Report, pp. 345–360 Narrative, pp. 361–371

2. Demonstrate command of the conventions of standard English capitalization, punctuation, and spelling when writing.	Capitalizing Sentences, Quotations, and Letter Parts, pp. 236–237 Capitalizing Names and Titles of People, pp. 238–239 Capitalizing Names of Places, pp. 239–241 Capitalizing Other Proper Nouns and Adjectives, pp. 241–243 Using End Punctuation, pp. 249–250 Using Commas I, pp. 250–253 Using Commas II, pp. 253–254 Using Commas III, pp. 254–256 Using Semicolons and Colons, pp. 256–258 Using Quotation Marks and Italics, pp. 258–261 Using Apostrophes, pp. 261–262 Using Hyphens, Dashes, and Parentheses, pp. 263–264 Using Abbreviations, pp. 264–266 Writing Numbers, pp. 266–268 Persuasive Essay, pp. 312–322 Response Essay, pp. 323–333 Multi-Paragraph Essay, pp. 334–344 Research Report, pp. 345–360 Narrative, pp. 361–371
a. Use punctuation (commas, parentheses, dashes) to set off nonrestrictive/parenthetical elements.	Essential and Nonessential Clauses, pp. 197–198 Using Commas I, pp. 251–253 Using Commas II, pp. 253–254 Using Hyphens, Dashes, and Parentheses, pp. 263–264

b. Spell correctly.	Spelling Rules, pp. 287–295 Improving Your Spelling, pp. 295–298 Persuasive Essay, pp. 312–322 Response Essay, pp. 323–333 Multi-Paragraph Essay, pp. 334–344 Research Report, pp. 345–360 Narrative, pp. 361–371
Knowledge of Language	
3. Use knowledge of language and its conventions when writing, speaking, reading, or listening.	Persuasive Essay, pp. 312–322 Response Essay, pp. 323–333 Multi-Paragraph Essay, pp. 334–344 Research Report, pp. 345–360 Narrative, pp. 361–371
a. Vary sentence patterns for meaning, reader/ listener interest, and style.	Compound Sentences, pp. 275–276 Compound Elements, pp. 276–277 Prepositional Phrases, pp. 277–297 Appositives, pp. 279–280 Adjective and Adverb Clauses, pp. 280–283 Persuasive Essay, pp. 312–322 Response Essay, pp. 323–333 Multi-Paragraph Essay, pp. 334–344 Research Report, pp. 345–360 Narrative, pp. 361–371
b. Maintain consistency in style and tone.	Persuasive Essay, pp. 312–322 Response Essay, pp. 323–333 Multi-Paragraph Essay, pp. 334–344 Research Report, pp. 345–360 Narrative, pp. 361–371

INDEX

Entries with bold page numbers represent terms and definitions in the Glossary of Terms, pages 4–28.

A

B

C

E

J

K

L

M

N

O

P

S

T

Y